Between Iraq
and a
Hard Place

Dan Lagassé

Kirk Legacy

ISBN 978-1-0980-1141-3 (paperback)
ISBN 978-1-0980-1142-0 (digital)

Christian Faith Publishing, Inc.
832 Park Avenue
Meadville, PA 16335
www.christianfaithpublishing.com

Many names in this story have been changed to protect individual privacy and security.

Printed in the United States of America

Dedicated to the orphans and widows of Kurdistan.
They have had to be fearless and courageous in
repeated wars and genocidal conflicts.
They have suffered greatly, many have perished, and all have been
undervalued as people. Yet they are precious in the eyes of God.

Between Iraq and a Hard Place is a vivid portrayal of a young couple who blazed a trail for the gospel among the Kurds of Iraq. Arriving at the end of the first Persian Gulf War, Kirk and Jane Legacy's story of enduring hardship will captivate the reader. They risked their lives in order to help save hundreds from starvation and dehydration. Over time, they not only introduced a people to the holistic love of Christ, but also found their hearts permanently attached to the Kurdish people when they adopted two baby girls on the brink of death. The insurmountable difficulties they encountered and the profound trust they developed in God's power are a needed salve for today's anemic church. The suspense was overwhelming at times, and I couldn't put the book down.

—*Chris Crossan, Senior Pastor, Gateway Community Church of Alhambra, CA*

Some serve Jesus overseas, return home and share how God provided for them on their field of service. But few are able to bring you along-side with such clarity, meaningfulness, and empathy as Kirk describes in this must read. You will travel along with him during the challenges, rewards, fears, victories, and, of course, moments of despair so often experienced by Christians who give their all.

—*Ron Wiebe, Retired Psychotherapist*

Kirk and his wife are not armchair theologians. They have thrown themselves into some of the gravest needs of the Middle East. In Kirk's book, you will read of some of the worst things that have occurred on planet earth. You will also meet people who at the cost of all comforts committed their lives to relieve the horrible suffering of the peoples of the Middle East. In the midst of it all, Jesus is high and lifted up. He remains the answer, whether you wrestle with the question of physical or spiritual healing.

—Dale Rhoton, Operation Mobilization

Kirk and Jane have long been heroes to me. The true-life story Kirk has penned here reflects perfectly the grace of the Lord and what it means to follow Him fully without being led by comfort or fear. God often shows up most clearly and deliberately in the fiercest of landscapes. As related in this compelling story those landscapes can be found in both locations and relationships.

—Paul Bradley, Division Director,
Foreign Armed Forces Ministries, Cadence International,
Chaplain Free Burma Rangers

Kirk and Jane brought hope and God's love to Iraq in 1991, when Saddam Hussein's anger against the Kurds exploded like a pyroclastic blast. Millions fled their homes for the mountains. Hundreds froze to death, every night. You lose your shoes, you lose your life. Just when things were looking blackest, a handful of visiting angels arrived.

Instead of asking, "What can we do?" they asked, "What needs to be done?" And so began one of the great stories of God's mercy and humanitarian rescue of our time.

You say you want to become like Jesus? You will become acquainted with griefs so heartrending that they will affect you, the rest of your life.

Desperate times called for desperate measures.

This book is about the future, about the kind of world that will come into existence if we have faith in God.

—Bob Blincoe, President, US Frontiers

This is the story of our remarkable God and his unfolding call on the lives of an ordinary couple. God's power, his presence, his indwelling, his compassion, his orchestration of the impossible, and many miraculous answers to prayer—all occur in the midst of incredible suffering and chaos. It is impossible to read *Between Iraq and a Hard Place* and not be moved to worship God and to believe intensely in Him and in His power and love. This true account relates God's hand of providence in the lives of countless people, in city after city and situation after situation. The story gives honor to the men and women of a forgotten race: the Kurds. They have lived so courageously against so many odds, and to this day, remain among the most fearless warriors, seeking their identity and freedom.

—Amy Mardock, Homeschooling Mom

Contents

"If a commission by an earthly king is
considered an honor, how can a commission by a
heavenly King be considered a sacrifice."

—David Livingstone

Prologue

"Get Out of Your Comfort Zone!"

"If God calls you to go to serve Him in another land and you are willing to obey Him, please stand." George Verwer, founder and director of Operation Mobilizaton, was speaking at Los Gatos Christian Church.[1] LGCC was a megachurch in California. I had been a member there for several years. George was giving a sober invitation, following a dynamic sermon on God's work around the world. He repeated himself as a few people stood. "If you are willing, should He call you, please stand and come forward."

It seemed a fairly straightforward appeal. I was a follower of Jesus, and I believed the Word of God, the Bible, to be true. I believed that He still guided Christians today, so if He, indeed, called me, then why not obey? I mean, I thought, with all seriousness, He is *God*. It seemed reasonable and honest to respond when God called.

Dozens of other people, mostly young adults, stood to their feet and walked to the front of the large hall.

I stood and went forward.

---

[1] Now called Venture Christian Church. During the 1980s, over 150 church members began training for overseas service. Twenty-four of them, eventually, were sent to every corner of the globe.

11

It was 1978. The church was very active in sharing the love of Jesus with the world and had begun a training program for people who wanted to pursue overseas service.

A pretty young girl also stood up somewhere in the vast auditorium during one of those invitations. Jane Stevens. One day, she was to become my wife, though I hadn't met her yet. And together we would embark on the experience of our lives.

Jane would go on to spend a year in training in the mountains of Peru, with Bob and Betty Whatley. And I, at the same time, would be traveling all over the Philippines with a great evangelist from Overseas Crusades, Ben Siaki. Upon my return, we became engaged.

After our marriage in 1984, we led a low-income inner-city ministry for three years. Our hearts, however, yearned to work with an unreached group of people, a people without any access to the gospel.

We attended courses at Fuller Seminary—including classes on Islam, cross-cultural orientation, and learning an unwritten language. Eventually, we applied and were accepted by Operation Mobilization. It had thousands of young people at work all over the world, but was most known for its literature distribution, emphasis on evangelism, and a large ship that distributed books to the third world.

We were specifically interested in joining a small training team in West Berlin. The team was learning Turkish, to love the many Turks living there. The team leader agreed to let us join their team, although our focus would be the Kurds. Kurds were the largest people group in the world (thirty million) that had no church. There were but a handful of known Christians. They also had no country. Their ancestral lands covered portions of Turkey, Iraq, Iran, Syria, and Armenia.

They would come to occupy the world's center stage at the end of the First Gulf War, in 1991. Jane and I would become caught up in the aftermath of that war. And we would come to relate in a most personal way to the dilemma of the Kurds, who are caught between a rock and a hard place. We were going to experience the biggest faith hurdles in our lives.

Part 1

Chapter 1

From Berlin to Diyarbakir

The Spirit of the Lord is upon me, because he has
anointed me to proclaim good news to the poor.
He has sent me to proclaim release to the captives and the
regaining of sight to the blind, to set free those who are oppressed.

—Luke 4:18

The mountains are our only friends.

—Kurdish Proverb

The Turkish/Iraqi border, Early April 1991

The dust-covered Ford transit loaded with supplies climbed the final stretch of dirt road from the Turkish village of Çukurca [*chuh-KOOR-juh*] on the Iraqi border. Our team was full of anticipation as we approached the barbed-wire fence along the mountain ridge. From a distance, one could see the thousands of tents of all shapes and sizes pitched haphazardly in the mountain valley. Small columns of smoke rose from cooking fires. We parked our vehicle and walked passed the Turkish guards holding their machine guns. They eyed us suspiciously but didn't stop us.

The sight was indescribable. To our right were dozens of mothers holding their babies, waiting to be seen at a medical tent. A seemingly infinite line of women and girls pressed forward to fill their water jugs from a makeshift pipe, and hundreds of men and boys crowded about the spot where food would soon be distributed. An ever-present flow of humanity moved up and down the filthy path that led from deep in the valley up to the Turkish border. Some 120,000 Kurds were reportedly taking refuge here in this one valley alone, and help was slow in coming.

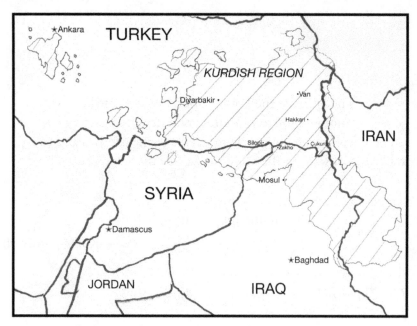

The historical region where Kurds live include parts of Turkey, Iraq, Syria, Iran, and Armenia.

Trucks full of loaves of bread arrived and were inundated by
men trying to get food for their families. It was complete chaos.

Most of the world began seeing news coverage of the Kurdish
refugees fleeing into the mountains early in March 1991. Few people
had even heard of the Kurds, and even fewer understood why two
million people would so suddenly flee their homes and country.

Kurdish leaders in Iraq, encouraged by the victorious US-led
coalition forces at the end of the Gulf War, had risen up in rebellion
against Saddam Hussein. Although he had been recently forced out
of Kuwait by the coalition, his vast military force was by no means
disabled. Yet Kurdish fighters, called *peshmerga* (translated: "one who
faces death"), rose up and successfully established Kurdish authority
in their regions of northern Iraq. Great victory parties were held as
town after town and city after city was liberated from the dominating
Arabs.

In Berlin, Jane and I had attended the Kurdish New Year fes-
tivities on March 23, 1991. A great map had been projected on the
screen depicting the Kurdish city of Mosul completely surrounded
by peshmerga. A deafening cheer had risen up as the three thousand
people anticipated freedom for their people—a Kurdistan free from
foreign domination. But their joy was short-lived.

A typical Kurdish wedding in Berlin.
Flute, drum, dancing and food.

Within days, the devastating news began coming in over the BBC. We sat in our small apartment and grieved as we heard of Iraqi helicopter gunships firing relentlessly on columns of fleeing civilians. The cities of Erbil, Sulaymaniyah, Zakho, and Kirkuk were reconquered by vengeful Iraqi troops. Entire cities were vacated as residents fled the merciless Iraqi army. Within the single short month of March 1991, the Kurds had risen up and established their freedom only to be subsequently ravaged. Their freedom has lasted but a few precious days.

As we listened to the radio during that time of chaos, our hearts were deeply moved. We had grown to love the Kurdish people during our three-year residence in Berlin, Germany. Berlin's central district of Kreuzberg had tens of thousands of resettled Turkish Kurds. They had tales of oppression, of political injustices, of suffering. Their language, which was forbidden to learn or even speak in Turkey, was taught openly at the Free University of Berlin. We were able to study their language Kurmanji, in the local cultural centers. This was all in preparation to better share the love of God with them. First, we had had to learn German, and then by speaking with Kurdish refugees, we wanted to learn Kurdish. Now as their suffering in the mountains of Iraq increased, we prayed, *Lord, how can we help? What are the needs?*

The front of our apartment house in Berlin (1988).

The view out the back windows of the apartment. Some of the buildings in Kreuzberg, Berlin hadn't been touched since the end of WWII when 50% of the city was destroyed.

Within days, the answer came during a conversation with an associate in Operation Mobilization. He phoned us from England and explained that several charitable organizations in Europe were combining resources to mount a relief effort. Franklin Graham, of Samaritan's Purse, had funded the effort and rented vehicles for the work. Drivers were needed for a convoy of trucks that would leave within the week. After a week's driving, they would arrive in eastern Turkey.

After talking with my wife and praying together, we decided it would be the best use of our energies and gifts to fly to Istanbul, join up with a local Canadian friend, Clarke Gourlay, and travel east by bus to the city of Diyarbakir. The team of volunteer drivers in their convoy could connect with us once we had surveyed the situation. We could then decide where the relief goods should be delivered, and how we could serve.

It took the volunteers and their trucks and Ford transits seven full days and nights of difficult driving from northern Europe to reach the remote eastern border of Turkey. Other organizations had flown supplies into eastern Turkey, only to have Turkish customs hold everything at the airport for four or five days. Meanwhile, children were dying from exposure and sickness in the snow-covered mountains.

The relief effort was renamed Mercy for All[1] to reflect the motivation for assisting. It was the seed of a new relief and development agency, a new nongovernment organization (NGO). Christians throughout Europe and America had responded with donations of tents, medicine, and food. As the relief effort got underway, personnel were needed to not only deliver the supplies but also to stay in the haphazard camps and help. It was an exhausting journey of thirty hours, made interesting only by the ancient sights we could make out through the dirty bus windows. Together with Clarke, we became part of this new NGO.

At four o'clock in the morning, the bus finally reached the ancient eastern Turkish city outskirts of Diyarbakir and pulled into

---

[1.] Pseudonym

the *Otogar* (bus depot) and discharged its weary passengers. Taxi drivers scrambled furiously as they competed for our fare into the city center. *Three North Americans in Diyarbakir*—that was a thing to behold. My wife and I crawled into the backseat of a dirty little yellow sedan and listened to Clarke. He was in the front passenger seat arguing vigorously in Turkish about the price for cab fare.

"The meter is defective," the driver seemed to be saying, as he pointed to the darkened device. Jane and I were too tired to care; we just wanted to see a pillow.

"Then stop the car," Clarke countered. "We will get out and get a taxi with a working meter." Amazingly enough, the meter was instantly fixed; it lit up and began clicking away. "I really enjoy this," Clarke said in English as he turned to face us. "It's great language practice." He didn't seem to enjoy the final price, however, which was increased due to the night rate and other unexplained surcharges. Clarke put on his best dissatisfied expression and paid the driver. The driver complained vehemently, of course, but accepted the payment and drove off, outwardly upset but inwardly content. It was all part of saving face, which is critical to all bargaining in Turkey. Even so, the twenty-minute ride cost us just 25,000 Turkish lira, or six US dollars.

We drug our weary bodies into bed in a run-down hotel (three US dollars a night) on the outskirts of Diyarbakir. It was a quarter past four in the morning. It mattered little to us that the mattresses were worn, the common shower ran with cold water, and the room was covered with a layer of dirt and grime. We were exhausted. Soon we would meet up with the convoy and discover the next step in the journey.

It seemed we had just slipped into bed when the sun began its rise. The silence was broken by a distorted loud speaker calling out in Arabic, for everyone to pray. It was another reminder just how different life is in a Muslim land. We listened to the recitation, "God is great… Prayer is better than sleep…," and then we bowed to pray from the depths of our hearts. It was not a ritual prayer we prayed but a groaning from our souls, a plea for the hundreds of thousands of refugees freezing in the mountains. They were without tents, blankets, food, and health care, and soon they would perish.

God, protect the downtrodden. Bring justice to the oppressed. Feed the hungry. Give shelter to the refugee. Lord, this is our prayer. In Jesus's name, amen.

Chapter 2

Eastern Turkey, Refugee Camps on the Mountain Border

This is the solemn pronouncement of the Holy One, the
True One, who holds the key of David, who opens doors
no one can shut, and shuts doors no one can open.

—Revelations 3:7

First Week of April 1991

Diyarbakir is the largest city in eastern Turkey, fondly called
the capital of Kurdistan by local Kurds, although Kurdistan
as a country does not exist. The ancient city is surrounded
by a black basalt wall dating back to AD 330 and is largely intact. Its
market is a bustle of activity every day of the week. As you get closer
to the central mosque in the old city, the crowds become so dense
you can hardly walk. A feel of excitement, of activity, and of the wild
frontier imbues the streets.

We found several United Nations High Commissioner for
Refugees (UNHCR) vehicles parked in front of a nice hotel at a
major intersection near the city center. The UNHCR had set up
a makeshift office in a hotel to coordinate its relief effort. A block
away, at the Turistik Hotel, a press office was installed. Over two

hundred journalists were reportedly in the city, trying to capture the latest news. But the closest refugee camps were over four hours away. I couldn't quite understand why the journalists were in Diyarbakir when the crisis was in the mountains. Then I discovered the reason; they did not want to stay in some remote village. So they hired taxis to take them on the four-hour trip to the camps on the border, where they would write their stories. Then they were driven back to the relative comfort of Diyarbakir. The big city was also the only place they could reliably communicate with the rest of the world. We were told to attend a UNHCR meeting that evening to get a briefing on the current situation.

"Where are most of the relief supplies going, and where is the need the greatest?" we asked at the meeting.

"Clearly," the official explained, "most groups are assisting at the most accessible location along the border, four hours south of here, near the town of Silopi. That is where all of the journalists are. There is a two-lane paved highway that leads there, making it relatively simple to truck in supplies. But further east, where there are no major roads, there is next to no one helping." It was obvious where we must go. As we talked with one another and then telephoned the director of Mercy for All, Julyan Lidstone, it was decided to send the convoy to the small town of Hakkari, located at the southeast corner of Turkey.

I had read a description of Hakkari in an old travel guide:

> The absolute, positive dead end of Turkey is Hakarri [hah-KAH-ree], (population 25,000, altitude 1,700 meters), 210 km south of Van, over a zigzagging mountain road. The scenery is spectacular. However, there is often trouble in these regions and the newspapers are full of items about Turkish border guards being killed by smugglers and Kurdish separatists.

Back in Germany, Jane and I, as we sought to understand Kurdish culture, had watched a 1983 film *A Season in Hakkari*. It depicted a teacher who traveled to this remote village, where there was no electricity, no paved roads, and no education.

This was our destination. We found the public bus and began the four-hour drive from Diyarbakir to Hakkari.

Along the bus route to Hakkari, we met a very helpful carpet seller in the ancient Kurdish city of Van. As he haggled with customers over carpet prices, I was amazed that he spoke over a wireless telephone. I'd never seen such a device. How on earth could a guy selling carpets on the edge of the earth afford such a luxury item? I wondered. We sat down on rickety wooden stools and had the customary glasses of strong tea, loaded with cubes of sugar, that always proceed a business transaction. At first, we were just interested in his amazing display of carpets. As we chatted, however, he quickly understood our purposes and gave us a single name to contact in Hakkari if we needed help.

"Go to the Fuji Foto shop in Hakarri," he said. "The man working there will help you."

The following day, after the rugged journey up through the mountains to Hakkari, Clarke, Jane, and I were desperate to find lodging. We sought out the contact in the photo shop. Not only would we need a place for the night, but we would need lodging for truck drivers and relief workers once the convoy arrived. We wandered up and down the dusty streets looking for a Fuji Foto sign where the friend of our friend worked. Men walking in Hakkari carried sidearms. Donkeys and crude carts crowded the dirt-and-mud streets. Buildings were made of rough stones, plastered with mud, and had crude poplar logs for roofs. It seemed every other person was a soldier.

"This really is the wild west," I said to Jane.

We found the photo-developing shop and went inside. It was dark and musty.

"We are looking for a place to stay," we explained in broken Kurdish to an elderly man. He wore a long beard and mustache. His face was lined with deep wrinkles.

It looked like it was going to be impossible to find lodging. The mountain town was overflowing with the Turkish police and military anxious about Kurdish rebel activity in the region. The few western reporters who had arrived were paying big money for the meager hotel facilities, and prices had been hiked accordingly. We had been told there were no vacancies for the three of us, not to mention for the many drivers and workers who were coming in the convoy. We had to plan for up to thirty people, considering not just the drivers but the additional aid workers coming.

In addition to lodging, we needed a place to unload and transfer all of the relief goods. The author of our guidebook considered Hakkari the utter end of the earth and apparently hadn't dreamed anybody would attempt to venture any further. But our destination was actually a good four-hour drive up dirt and gravel mountain roads to the tiny village of Çukurca. And we faced another problem. There was simply no way the large trucks carrying supplies, could maneuver up the steep dirt switchbacks fully loaded. That meant we had to find a small shop in Hakarri to serve as a warehouse. The large trucks could then off-load their supplies in the warehouse in Hakarri, and our team's smaller Ford Transit vans could make multiple trips up the mountains with the relief supplies.

"We came to help the Kurds," I told the old Kurd in the photo shop, quietly praying he could lead us to some sort of housing. Slowly and painstakingly, I explained in Kurdish who we were, what we were doing, and, finally, what we needed. His face began to light up.

He reached underneath the dusty counter and produced stacks of freshly developed pictures of the camps. There were photos of big vegetable trucks with men clamoring all over them and fighting for loaves of bread. There were children without shoes wading through a sea of mud. Weary women were wearing all their clothes and carrying huge bundles of belongings as they climbed the hillsides. It was a disaster that pictures and words simply could not begin to convey.

The human crisis was very much on the heart of the old man, and he was personally involved doing all he could to alleviate the suffering, as were many of the Kurds in Hakkari. He spoke to his colleagues in the tiny shop for some minutes.

After some discussion with them, he said to us in Kurdish, "Come, you will stay in my home." I was at once surprised and grateful. But then I thought of our team of truck drivers and their convoy of trucks, which would arrive the following day.

Without my saying a word, he continued, "When you need more space, my family will move up into the mountains, and you can use the whole house." Unbelievable!

The day before, we had asked dozens of people if there was a place available and had been told repeatedly there was nothing whatsoever.

"The Turkish army and police are using every empty building," we'd been told. But Clarke had been asking people these questions using Turkish. Clarke had lived in Turkey for a number of years and spoke Turkish fluently. People could understand him because all Kurds living in Turkey are required to learn Turkish, the national language, in school. Speaking Kurdish was forbidden and punishable by imprisonment. It was unlawful to even utter the word *Kurd*. The people living in eastern Turkey were called "mountain Turks" by the media and the government.

On the second afternoon, when my wife and I were wandering the streets together, we began conversing with some locals in the local dialect of Kurmanji, Kurdish. We knew the language was strictly illegal, but we didn't speak or understand Turkish, and the locals certainly didn't speak English or German. So how else were we to communicate? They were so enamored by the foreigners who spoke their forbidden language they insisted on finding a solution to our problem. Small crowds gathered around us and were eager to help.

One man offered us the use of the only remaining empty shop in town so we could unload and store the relief supplies. That would also give us space to organize the materials. It had all been stuffed into the big trucks and needed to be sorted. Then we could split the material in half so that we could send two teams in the smaller vehicles to operate in two separate encampments.

While we stood in the dirt roadway talking to these strangers, a dump truck drove up and stopped. We were at first confused. The driver indicated we should climb up into the cab, which we did. We had no idea who he was and where he would take us. But we felt God was guiding us.

He drove a few blocks to a shop on the outskirts of town. We climbed down and met an older Kurdish man, who directed us to a dusty storefront shop. The glass store front was probably only sixteen feet across, but it was a deep concrete structure that would hold everything we had transported from Europe. He explained to us that we could use it for as long as needed, without cost. We were amazed at the hospitality and generosity of people who possessed so little.

We were then driven up into the hills on the outskirts of Hakkari and let out at a simple Kurdish home, where we were welcomed to stay. It was a five room house, constructed with rock and mud, and the flat roof was made from huge poplar poles laid across the outer walls. The surface of the gently slanting roof was flat hardened mud and was used in the very hot summers as a place to dry vegetables and also to sleep. In the center room was a wood burning stove for cooking and also for heating during the freezing winters. There were just a few small windows to allow light to enter. All the floors were covered with beautiful hand woven wool carpets. The walls had no decorations and there was virtually no furniture. It was perfect.

Having established a place for the team to live; and for the supplies to be warehoused, Clarke, Jane, and I boarded a bus for the long journey back to the northern city of Van. We had established the Kurdish city of Van as a good location to rendezvous with the string of trucks bringing relief. We rejoiced at God's provisions. There is no feeling like coming to God with an enormous challenge and seeing Him supply in an indescribable way.

As the bus dropped us at a major intersection in Van, we began our search for our agreed upon meeting place, the Hotel Asur. We had no maps or directions.

"There are two kinds of hotels in eastern Turkey, Jane," I said. "One star and two star."

"What's the difference between them?" she asked.

"The two-star hotels have clean sheets." The Hotel Asur was a two-star by this definition. It also had a decent shower, for which Jane was especially grateful. Had she known it would be her last decent shower for the next five weeks, she might have felt different about it. She certainly would have showered longer. After cleaning up we went down to the lobby to ask about our passports, which are routinely taken from guests by the hotel clerks in Turkey when they lodge.

"I hear English being spoken," Jane exclaimed. We rushed outside and saw the first of the weary truck drivers climbing from their vehicles. Joyfully, we welcomed them and gathered together to discuss plans. A traveling team member then explained to us that one of the Ford transit vehicles had driven on ahead of the rest of the convoy. The Ford was an excellent vehicle for carrying seven adults plus some luggage. It could navigate the gravel roads and the sharp switchbacks in the mountainous terrain. They wanted to scout out the roadway to two needy encampments besides two Kurdish villages: Çukurca [*choo-KER-jah*], [Çelê in Kurdish] and Uzumlu [*oo-ZOOM-loo*]. These are the Turkish names given to them. Villages in eastern Turkey have two names: the Kurdish names of origin which the residents use and the Turkish names that have been officially assigned them. All the signs and maps use the Turkish names of course.

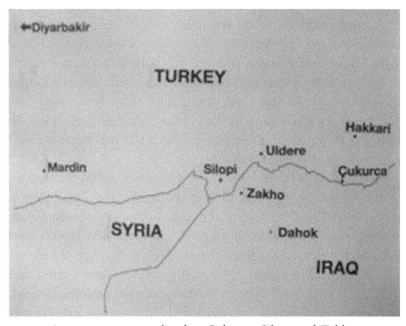

At various times we lived in Çukurca, Silopi and Zakho.

Mercy for All was able to use several of these Ford Transit vehicles
to ferry people and supplies to the mountain villages of Çukurca
and Uzumlu. They drove all the way from Belgium to Iraq.

It was midnight when the relief workers returned from their
scouting trip to Uzumlu and Çukurca. Both villages sit right on the
Turkish/Iraq border. It was reported that both places were in desperate need of help. Taken together, there were well over two hundred
thousand people in these two camps alone. Our mountain of supplies would be but a drop in the bucket considering the incredible
need. But it would be a beginning. About ten volunteers would be
sent to each of the villages to live.

Our next consideration was travel permissions. We couldn't simply drive a convoy of trucks up into the mountains. The region was
under martial law, because of the ongoing battle between Kurdish
separatists and the Turkish army and local police. The further southeast one traveled, the tighter the restrictions became. There were
military checkpoints all along the route, at every intersection, river,
bridge, and settlement. They were designed to inhibit movement of
the Kurdish resistance. In fact, it was forbidden for foreigners to travel
here. Locals were routinely searched and arrested if their IDs were

insufficient or if they were carrying contraband. The US embassy in Ankara, Turkey's capital, regularly issued warnings for Americans to stay out of the region because of terrorist activities, hostage taking, and the perpetual state of war.

Because of the refugee crisis on the border, however, we hoped the Turkish officials would permit us access. It was in the city of Van where we would try and learn as much as possible about travel restrictions and security prior to beginning the journey with an entire team and tons of supplies. A trail of conversations with locals led us finally back to the same shop full of dusty carpets and our old friend with the fancy phone.

The city of Van is famous for its beautiful handwoven Kurdish carpets. We sat again on the same low bench surrounded by carpets of every size and description, waiting patiently for the proprietor to assist us. He was extremely busy seeing customers and pacing back and forth as he talked on his wireless phone. Tea was brought in shortly, and we sat together, making small talk in Kurdish.

In the market areas, young boys were employed to carry hot tea and bowls of sugar cubes to the various businesses in their vicinity and return later for the glasses. The store owner pays the boy for the tea the customers consume. We felt we had drunk gallons of tea, as we went from shop to shop making our purchases in preparation for our extended stay in the mountains. There were no department stores, and each item we needed was found in a different shop. The gas stoves were in the stove shop, the gas bottles in a different shop, the aluminum pots in a special shop, and the plastic bowls in the plastic shop. And on and on it went.

Since we were foreigners and guests in their city and were visiting their shop for the first time, it was imperative we sit and accept glasses of tea. They were especially insistent when we spoke Kurdish with them. They had never met a foreigner before who spoke their mother tongue. In Kurdish culture, it is the host who is honored when he receives a guest. And it was most important for us to joyfully receive their kindness and hospitality to establish friendship and trust. Gift-giving and receiving is foundational in establishing a relationship in Kurdish culture.

As it turned out, our friend the carpet salesman was also responsible for a relief effort mounted by the Kurds living in Van. They were making great sacrifices to assist the Kurds from Iraq. They considered them kin, more so than the Turks who reigned in their region of Turkey. Since the Turkish media is controlled and censored by the government, the work of Turkish Kurds in assisting the relief effort was not reported in national papers. The people of Van drove their own trucks on the sixteen-hour trip to and from the border to deliver supplies flown in to the Van airport. That was the nearest large Turkish airport to the crisis. These local volunteers charged nothing for their services. We asked the carpet salesman if he could help arrange travel papers for us as we drove into the region.

"I have an appointment with the subgovernor of Van in two hours," he said. "I will bring it up."

We were awed at how quickly everything was happening. Truly, God was guiding us in a unique way. He was opening the doors in a region that was truly closed. We got the papers that very afternoon and then continued our major shopping spree to outfit our two teams for survival on the border. We decided we would camp in one of the tents the convoy had brought from Europe; cook our food using small Turkish propane stoves; and eat rice, beans, spaghetti, and other local foods. A few simple vegetables, in season of course, would be available in the village near the border, and we could send someone to Hakkari to buy other essentials as needed. Even if Hakkari was "the end of the earth," it still was a far cry from Çukurca or Uzumlu. In Hakkari you could buy gasoline, propane for cooking, and things like a can opener.

Buying gas for the trucks was going to be a major problem. With no automotive gas for sale in the village of Çukurca, we had to drive four hours to the nearest station and four hours back just to fill the tank up! And that left very little to use if we had an emergency trip to take. We solved the problem by getting a five-gallon gas can. Then the supply team would deliver it to us, full, when they brought us other replenishments.

The second village where Mercy for All was working, Uzumlu, had a road that was so deteriorated that the team had to hitchhike on a dump truck or borrow a four-wheel drive pickup just to get to the camp. The official Mercy for All headquarters in Uzumlu was set up in a tent in a field adjacent to large overcrowded hospital tents. When the volunteers arrived, they set to work immediately.

"What needs to be done?" they asked those already at work. The field hospital requested help with all sorts of tasks.

"Clear away all this medical waste," a nurse requested. The urgent needs were unending.

Airdrop relief sometimes landed in minefields, where children and adults were injured trying to get to the supplies.

The team coordinator wrote in his journal, "We rejoiced on this our tenth day because twenty-four hours have passed without anyone being blown up. The whole region had been mined by the Iraqis."

But, at times, the greatest adversary seemed to be the weather. A week before our arrival, snow had covered the mountainsides. The snow had melted and drenching rains began. It was still nearly freezing at night, and the rains made everything a horrendous muddy mess.

A terrible wind and rainstorm blew up around midnight during the first week of our stay in April. Winters in the Kurdish mountains are harsh, with snow, wind, rain, and ice. One of the hospital tents, although staked to the ground, blew clean away, exposing its inhabitants to the vicious storm. Those lying on army cots were drenched in the icy rain.

The adjacent tent was full of infants. They were all receiving intravenous feedings because of dehydration (the results of diarrhea), and the IV bottles were hung from the tent frame above their cots. There were no IV poles available for so many patients. The IV bottles with their tubing swung back and forth violently as the tent shook from the powerful winds. Team members rushed inside just as the entire structure began lifting off the ground. If it blew away, the needles and bandages from all the babies would be ripped from their little arms. Volunteers jumped up and grabbed the overhead poles of the tent and hung on with their combined weight. The winds blew, and the tent still began to rise. One inch, two inches…

"Oh God," they cried out, "You are over heaven and earth. You can stop the raging storm! Spare this tent for the sake of these children!" The moments seemed eternal as the winds continued to blow.

Slowly, the torrent died down. Had the gusts been but a bit stronger, the tent would have disappeared down the mountain. God had, indeed, heard their prayers and spared the infants.

The Village of Çukurca, Turkey.

The Çukurca team was located further east along the border. It set up its tent on a level slip of earth against a hillside, just below the barracks of the Turkish army. A small creek ran along the east end of the plateau. Meals were cooked out in the open. A makeshift latrine was made by digging a hole and then pounding in four six-foot poles into the earth. These were wrapped with some of the plastic that was transported in the convoy, for a sense of privacy. The Turkish soldiers were constantly overlooking our camp, making it impossible for the women on the team to bathe. We had absolutely no privacy.

Jane and Kirk on the Iraqi border with the Mercy for All team.

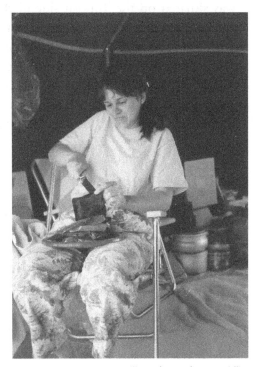

Jane opens an MRE ("meal, ready to eat").

Kirk finds a quiet spot for some time in the Word.

The team was situated on the Turkish side of the border; we were not permitted to set up camp inside Iraq. But we could walk over the ridge, which was the actual border, pass through an opening in the barbed wire and enter the valley where the refugees were living.

The team's first task amidst the refugees was to help people dig latrines. The mud and waste problem was even more acute in that enormous valley because people's makeshift shelters were so closely situated. Nothing could stay clean. Within a three-kilometer-long valley resided an estimated 120,000 refugees. Our team began coordinating garbage pickup and began visiting refugees in their makeshift tents.

In both camps, people requested prayer for help from God. Kurds are a very spiritually oriented people and believe that God had allowed this to happen to them for a reason. Everyone who suffers invariably asks God, "Why?" Kurds believe that everything in their daily lives has spiritual, as well as physical, implications.

No other relief group working in the camps were addressing their spiritual concerns. There were a dozen relief agencies stationed in Çukurca. Their worldview was humanistic and secularized, acknowledging the natural world but denying the supernatural. They provided physical bread but refused to offer spiritual bread. As our team members prayed for the suffering Kurds and showed spiritual concern for their trauma, many requested Scriptures in Kurdish, Arabic, and English. They recognized that our volunteers—who came from America, Canada, Holland, England, Germany, Switzerland, Belgium, Korea, and other nations—had sacrificed personally to give to complete strangers. They wanted to know our motives; they wanted to hear our hearts. They could see that though we were all from different countries we were united as a team.

Mercy for All team: camped about Çukurca, Turkey. Pictured here are Koreans, Germans, a Dutchman, Americans, and a Turk. Members came and went as they were able.

Mercy for All also established a Food for Work program and distributed commodities as payment to over 250 volunteer refugee employees. Refugees worked throughout the camps as translators, doctors, nurses, education workers, etc. with other agencies. But there had been no system of remuneration for their work; they had been unpaid volunteers. This worked fine during the first weeks of the crisis, but as systems began to develop, it became imperative that they be paid somehow. The UNHCR forbade cash payments to refugees because it would offend the Turkish authorities and had historically proven to create more problems than it resolved. Some suggested that rice, flour, beans, tea, and sugar be used as payment. This suggestion received approval. The refugees that were working for the nongovernment agencies during the day were unable to stand in lines to collect their rations so they were paid in food subsidies. Practically, however, the food as payment served as a supplement; there was always some relative who collected the family's food ration for them if the head of household was occupied.

During our second week in Çukurca, there was an outbreak of cholera in the camp. Sanitary conditions were deplorable, and the risk of an epidemic was high. The cold rains of April were gone, and, suddenly, it was getting very warm. The unsanitary filth (there were few latrines) led to contaminated water. A French medical team was consumed with the task of establishing an isolation unit to contain the disease. Mercy for All members went to the areas where cholera patients were living, and sprayed a liquid chlorine solution on bedding and their tents, to suppress the bacteria.

Mercy for All team member prepares to spray
chlorine after the outbreak of cholera.

Additional medical services were needed, particularly deep in the valley within Iraq. Mothers were too weak to carry their sick babies the three kilometers up the mountain to the clinic. The heat during the day became unbearable; the terrain was difficult, and resting along the way was impossible with no shade. When the sick did reach the medical tents at the crest of the mountain, just inches from the Turkish border, they had to wait at least forty-five minutes to be seen.

No Iraqi Kurds were allowed to cross the border into Turkey. Our international team could walk up the hill from Turkey and enter into Iraq through the guarded gate in the barbed-wire fence, but Kurds could not leave Iraq. The Turkish military had established machine gun nests and armed guards all along the barbed-wire fence to insure no one crossed illegally. These Kurds were literally caught between Iraq and a hard place. Turkey is a hard place to be a Kurd. It is even harder if one is a Kurd from Iraq trying to get into Turkey.

A Kurdish woman prepares flat bread, surrounded by her family. An estimated 120,000 people had filled this valley at the top of the mountain between Turkey and Iraq.

American army medics, stationed there with the US Special Forces, were doing everything in their power to alleviate the suffering in the camps. Several medics were treating patients in a crude shelter three kilometers down the valley into Iraq. When we asked them about safety for the Iraqi Kurds camped in the valley and NGO's at work on the border, we were told that Iraqi tanks were twenty-five miles away. We were assured that the US Army was also out there pushing the Iraqis further south.

Some medical procedures require unique skills the army could not address. Such was the case with an infant brought to a make-shift shelter deep in the valley. It was no more than a blanket on the ground and a shade tarp tied to trees overhead. The medics were attempting to treat the sick here because patients were too sick to climb mountain slope up to the Turkish border where the French medical team was working.

"Medics are great," said one US soldier to me. "And we get lots of training in a broad variety of things. But some things are better performed by a specialist." Starting an IV in a seriously dehydrated infant was one of them.

That very day a specialized medical team arrived with Mercy for All and set to work. The team had come from Seoul, Korea, sent out by Yongi Cho's[1] enormous church. The Korean team leader was the chief pediatrician at the largest hospital in Seoul. The very afternoon the Koreans arrived, they surveyed the camp and found three babies dying of dehydration. The army medics that had been unable to start IVs in them rejoiced when the pediatrician succeeded. It meant a chance to survive for those babies. The army medics present quickly radioed in for a Chinook helicopter. They had a landing zone (LZ) up on the hillside inside of Turkey. The chopper flew over the ridge into the valley in Iraq near where the babies were located. Then they flew the infants with their mothers to a simple medical clinic over the hill and down the mountain to the town of Çukurca.

[1.] David Yungi Cho (formerly known as Paul Yungi Cho) is a South Korean Christian minister. He is a senior pastor and the founder of the Yoido Full Gospel Church (Assemblies of God), the world's largest congregation, with a claimed membership of 830,000 (as of 2007).
http://en.wikipedia.org/wiki/David_Yonggi_Cho

Inside a chinook helicopter. Jane at left, Kirk in the center.

Remarkably, Turkish believers from Istanbul also joined Mercy for All to work alongside the other volunteers and minister to refugees. Considering the strong animosity of Turks for Kurds, and vice versa, it was truly a miracle of grace that these men left their jobs, traveled fourteen hundred miles, endured the harsh conditions, and ministered in love to a people their fellow citizens feared and hated. Turkish television always identified Kurds as terrorists. "Mountain Turks" were enemies of the state. Everyone knew, however, Kurds were actually a different race, spoke a different language, and had a different culture. For these Turks to reach out in love to Kurds was a very powerful testimony.

In stark contrast the Turkish doctors of the Red Crescent, which is the equivalent of the Red Cross in Muslim countries, had refused to enter the refugee camp to conduct immunizations.

"We will go under one condition," they said. "US soldiers must be with us to offer us protection." It was a ridiculous demand, but it showed the genuine fear that even educated Turks have of average Kurdish people.

A Turkish Christian, however, a pastor and Assyrian by birth, traveled by himself from Istanbul to help Mercy for All's work in the camp. He was especially concerned for the spiritual nurture of both the Assyrians and of the Kurds. Perfect love casts out fear.

"I would like to hold a church service in the camp," he told me on the day of his arrival. "God be with you," I said. "With the secular forces of the relief committee arrayed against any spiritual input in the camp, I truly doubt if it can be done." His English was not very good, so he probably didn't even understand my skeptical response. As the team leader for Mercy for All in Çukurca, I met each afternoon for a briefing with the heads of the other agencies working with the refugees. Their cynicism and disdain for the values of Mercy for All were openly discussed. Christians were not welcome.

The following morning, he went straight to the refugee tribal leaders within the camp. He talked with the Orthodox priest who himself was a refugee and obtained his permission. I suppose it never even occurred to our Assyrian coworker to ask the UNHCR. It was just as well. They would surely have suppressed his plans. On Sunday morning, three hundred people gathered around a large tent to hear him preach. The refugee priest gave an introduction and a welcome; they sang some hymns, and the Istanbul pastor preached the gospel. Perhaps two-thirds of the crowd were Kurds, listening in as the service progressed. It was likely the very first time they had heard the message of Jesus's love.

One of our team members named Joop was from Holland. He was fluent in Arabic, and he gathered dozens of children about him and told them Bible stories. It was clear the refugees were longing for a supernatural explanation for their crisis. As I heard stories of hearts opened to the love of God, I was reminded of the ending in the life of Joseph. He'd been sold into slavery by his brothers, falsely accused and thrown into prison by the Pharaoh of Egypt, and then later rose to save both Egyptians and Hebrews from a seven-year famine.

"You intended to harm me, but God intended it for good to accomplish what is now being done, the saving of many lives."[1] The genocide perpetuated by Saddam had done great harm, but had also

---

[1.] Genesis 50:20, NIV

opened the door for the preaching of the gospel to a people scattered by war.

A US chinook helicopter prepares to lower a pallet of food.
Initially food and water were dropped with parachutes.
Sometimes, in people's eagerness to get to the falling
food, they were injured or killed by the heavy pallets.

President George Bush ordered the largest relief effort ever
to feed the refugees fleeing from Saddam Hussein.

Looking toward Turkey (Çukurca) from the Iraqi
border where the refugees were stranded.

At the beginning of May, the weather began to change rapidly in the mountain valley. The extremes of winter gave way to the
extremes of summer with little cushion for spring. By midday, it was
quite uncomfortable. Fires for burning garbage were lit only at night,
filling the valley with a gray smoky haze.

Many refugees began to think more and more about returning
to their homes, but they were anxious about the vengeful Iraqi army.
Many had seen their homes destroyed three or four times during
their lives. Their fields had been burned, their orchards destroyed.
Even their wells and been poisoned.

Each morning since Mercy for All had come to help, I joined the
Kurdish community leaders for a joint leadership meeting in a long
low tent, pitched in Iraq near the barbed-wire border. Each Kurdish
tribe residing in the camp sent their leader to represent them. The
US Special Forces captain was also present. None of the other NGO's
came; they had their own meeting in a building in Çukurca in the

afternoons. Inevitably, the talk would turn toward guarantees for safety.

"Is it safe for us to return?" they asked the US Army captain repeatedly. They wanted concrete assurances. "Will the American military stay and protect us if we bring our families back to our bombed-out villages?"

And each morning, the captain gave a carefully worded response. The captain was conscious of their fears and yet wise enough not to make any promises that he could not fulfill. "That is a political decision, which will be made in Washington by people much higher than me," he replied. "I am just a military man on a mountain in Iraq, and what I think matters very little. But I will convey your concerns to my superiors." He did not want to raise their hopes too high, for there was no indication that Washington would offer any protection at all for the homeless Kurds. US President George Bush had launched Operation Provide Comfort to help stave off the disaster of two million Kurdish refugees. The Iraqi Kurds had risen up against Saddam at the end of the Gulf War at the behest of the US (according to the Kurds). But they had been savagely slaughtered and forced into exile. But what next? Where were they to go from here? How would Washington respond?

Finally, one morning the captain had progress to report.

"Tomorrow, we will fly two helicopters to your villages so that you can see that they are safe. You choose reliable men to represent your people, and they can report to you themselves what they see. Then you can decide if it is safe to return."

It was an excellent strategy that could not have come a bit sooner. If the men could at least see with their own eyes that the Iraqi army was gone, they would feel better about returning to their homes. People could begin to leave the mountains before the extreme summer heat set in and before water shortages became severe.

"But what guarantee do we have that Saddam will not turn right around and attack us once we are home again?"

"My home has been bombed five times," said one man. "How can you promise me Iraqi planes will not come and destroy it again if I rebuild?"

"I cannot promise you that Saddam will not return," replied the captain. "And anyone who says he can promise you that is deceiving you. No one can offer that kind of guarantee."

Eventually, however, the idea of safe havens was agreed upon in Washington and by the UN security council. They prohibited Iraqi aircraft from flying north of the 36th parallel to protect the Kurds, and south of the 32nd parallel—to protect the Shiites [*SHEE-ites*], who lived in the south of Iraq. The US, Britain, and NATO troops also established major transit camps outside the Iraqi city of Zakho, which lies just across the Turkish border town of Silopi. Additional transit camps were built along the routes to the Kurdish north. These gave Kurds an assurance of safety and logistic support as they returned to their homes.

The transit camps were key in solving the logistical nightmare of moving a million people back to their homes. There were neither roads nor vehicles that could carry the people directly back to their homes in Iraq. The Caucasus mountains stood in the way. They had walked through the mountain passes on trails from the mountains in northern Iraq, to get to the Turkish border. The only way for them to travel safely back to Iraq would be in vehicles. So they would have to board buses, dump trucks, or whatever vehicles were available and make an eight-hour circuitous trip through southeastern Turkey, crossing back over into Iraq near the Turkish town of Silopi, where there was a bridge that crossed the river.

A transit camp would be built outside the small Iraqi city of Zakho, where they could rest, obtain supplies, get medical treatment if needed, and even remain for a longer period of time if their village were not yet secure. Many wells had to be decontaminated, towns cleared of mines, and, of course, homes reconstructed before the following winter.

As news of the Zakho transit camp spread among the refugees, more and more families decided that the risk of returning home to Iraq was better than dying of disease or heat exhaustion in the mountains. Dawn of each new day saw convoys of vehicles winding their way over the treacherous dirt roads on the Turkish-Iraqi border. From the mountain ridge, I looked down at the huge open trucks in the valley below that were full of people and their meager belongings. The Mercy for All leadership, including Jane and myself, began considering how we could support the returning refugees on their journey.

After consulting with other agencies, talking with our Mercy for All leadership, and praying for guidance, Jane and I desired to turn the leadership of our Çukurca team over to others and go to northern Iraq.

Late one afternoon in early May, Julyan Lidstone traveled to Çukurca from Ankara, where he was directing much of the recruiting of volunteers. He was my direct supervisor within Mercy for All. I told him of my heart's desire to go with the Kurds to their homes in Iraq.

He said, "Let's go for a walk." That was Julyan's way of having a serious talk.

As we walked along the dirt roadway and looked upon the mass exodus of people, I told him how we could see the camp shrinking and how the need was now in Iraq. Mercy for All was a new organization and was just finding its feet. Turkey was the only place it was working. Julyan had lived and worked in Turkey and felt good about the work we were doing. He said he wanted me to remain in Çukurca to train and lead volunteers as they arrived. He could read the disappointment on my face. (I have never been able to hide my feelings in my facial expressions.) He and I concluded our walk by standing side by side, looking out over the mountains, and praying about the immediate future of the work. Jane and I accepted the disappointing decision; however, we believe in submitting to authority.

The following morning, Julyan brought me surprising news that Mercy for All had cleared us to move across into Iraq. It would be the second country that Mercy for All would operate in. He had been in contact with the head office, which had been established in Sweden. Mr. Bertil Engqvist, of OM Sweden, had worked from the beginning in gathering relief material. Julyan and Bertil had decided they wanted Jane and me to lead the effort into Iraq. We would depart as soon as possible. We did not have much to pack since we'd been living out of one duffle bag and sleeping on the ground in a tent.

The US Army and others were constructing the transit camp in Zakho, Iraq, at record speed, but they intended to withdraw and turn the work entirely over to nongovernment organizations (NGOs). And that meant us and others like us. But what would we do? Where would we live? How would we live? Those were all unanswered questions.

We had, providentially, landed right in the middle of a joint-forces effort to alleviate the suffering of the Kurds. We were not alone in working with the Kurds. There were at least ten other NGOs working in Çukurca alone. On top of that were all four US armed services and a broad multinational force. This joint endeavor did everything possible to facilitate NGOs in their work. Mercy for All received all types of logistic assistance, as did other NGOs. For example, the Korean medical team was flown in by a military helicopter from Diyarbakir—right into the rugged mountainside above Çukurca! They landed in the LZ that had been set up in a circle with rocks painted white. I was privately jealous as I reflected on our own lengthy overland journeys.

On May 13, 1991, Jane and I were also blessed by the military's assistance. We climbed aboard a German mosquito helicopter and lifted off about midday. The helicopter had room for just six people, or it could be outfitted to handle their crew of three and a stretcher. It had no armaments and was equipped for medical evacuation flights (medivacs).

Our pilot had never flown in the region along the Turkish and Iraqi border before and was pleased that we could speak German. He had, in fact, had some trouble finding Çukurca on his way into the crude landing zone on the hillside. His navigator was even more pleased to see that I had hand-drawn maps with the refugee camps on them. His topographic maps were useful, but the mountains were so remote that there were no navigational aids like towns, lakes, or roads to establish one's bearings. He especially didn't want to fly over Iraqi territory. The German constitution at the time forbade the German military entering any airspace of non-NATO countries.

Peering out the convex window of the tiny helicopter, we could clearly see a convoy of vehicles winding their way along. I counted forty-two dump trucks and thirty-one buses, all packed to the gills with people and the few belongings they'd been able to carry. After forty-five minutes of the most spectacular scenery I have ever seen, we touched down in the parking lot area of an abandoned warehouse that had been converted by the combined military effort into a landing zone for a major military operation. The warehouse was just outside the rustic town of Silopi, Turkey. We gathered our bags and moved out from under the blast of the spinning chopper blades.

Across the two-lane highway from the warehouse, a US military tent city had gone up. The Iraqi border was just eight kilometers away. A Humvee sped by us, raising a cloud of dust. Directly before us was an enormous stockpile of meal-ready-to-eat (MRE) rations covering the entire end of the parking lot. I approached the soldier manning the crudely erected gate.

"We are from Mercy for All and headed to the city of Zakho. Can you give us some directions?" I wondered how far we would have to walk in the furnace-like heat. Shifting the two shoulder bags a bit, I set our suitcase with the laptop on the asphalt. It was the lightest computer on the market and weighed over twelve pounds. We were going to have to learn to travel lighter, I reminded myself for the zillionth time. The Iraqi city of Zakho was sixteen kilometers away.

"Go past the razor wire here." He waved his hand to the left. "Cross the street and wait by that sign down the road. A dark-green bus will be coming along anytime. It'll take you there."

I was dumbfounded. Bus service here, at the edge of nowhere! It was a US Army bus, and it only carried army personnel. They had made an exception to assist NGO personnel, however. Jane and I were grateful. We boarded and found seats.

As we sat down, I was impacted with the risk of the situation. The uncertainty of it all. The danger. The bus bumped along, approaching the Iraqi border. Looking through the front window of the bus, I could see a large concrete arch high above our heads, that spanned the road. It had Arabic letters on it. It was just a hundred or so yards ahead.

It suddenly hit me, *I didn't really know where we were going.* "Zakho" was little more than just a name. It meant no more to me than to most of the people who read this page. Where would we sleep? What would we eat? And of more immediate concern, where should we get off the bus? And then the final thought that hung in my mind, *What am I doing bringing my wife into Iraq, a country with whom our country just fought a war?* I looked at my beautiful petite wife. Her brunette hair, her lightly tanned skin and brown eyes, her pleasant trusting face. Silently, my heart turned to God as I questioned the wisdom of it all.

But then a peace settled over me, which I can only describe as the "peace that passes understanding."[1] I was confident that the God who had led us this far would not abandon us now. He is faithful.

I leaned forward to speak to the soldier seated in front of me. "Do you know where this bus goes?" I sheepishly asked.

"It makes several stops," he replied. "There are several camps set up, as well as the headquarters and army encampment. It's all spread out over four or five miles." I pictured Jane and myself with our seven bags walking for miles in the desert heat.

Then I remembered another organization that was setting up an outpatient dispensary. "Have you ever heard of a group called Global Partners?" I asked in a loud voice, hoping someone on the bus might overhear and respond.

Much to my surprise, the same soldier responded with a smile on his face, "Why, they are staying in the tent right next to me! Just get off when I do. I'll show you where they are."

---

[1] Philippians 4:7: "And the peace of God, which surpasses all understanding, will guard your hearts and minds through Christ Jesus."

Chapter 3

Baby George

We do not give anyone an occasion for taking an offense in anything, so that no fault may be found with our ministry.

—2 Corinthians 6:3

Zakho, Iraq, May 14, 1991

The heat of the early summer blazed down on the canvass hospital tent, pitched across the makeshift road from Camp Redeye, home of the 432 Army Reserves. After disembarking from the army bus, we had been welcomed by an energetic young man with eyes that spoke intensity and love of life. Chris Crossan was from Southern California, where he had developed a love of Jesus, and then a love for Turkey and its Kurds. His home was also in Germany, where he lived with his wife, Karen, and four lovely daughters. Chris was to become one of my dearest lifelong friends.[1] He invited us into a large twelve-man army tent. Low cots were set up in two long rows.

[1.] When, years later, I needed a lung transplant, Chris helped me find the best transplant hospital and then later offered to give me one of his own lungs! (But I needed two.)

"Take your pick," he said.

Camp Redeye, as it was affectionately called by the marines who were building it, was also home to the many NGOs who had come to aid the returning refugees. They were working round the clock in eight-hour-on and eight-hour-off shifts to set up tents, latrines, water supply, medical facilities, and a transport center for an expected twenty thousand Kurds being transited from Turkey onward toward their homes in northern Iraq.

The "Town Hall" in Camp Redeye, Zakho, a transit camp
to accommodate 20,000 people. Later a second camp was built.

One morning, we were notified of a days-old infant that had been abandoned and was struggling for life. Jane had trained as a nurse and was using her knowledge to help wherever she could. We walked through the wheat fields and freshly created dirt roads to a large green army hospital tent. A medical assistant greeted us as we entered the tent.

"Excuse me, sir," I began, "we are here to visit the baby found under a tree." It sounded like something from a fairy tale, but it was real life. And it was tragic.

"Oh, you mean Baby George?" the soldier said. He had been so nicknamed in honor of the US President George Bush. He was not a day older than six weeks. Canadian army medics had discovered his little form high in the mountains of northern Iraq, outside the village of Kani Masi. He appeared healthy and lively. His crying attested to that. But there was nobody in the area; he had been abandoned there, his family perhaps killed. The medics searched for relatives or anyone who could give them any information about the child.

"How could anyone leave an infant exposed like this?" the medical assistant wondered out loud. His little eyes blinked as he looked up helplessly.

"How is he?" I asked, as I peered into a cardboard box. Its side was cut away to form a crude bed.

"He is the healthiest baby we have seen," he replied. The tiny hands and feet seemed to wave a greeting. "The problem is this tent." Inches away behind a plastic sheet were the cots of seven patients with typhoid. "This is no place for a healthy baby." I looked into his little eyes. "Can't he be brought somewhere else?" I asked. "My wife is a registered nurse and is working here with me. She could take care of him in our tent. It's not fancy, but at least there isn't any infection or disease. We are in tent number H7, just a hundred meters down that path." I pointed to our tent across the dirt road.

"I really don't have the authority to release him. Why don't you come back this afternoon after I've asked the doctor?" It seemed reasonable enough. But I hated to see the infant exposed to such deadly disease for even a minute. Our hearts were full of compassion for the little boy; we knew we would be willing, if asked, to raise him as our own.

I returned after lunch and met the doctor. "Can you release Baby George into our care so that he doesn't become infected?" I asked. He frowned.

"This morning, I would have gladly done so. But the UNHCR came by and instructed me not to let the baby go anywhere." The United Nations High Commissioner for Refugees had raised their flag in Zakho a few days earlier, and nobody was sure just what kind of authority they had.

"Why would they say that?" I asked him

"I don't really understand it myself," he replied.

"Do you know who it was that talked to you?" I asked him.

"Her name was Janet, or Ganett or something. She said she was in charge of social services." He didn't know where I could find her, but I knew they were just setting up their offices across the border in Silopi, Turkey.

I hitched a ride with another NGO worker who wanted to use a phone; he had to travel twenty-six kilometers back to Turkey that afternoon to find a phone. There was no phone service in Iraq; precision bombing of the AT&T building at the start of the air offensive on Baghdad had taken care of that. All of the NGOs relied on the PTT, the Turkish Phone Company, to keep contact with the outside world. The telephone lines in the whole region of eastern Turkey were terribly inadequate and poorly serviced. One could wait hours for a call to get through.

It was a good half-hour before we reached the border, an hour's wait for the driver to use the pay phone, and another twenty-minute drive into the sleepy town of Silopi. We pulled up at the two-story concrete hotel on the outskirts of town where the UNHCR was setting up offices. The lobby was empty, and there was no sign of life on the first floor. At last, a tired-looking man appeared. I asked him where I could find the UNHCR.

"They moved," was the reply. So we climbed back into the car and drove around the small town looking for the shiny new white Suzukis with the blue-lettered UNHCR emblazoned on them. They stood out so dramatically among the local vehicles, which were mostly dirty vegetable trucks, small worn-out cars, and donkey carts. We found a new Suzuki on the main road, parked before the stationery shop.

A German was inside trying to purchase ten boxes of paper clips. Having come straight from the refugee camps where people were fighting for water and bread, it struck me as strangely ludicrous. I asked him in German where his new office was, and we were soon on our way. There were only two main streets in the town of Silopi, and the majority of traffic was pedestrian, so we had no problem finding it.

The UNHCR Silopi offices were on the second floor of a recently built residence. The exterior was freshly whitewashed. The interior floors were concrete, a bit uneven, but very modern for Silopi. The steel-framed windows had wrought iron bars over them to discourage unwanted intrusions. As I reached the top of the narrow concrete staircase, I peered inside the first door on my right. It was the toilet, only it was a bit extraordinary. They had torn the Middle Eastern-style toilet out of the floor and had a Western toilet installed. It was undoubtedly the only one in town. I was impressed.

I entered the next room. "Excuse me," I said. "My name is Kirk Legacy. I work with the group Mercy for All, across the border in Zakho. I am looking for a UNHCR staff person by the name of Janet, or maybe it's Ganett."

"Why?" a short woman asked.

Why are they so distrustful? I wondered. "I have a question regarding social services in the Zakho, Iraq, transit camp. I understand she is working there."

"Well, she isn't here now," the woman said abruptly.

"May I ask what her correct name is?"

"Ganett," she said.

"When might I find her?" I persisted, having spent two hours to get to their offices I wasn't about to give up so quickly.

"She should be at the NGO meeting tonight." That meeting took place every evening in the tent village outside of Zakho, where all the refugees, the NGOs, and the military were camped. I returned back across the border into Iraq, with growing frustration that such bureaucracy was impeding relief.

At the evening meetings, a representative of each NGO attended as well as representatives of the military. For several days now, UNHCR staff had been coming as well. A general assessment was given of the camp situation; there was an update on the movement of refugees; security concerns were raised, and unmet needs brought up. It was generally at these meetings that I learned of the areas in which Mercy for All could be of assistance. After the meeting, I asked several people if they knew Ganett.

"I am Ganett," said a short dark-haired woman. Her skin was olive toned; she couldn't have been more than thirty. Her accent didn't betray her nationality; it sounded close enough to an American accent to almost be unnoticeable. *Perhaps she is from India*, I thought. I had yet to meet an American among the UNHCR personnel. They seemed to come from everywhere but America. I had met French, German, Swiss, Guatemalan, Ethiopian, Kenyan, Greek, and an Indian—all wearing the light-blue UNHCR armband, but no Americans. I guessed there weren't too many Americans who were keen on working in Iraq immediately after the Gulf War. More likely, it was UNHCR policy since American had led the coalition that invaded Iraq.

After introducing myself, I asked her about the abandoned baby whom the medics had called Baby George.

"What about him?" she asked.

"Well," I began, "he is living in a tent with seven typhoid patients. The doctor feels he is in very good health, but that it's unwise to leave him there. Don't you think it would be better if he were placed in a different tent? I am here working with my wife, and she is willing to stay in our tent and look after him. She can provide everything he needs until another solution is found. We are even willing, if necessary, to adopt him if his family cannot be found."

"I have just arrived here," she began. She spoke slowly, choosing her words carefully. "I want to travel to Kani Masi, where he was found, and begin a search for the child's family."

"Couldn't the baby live with us in the meantime?" I suggested. "And if relatives are found, he could then be placed with them."

Her answer shocked me. It seemed to reflect a general distrust the UNHCR had for NGOs.

"You would bond with the child and then perhaps disappear with him. Anyway, it is against UNHCR policy for refugees to be adopted by people outside the refugee group."

It seemed like a reasonable policy. But there had to be some other viable alternative for the infant. I realized there would be no chance of our even temporarily caring for the helpless infant. The woman looked uneasy; she was anxious to get away.

"I need to join my colleagues for a meeting. Excuse me." She stepped out of the tent into the night. I was so frustrated I could have screamed. I followed her out.

"Listen, here is my card," I said. "I am in tent H7 in the NGO camp. Please, if there is any way I can help, let me know." She turned and walked away.

Chapter 4

Kurdish Refugee Transit Camp

Zakho, Iraq, May 1991

The days passed quickly in the camp in Zakho. The needs were so immense, and there just never seemed enough time in the day or people to meet the demands. The care for Baby George had been taken from our hands by UNHCR officials, but there were many other pressing concerns each day.

Jane began giving her time each day working in a medical dispensary. She was evaluating the needs of patients, sorting out the medicines that had been donated from all over the world, and figuring out how to translate them so volunteers knew what they were. The canvas of the dark-green tent absorbed all the blazing heat from the sun, making the inside of the dispensary like an oven. She had sewn outfits like Kurdish women wear for herself, but even the light cotton fabric was too hot.

Her team had to do their best to explain to people the correct way to take the medicines. Jane said that most of the women asked for pain relievers for their constant back pain. It is the Kurdish woman's job to carry all the heavy burdens, like water and firewood each day.

As the exodus continued, we became aware of the needs of the Kurdish villages to the east. Most of these villages had been completely leveled by the Iraqi army to force the Kurds from their mountain homes. There was one village, however, Begova, whose buildings had escaped destruction by the Iraqis because their soldiers needed a place to live. It was located up in the Taurus mountains, ironically quite close to Çukurca, only it was on the Iraqi side of the mountain range. No doubt many of the Kurds with whom we'd worked in Çukurca had fled by foot via Begova on their way over the mountains to Turkey. No roads connected the two towns; the mountains are too steep. Access to Begova from within Iraq was only by a narrow sometimes-paved roadway that led eastward from Zakho and then turned north toward the Turkish border. The buildings in the small town and the roadway leading to it had been preserved, but not Begova's inhabitants. They had all either fled or been killed. I was asked by an officer in the military to ride along with him for the fifty or so kilometers and visit the town to see if I would bring the Mercy for All team up to work there.

Jane and I climbed aboard a US Humvee and headed for Begova in the early afternoon. We hadn't much time. It was inadvisable to travel after dark; army intelligence expected a counterattack at any time. As we climbed the switchbacks toward Begova, the remains of Iraqi military vehicles were everywhere. Local Kurdish fighters, the peshmerga, had sabotaged and attacked the Iraqi soldiers as they retreated. Now we saw children playing in the discarded burned-out vehicles, swinging from sagging telephone wires, and climbing upon an abandoned tank.

The air was cool as we crested a low ridge. We had left the hot plains of Zakho. One-story flat-roofed homes with walls made from mud and stone dotted the hillside. A few poplar trees stood as tall silent witnesses to the atrocities that had occurred there. A mass grave of 250 women and children had been discovered, located just outside the stone fortress Iraqi soldiers had built for their protection. The inhabitants of Begova were all gone.

Working with the coalition forces, the elite Fortieth Commando Royal Marines from Great Britain, had forced the Iraqis out of Begova and the surrounding region after the failed Kurdish uprising at the end of March 1991. With the Iraqis gone, British marines moved in to assess the remains of the villages and provide protection and assistance to the returning refugees. It was a massive undertaking, and the marines welcomed the aid of any NGO willing to take the risks of living in the area.

The enormous mountains were beautiful, snow still visible on the peaks in the distance. I knew much of the region was totally inaccessible in winter, the snow too deep and roads too poor. Most of the mountainous region was uninhabited.

Saddam Hussein had sought to seal the Kurds off from Iraq's neighbors Syria, Turkey, and Iran by creating a sixteen-mile-wide area, appropriately named the "death strip." Thousands of villages had been bombed, many with poison gas. Orchards had been burned, fields salted, wells and streams poisoned, even beehives destroyed. The intent was to prevent the Kurds from living where they had lived for a thousand years and to divide them from the other Kurds in neighboring countries. As a further deterrent, the entire area was mined. Turkey had also mined its mountains to prevent its Kurdish population from crossing the mountain borders into Iran or Iraq to meet with Kurds from those countries.

The world remained basically silent when Sadaam bombed the large city of Halabja, Iraq, with poison gas on March 16, 1988, killing well over five thousand Kurdish civilians. That atrocity has become a symbol of the ongoing genocide carried out for two generations. Every Kurd knows and refers to Halabja; it is a symbol of the decades-long attempt to annihilate them. The official word for this genocidal campaign in Arabic is Al-Anfal, or simply the Anfal. Ali Hassan had designed the plan for the Kurdish genocide. Known as Chemical Ali, he was Saddam Hussein's first cousin and the minister of defense.

To speak of Halabja to a Kurd is like saying "9/11" to an American. It evokes a gut-wrenching feeling of thousands of innocent people dying in a horrific slaughter. The much-publicized image of a dead mother and infant, lying together in the street, their faces spattered with blood, is the image of a suffering people. It is the story of the Kurds under Saddam Hussein. There are grisly and well-documented reports of the effects of the gas. It led to burning lungs and eventual death. The gas caused burning and blistering sores, blindness, and lifelong debilitation, for those who were fortunate enough to get away from the deathly cloud. Every Kurd knows the meaning and the nightmarish fear of "weapons of mass destruction." It is exactly this fear that led all of Iraq's Kurds to flee for the mountains in March 1991. They knew what Saddam was capable of.

We continued to drive in the Humvee around the small town. Begova had, at one time, perhaps four thousand residents, if one included the homes in the surrounding valleys. Its well had not been poisoned, since the Iraqi soldiers needed clean water, but the pump had been ruined. Volunteer engineers went to work, repairing an old generator to pump water up to what had been a hospital clinic. The clinic itself had been completely looted and trashed, its windows broken, the toilets ruined. The wiring and all the lights had been ripped out, the walls soiled, and the rooms littered with trash.

A group of local Kurds undertook the first cleaning of the rooms, and then a group of Germans cleaned and scrubbed the place. We were shown inside the ruined hospital. I saw immediately that lights, paint, and glass would have to be purchased and the toilets repaired to make the place functional. The commander of the Fortieth Commando Unit invited me to bring the Mercy for All team of ten to live inside their encampment. Their tent-camp was encircled with razor wire and had been cleared of mines. A twenty-four-hour guard at key locations provided some security. We knew, of course, that our security was in the Lord. Otherwise, we would never have come that far in the first place.

The peshmerga had also posted their guards at bridges, crossroads, major buildings, and along the highway. The peshmerga cooperated well with the British, and although there were no formal agreements, there was mutual respect and admiration. On one occasion, a British helicopter had spilled a load of military hardware. "There were one hundred and fifty class 1 items lost from the chopper," the commander told me. "That includes weapons, radios, and essential fighting equipment. There is no doubt the peshmerga could have used it and, in fact, badly needed it. But every single item was returned to us. Not a thing was missing." It was clear that the peshmerga were honorable men and wanted the British to remain.

Returning to Zakho, I shared the needs of Begova with the ten or so team members of Mercy for All. They knew there were additional risks of leaving the large settlement in Zakho, but they also could see that no other NGO was going to work there. It seemed, in comparison, that the huge camp in Zakho would not miss us. The hundreds of military who lived beside us had even built an indoor shower (out of plywood) with hot running water. It was feeling like luxury.

Mercy for All agreed to pack up and relocate to Begova. The following day, we moved fifty kilometers up into the Taurus Mountains and were greeted by the British marines in their khaki shorts. (Kurdish men never wear shorts.) We began by making makeshift accommodations in an army general purpose (GP) small tent in the encampment of the marines, and then got busy at work in the clinic. In the coming weeks, doctors and nurses came from as far away as Korea to join us. Over a hundred patients were lined up each morning waiting to be registered. There were, of course, no files, medicines, or medical equipment; everything had to be brought in from the outside. Furniture had to be constructed; the wood to construct it scavenged. One team member was in charge of finding medicines and equipment at the various NGO and UNHCR facilities in Zakho, or even from Turkey. Another two members made repairs on the building. One assisted in registration; and then there were nurses, a surgeon, a pharmacist, and a pediatrician. Together with two marines, two team members opened a feeding center, where mothers could bring their undernourished babies and receive a portion of porridge made from heated rice and sugar.

Eventually, a general practitioner arrived from England who was skilled in administration. He took charge of the clinic and met with the local leaders to plan for rebuilding other areas of their community. A local resident who had been a nurse, before the village had been forcefully evacuated, returned and worked each day, without pay.

"There is one thought that keeps burning in my brain," I said to Jane. "Saddam has destroyed some villages repeatedly, even five times, when the residents sought to reestablish them. We both know that

Begova lies in Saddam's so-called death strip. There is no doubt in my mind that he will return and destroy everything here the moment he can. All the work the others and we are doing to rebuild and resettle will in all likelihood be destroyed in a moment. He doesn't want the Kurds to live in Begova, and he will savagely destroy it as soon as the Brits are gone." Her answer made me reflect even deeper.

She said, "I guess we have just a tiny idea of what the Kurds are experiencing. These are their homes, all that they own, their history, their future. Think of what they have invested here, of what Begova means to them. We are experiencing just a taste of what it means to be Kurdish. Think of the unending suffering they have experienced. That is, after all, what it means to suffer as Jesus suffered. To be Christ to the Kurd means to suffer with them as Jesus suffers with them."

Little did we realize at that moment how we would share in another part of Kurdish suffering, the meaningless and preventable death of a loved one.

Chapter 5

Begova, Baqtiar

With such affection for you we were happy to share
with you not only the gospel of God but also our
own lives, because you had become dear to us.

—1 Thessalonians 2:8

Zakho, Iraq, May 1991

After several days of organizing the Mercy for All team in Begova, I prepared to catch a ride back to Zakho. Julyan Lidstone was sending new volunteers all the time, and I needed to orient them to life in Iraq. Following a quick British military breakfast out of a plastic envelope, I packed a few things for the day. It was 9:00 a.m. when the Royal Marine and I passed through the serpentine wire that the marines had laid around the perimeter of our camp. We climbed into his vehicle. Mud spattered up the sides of the Land Rover as we lumbered up the switchbacks leaving Begova. The asphalt had broken and disintegrated on the steep turns along eroded hillsides, leaving slimy and potholed sections of roadway. A large truck groaned hopelessly back and forth as its wheels spun in the mess. A tractor worked to clear a landslide before we could pass. Off to my right lay the bombed remains of several East German-made army trucks, which had been cannibalized for their useable parts. It was only fifty kilometers back to the tent city in Zakho, but the trip was seldom boring.

US troops were encamped at the crest of the hill; and at critical junctures—such as crossroads, bridges, and buildings along the route—were British and peshmerga guards. In the valley ten kilometers outside of Zakho was a formal coalition forces checkpoint manned by soldiers from Spain. They were clad in green camouflaged uniforms and wore dark sunglasses and burgundy berets. With weapon in hand, they examined each vehicle at the stop. Having recognized our white Land Rover, in spite of the mud, they waved us through. A few kilometers further, children clambered over a partially demolished Iraqi tank, swinging from the gun turret. Others created a makeshift swing from another downed power line. These were the toys of a war-torn land.

As we pulled off the narrow highway into dirt pathways in the wheat field that we called home, I reflected on the tasks that lay before me. First was the NGO meeting later that afternoon. Many things would be discussed, including legitimizing everyone's presence in the country with Baghdad. None of us possessed a legitimate visa. A three-party agreement had been written up between Baghdad, the United Nations, and the NGOs. The agreement was supposed to give us some kind of legitimacy.

We were to provide Baghdad all information about our activities, about ourselves, and the individual organizations with whom we were affiliated. Then Baghdad would issue a temporary visa. Many people had objected to giving their personal data, and few wanted to surrender their passports to be brought to Baghdad for processing. The recent hostage crisis preceding the Gulf War was fresh in everyone's minds. Three thousand and one hundred Americans had been trapped in Iraq and Kuwait at the end of August 1990, as the US was building its military in the dessert of Saudi Arabia in preparation for the invasion of Iraq and Kuwait. Saddam had threatened to hold foreigners as prisoners at Iraqi military bases and other targets. None of the NGO leaders gathered in the tent in Zakho wanted to hand Baghdad information that could backfire on them.[1]

Then there would be an update given on each of the camps where NGOs were at work. I would report on the work in Begova. An ongoing assessment was made regarding the needs and numbers of the migrating population. A sanitation report, a health report with its gruesome death count, and a security report would be given. New problems would be addressed, such as the thousands of kids who were playing on the highway, and solutions suggested. The briefing was a vital tool for the ongoing work of our team. It was at one of those meetings where I had learned of the needs in Begova. That had led to the placement of the medical team there.

Just recently, I had learned of another area where Mercy for All could assist. Countless individuals had been separated during the tumultuous days of the flight to the mountains, and many had been airlifted out of the mountains to various hospitals to receive emergency care. These people had lost track of their families. Some were in a refugee camp in Turkey, some were in a transit camp in Iraq, and perhaps some had returned to their villages. But nobody was providing these people assistance to locate their loved ones. There were also disabled people, elderly people, widows, and orphans, who were alone because of the tragic flight. They were in desperate need of assistance. Without someone healthy and strong in their family, who could fight for food, or someone to find them a tent, bring them to the health dispensary, or whatever, many of these people would perish. I remembered a verse from the Bible I had memorized as a youth, "True religion is this, to visit the widow and orphan in their affliction and to keep oneself unspotted from the world" (James 1:23). There couldn't have been a more appropriate way for our team of Christians to aid in the relief effort.

I thought of Baby George, the healthy infant who had been left in the hospital tent. Besides attending the meeting and networking with the other agencies back in Zakho, I was determined to find out

---

[1.] http://www.newsweek.com/crisis-gulf-war-path-206032

what had become of the little fellow. Perhaps there was still some way we could help him.

I also needed to telephone Julyan, our Mercy for All director in Ankara, Turkey. Since the telephone system was entirely out of commission in Iraq, I would have to drive to the Turkish border, maybe even into Silopi to make the call. The director needed a report of recent events, and I needed to know who was coming and when they'd arrive. I knew another group was expected to arrive the following morning, but the journey was so long that things often went awry.

Jane and I would have to prepare for their arrival. We had a large tent in camp Redeye, which could sleep twelve, but it had only two cots. The remainder of the giant space was empty with nothing but white plastic sheeting. It would be a scramble to locate ten more cots. The new team members would be able to live in our large tent and join the 432nd of the US Army for their meals. The military had erected a huge mess tent and were serving real meals with real food! We no longer had to shop for food and cook it ourselves.

"Just stand in the chow line and eat all you want," we were told. It was a real luxury. On one occasion, they had barbecued hamburgers and served ice-cold pop. That seemed like a taste of heaven.

When the team arrived, I would need to first see that they were suitably accommodated and then orient them to the camp and work. Team members often didn't know one another; it was the common bond of Jesus and His love that gave us purpose and motivated us to action. Still, there could be conflicts, and it was important to resolve these before they began to affect our relationships. Sharing a tent, even a big one, with eleven people, is not easy even under the best of circumstances. I strung up several dark-green US Army blankets to create an impression of privacy, but it was second rate at best.

I lay on the cot that night, exhausted and yet content. I was beginning to see that our efforts, though seemingly so small in comparison to the overwhelming need, were, in fact, making a difference. Jane and I prayed together—thankful for safety and health and for the simple joy of having the tent to ourselves for one night. I fell into a deep sleep, which was unfortunate, because I didn't hear the massive rains begin.

Jane didn't sleep so well as I. In fact, she had the worst night in her recent memory. Something she had eaten made her violently ill. The outhouse was about seventy-five yards away, which was much too far to hike in the torrential rain, and besides, the trampled wheat field had turned into a treacherous muddy mess. She was especially thankful we had the tent to ourselves as she utilized the blue plastic basin in the corner of the tent. To exacerbate matters, she ran out of toilet tissue on the fifth of ten episodes.

"The word *misery* doesn't come near to describing it," she told me in the morning.

I suggested she stay "in bed" (the army cot), and then volunteered to bring her a cardboard tray with breakfast from the chow line; but she politely declined, opting instead for a small plastic bowl of fruit cocktail. The two rain flaps in the tent roof had been left open all night, and the sides of the tent had been partially rolled up to allow some air circulation during the oppressive afternoon heat of the previous day. Now there was one to two inches of dirty rainwater over most of the plastic flooring. It needed to be cleaned before new volunteers arrived...

With the tent cleaned up, I left Jane to rest and headed off for the main US Army base outside of Silopi. An army chaplain in Zakho had heard my request for cots for the relief workers and had directed me to the supply depot outside Silopi. A "quick strike force" of five thousand US servicemen had set up camp near a dry riverbed outside Silopi in Turkey. Their mission was to be ready to cross into Iraq at a moment's notice to respond to Saddam's forces, should they move north and attack the Kurds. It was an impressive display of force and support for the beleaguered Kurdish people of Iraq, but a bit too late. If there had been that kind of support a few months earlier after the Kurdish uprising, there would have been no flight into the mountains. There would have been no refugee crisis. But one can't change history.

I approached a soldier at the supply depot and explained my situation. He opened a container full of army cots and said simply,

"Take what you need." It was a tremendous provision. We now had beds for another ten volunteers!

"Hello, anybody in there?" A balding sunburned head poked through the canvas door into the tent. Sandy stepped in, a broad smile on his face, reached for my hand, and said, "You must be Kirk. How's it going?" His cheerfulness never stopped. At the end of an exhausting day in the sun, Sandy still had energy. "Let's organize a soccer game for these kids. They love soccer. That'll keep 'em out of the streets." And he went out and did it. He was a man of ideas, of energy, and of action. He had compassion for people, a zeal for living, and he loved to tell people why. "I was lost, and Jesus found me. I was a sinner, and He saved me." He was invaluable not only because of his incredible energy and love for people but because he spoke fluent Arabic. Most of the Kurdish men and some of the women knew Arabic from studying in Iraqi schools.

He was just one of the team that arrived that day and the next. Altogether, there were six that began to work there in the transit camp. They were officially called social services by the UNHCR. Soon, we were asked to provide the services not only in that camp with its twenty thousand people but in a second camp as well. The military bulldozed more roads in the wheat fields, to accommodate another twenty thousand people. For lack of a better name, it became simply Camp Two. Our team members were trained linguistically with knowledge of Arabic, and even Kurdish, and were, of course, sensitive to the special needs of this vulnerable group of people.

And who was more vulnerable than the infant they'd affectionately named Baby George? Later, he would be given the name Baqtiar by a Kurdish couple. I decided to check in on him. The large green tents housing the NGOs were lined up military style in Camp Redeye. A space of about thirty feet separated these rows of tents from a special tent, which was serving as a hospital ward. I stood outside the main flap to that tent and gave a gentle shout.

"Hello, is anybody there?" A moment passed, and a woman pulled the flap aside.

"Come in," she said. I stepped inside onto a piece of plastic, which due to the recent rains was still covered with dirt and mud. It was the stickiest mud I have ever experienced. With each step, more mud would adhere to my boots, so that eventually each leg had an extra ten pounds of weight attached to it.

"I've come on account of Baby George," I began. "How's he been getting along? Any word on the search for relatives?"

"Just a moment please. I will get the doctor." I was amazed how pleasant the volunteers treated one another, especially considering the lack of good sleep, the daily stresses, and the unrelenting work schedule.

Several minutes passed. I looked around the dark interior. The air was stifling hot and smelled like a mixture of antiseptic and dusty wheat field. Across from where I stood, not eight feet away, was the familiar cardboard box sitting on a foldout table. Behind the table hung a sheet of plastic forming a crude divider in the tent. From the top of the cutaway box, a blanket protruded. I stepped forward and peeked inside. The tiny infant lay stretched out in a contented sleep. My thoughts were interrupted by the doctor's voice.

"How can I help you?" he asked. I inquired if he had heard anything further from Ganett. "Has there been any success in the search for relatives?" I asked.

"They flew up to Kani Masi but could not locate anyone. Apparently, the infant was abandoned. It's hard to imagine such a thing happening." I had driven by Kani Masi with the British Royal Marine. There was nothing left of the village but charred rubble. Not a single building was standing.

"What will be done now?" I asked. "Is this where the baby will remain?"

"Regrettably, these are not the best circumstances," the doctor said. "Behind this plastic curtain are the cots with our typhoid patients. "I agree that he would be better off in your care, but, unfortunately I have been told to keep him here."

"What do they plan to do?" I asked.

"They are looking for a Kurdish family here in the refugee camp who will take care of him or maybe adopt him."

"Well, that sounds like a good idea," I responded. "I just hope it doesn't take them too long." It had already been a week since he was first flown in to Zakho.

A second week passed before I heard from a team member that a Kurdish couple had been found to take in the baby. The pair had been married for some time but as yet had no children. A child brings great joy and prestige to a couple in Kurdish society, particularly a son.

A nurse from Mercy for All made certain the young couple had adequate supplies, cooking gas, utensils, training in preparing milk, and general infant care. I joined her one morning and visited the young couple and their tiny infant in their little tent. The label on the flap said "Sears." It had been set up, along with thousands of others, by US serviceman. It's funny how a small reminder from home, like the sales tag on a tent that was shipped around the world, reminded me of my home thousands of miles away. I pictured the Sears store in San Jose and thought of some of the things we'd purchased there. But there was no time to reminisce. This little baby boy needed attention. The Mercy for All nurse made sure they had everything they needed to care for their boy. Little Baby George had a new name now. A Kurdish name. Baqtiar. It sounded like a prince's name. The family seemed genuinely happy. Indeed, everything seemed ideal.

The third week of Baqtiar's life in Zakho took an alarming turn. Jane and I got word that he was sick. *How could this be?* we wondered. He had been declared perfectly fit when brought into camp. But then that was before he was put in the tent with the typhoid patients.

I was on my way to meet with the camp leaders in the early morning when Baqtiar's new father found me in a clearing and gripped my arm in urgency. He began explaining in Kurdish that his child was sick—*very* sick. I went with him to the Dutch hospital tent, which had been set up in the field in the middle of transit camp one. Jane joined me as we approached the entrance.

No sooner had the three of us stepped inside when a military doctor stepped up and demanded in a loud voice, "Who is going to fill out the death certificate? That's what I want to know. Who is going to fill it out? Are you?" He thrust a document in front of me. I stood there dumbfounded, looking at him.

We were stunned. The doctor's words echoed through my mind. *Death certificate. Death certificate. Surely not Baqtiar's death? Surely not!*

"We came here to inquire about a sick infant by the name of Baqtiar. This is Baqtiar's father," I said and motioned to the Kurd beside me. "My wife and I have also taken a personal concern in his case."

A nurse, realizing what was happening, ushered the doctor away from us toward the rear of the tent. A second, much younger, doctor appeared, who seemed visibly shaken.

"I was holding him in my hands," he said with a thick Dutch accent. "I was examining him, and just like that, he stopped breathing." Tears flooded his eyes. "He died in my arms. I was holding him, and he died." Baqtiar's father looked at the young doctor's tears and knew, without any English being translated, what had transpired. For a long moment, we all just stood there in silence as the tears flowed. Then they went together into the back of the tent, and Baqtiar's father returned moments later, cradling the lifeless infant in his arms.

Grief welled up inside of me so that I could hardly speak. I turned to the attending nurse. "What is this about a death certificate?" I asked.

"I will take care of it," she said. I thanked her and left the tent.

Jane and I decided we would do whatever we could to help the young couple through this terrible grief. The US Army had given our NGO a discarded Dodge truck. They didn't have a key for it, so I had to hot-wire it each time to start it. It was a Godsend. In the afternoon, we drove the couple with their deceased child from the refugee camp into the city of Zakho where their relatives lived.

We were led through a metal gate in a high concrete wall. A small yard with closely cropped grass and a variety of large shady plants made for a cool and pleasant respite from the oppressive heat. I was ushered into a room where the men sat and talked. Jane was taken off to join the women. This is typical Kurdish hospitality. Male guests join the men in the sitting room and sit on cushions on the floor with backs to the walls, and women chat in the kitchen or show off clothes and jewelry in the bedrooms with the women of the house. Today was different; it was somber. The women worked quietly preparing food; the men spoke very little. Jane and I felt honored to be present in their grief.

Baqtiar was prepared for burial in the traditional Muslim fashion. His body was washed carefully, and he was placed in a bag made from uncut linen. He would be buried that afternoon in the local cemetery in Zakho; time and circumstance wouldn't permit a coffin to be constructed.

The women of the house spent the next hour or so preparing food, and when it was ready, the men were served, followed by the women. Seated cross-legged on low cushions, we gathered around a plastic tablecloth, which was spread out on the floor. Each of us was served a bowl of meat and vegetable soup. A heaping platter of rice was served from which each person served himself. Generous portions of Kurdish flatbread were passed around. The host was especially honored if his guests eat a lot, and I did my best to honor him. Hot tea was served, sweetened with heaps of sugar. I drank lots of tea not just to be polite; it was a necessary prevention against dehydration. In the 110 to 120 degree midday heat, the body lost lots of water.

Toward evening, we drove through the dusty backstreets of Zakho toward the cemetery. The streets were heaped high with garbage—evidence of the lack of infrastructure in the Kurdish areas. There were also no policemen at work, no banks or schools open, and no government offices in existence. All government officials were part of Saddam's regime. They had fled when the Iraqi army lost control of the north. I turned the white pickup into the driveway of the cemetery. Rows of fresh mounds of dirt gave silent testimony of the recent losses during the failed Kurdish uprising.

Baqtiar's parents selected a corner of ground near several other tiny little mounds, evidence of the many children who had perished that spring. I thought back to the hillside above Çukurca in Turkey. It was the very young and the very old who suffered the most, and who contributed to the high death count each day. The US Army was

73

saying that over thirty thousand Kurds died as a result of the fiasco in the mountains of Turkey and Iran. In the early days around April 9, when the airdrop of food crates first began in Çukurca, six hundred people were dying of starvation and exposure each day. Those numbers suddenly felt very personal when I looked at the small form in the white linen cloth. Was there any Kurd who was not affected? Anyone who had not lost a loved one? I looked at the grieving family around the tiny hole dug in the ground. Carefully, they laid stones and scraps of wood in the earth to protect their little relative. Such care and concern. Such love and loss. It was a microcosm of the suffering people. A needless death. *How unfair and cruel!* And yet so typical of life in Kurdistan. It was typical of their whole history, for that matter.

I did not know how to express my grief. Nor my outrage. I lifted my hands as I had seen them do. We stood in a circle around the grave. I prayed in Jesus name for peace, for hope, for a future for these people, for salvation both temporal and eternal. My Kurdish language ability was far too limited to express what was on my heart, but God understood my tears and the burning in my chest. They, too, prayed with lifted heads and outstretched hands, silently. It was so difficult to say goodbye. I fashioned a crude sign from a piece of cardboard for the tiny grave, with Baqtiar's name and the date of his death. We drove them to their home in town, speaking very little. Our hearts were so heavy. Jane and I returned to our twelve-man tent in Camp Redeye, in the field outside the city.

I thought of the events of that one day. Baqtiar had been sick in the morning, was brought to the Dutch hospital tent, and then died in the arms of the doctor. He was then given back to the young couple and brought to some relatives' home in town and prepared for burial. Finally, he was buried in the Zakho cemetery. That one day seemed to have lasted forever.

There was no cause of death ever given to the family.

Baqtiar's grave. (Jane at right)

One morning shortly after the tragedy of Baby Baqtiar, we were informed of an important visitor who was coming to visit camp Redeye. The Chairman of the Joint Chiefs of Staff, Colin Powell, was flying in to Zakho, Iraq to assess the progress of Operation Provide Comfort. Colin's post was the highest military position in the Department of Defense. Powell had been a key figure in Desert Shield and Desert Storm. Desert Shield was in response to Kuwait's invasion of Iraq on August 2, 1990, and resulted in the huge build-up of US and coalition troops in the Saudi Desert. Desert Storm was the rapid invasion of southern Iraq and also Kuwait. Powell had advocated the use of overwhelming force in military conflicts, something which resulted in very few casualties during Desert Storm. It became known as the Powell doctrine.

We watched as three black hawk helicopters flew in from the west. Nobody knew which of the three had the Joint Chief of Staff inside; that was the point. As one of the choppers flew across the top of a hill in its descent we heard an explosion and saw a puff of smoke. The rotor blades had exerted such downward pressure that a mine had exploded on the top of the hill above our camp. It did not damage the aircraft.

A large camouflage net had been erected in the dusty field and rows of chairs set up. A defensive perimeter had been set up with various Humvees and equipment also under camouflage. The military leadership were all gathered and were taking their seats in the semi-shade as Powell climbed out of his helicopter. After greeting several of the generals he stepped up to a podium and gave a short talk. A white board was also on display indicating the number of refugees that were in transit, how many had been assisted, etc. Jane and I were seated a few rows back, and other NGO volunteers were present as well. It was a special honor to meet this man whom we all esteemed.

A few days later it was time for Jane and I to return to Berlin. On the way we stopped in western Turkey for a two day break in a *pension*, a simple bed and breakfast outside of Bursa. There were hot springs there; it was a welcome rest. It was also home to dear friends of ours, Ken and Trudi Berding. Then it was on to Germany to recover both physically and emotionally. We had experienced so much in such a brief time. Jane was also expecting a visit in Berlin of her two sisters. It was a refreshing time.

But the call to help the suffering weighed heavy upon our hearts. There was still a need for leadership on the Mercy for All teams deployed in Turkey. So in September of 1991 we traveled back to Turkey. This time we headed for the border town of Silopi, where refugees had been allowed in to Turkey. We were welcomed into a house the Blincoes had rented on the outskirts of town. Life was about to get very interesting.

Chapter 6

Border Riot

Iraq/Turkey Border, November 1991

The four-wheel drive Mitsubishi slowed in the darkness as it approached the Turkish/Iraq border near Silopi. Bob Blincoe was driving his SUV, and I was riding shotgun. Bob stood an imposing six feet five and his voice had a deep commanding tone. The average height of a Turkish man is five feet eight inches tall, and of an Iraqi male five feet five inches. Most people listen when Bob speaks. His job in America was a presbyterian pastor. In Iraq, he headed up a team of veterinarians who were tasked with immunizing all of the flocks of sheep and goats of the Kurds, a herculean task. Bob has a heart of gold, a warm smile, and is married to a kind and soft-spoken wife, Jan.

We were driving from Zakho, Iraq, to Silopi, Turkey. A five-kilometer line of trucks stretched ahead of us and blocked the roadway entirely. We pulled up behind the long line. We wanted to make it over the border and to Silopi. On either side of our vehicle was an enormous parking lot that had been converted recently into a welding center, to construct illegal fuel tanks that fit between the wheels of cargo trucks. Originally, the lot had been used by all the trucks that would wait to cross this international border point. Since the international embargo now forbade any type of trade with Iraq, the prices of both diesel and gasoline had risen sharply in Turkey, as elsewhere in the world. Along the highway, one saw tanks from oil tanker trucks, temporarily out of use. But the ingenious entrepreneurial spirit of the Turks had discovered a way to profit in spite of the embargo.

Regular cargo trucks were in great demand, to supply the north of Iraq with precious food and building materials. These trucks were permitted to cross the border into Iraq, whereas the oil-tank trucks were not. Makeshift tanks were hastily constructed along the route to the border and welded, or sometimes tied, onto the cargo trucks. Some tanks were simply laid out in the empty bed of the open vegetable trucks. On top of these empty tanks, Turkish legal exports were piled. Once the delivery of timber, flour, or whatever had been made in Iraq, the truck driver could fill up his boxy tanks with super cheap fuel in Mosul, Iraq, and then drive back into Turkey. It cost him about two cents a gallon for diesel in Iraq, and he sold it for $3.50 a gallon in Turkey. In just seven trips across the border, a trucker could earn enough to buy a new truck. It looked as if every truck in Turkey was at the border trying to get in or out of Iraq.

An endless line of trucks waiting to leave
Iraq. Fuel barrels at right.

Things had gotten out of hand, however. Convoys of supplies destined for the Kurds in the north were being held up for between seven and ten days at the border, as truck drivers waited to have tanks welded onto their trucks. An additional wait of a week could be expected at the border on the return trip. The border police demanded a high bribe to bring the illicit fuel into Turkey. It was not unusual to see what seemed like a thousand trucks lined up at the border on the Iraqi side, waiting until a deal was struck. Each of the hastily constructed tanks leaked, and pools and lakes of diesel formed under the parked trucks all along the road between the Turkish/Iraqi border and Zakho. It was risky to drive even fifteen miles per hour along the slick surface. The four lanes had been reduced to one and a half lanes for most of the route. More than one truck exploded in flames along the mountainous road into Mosul, incinerating their drivers.

The stench of fumes along this stretch of roadway was stifling. Truck drivers gathered in small groups along the road, waiting sometimes days in Iraq for Turkish customs officials to permit them to cross back into Turkey with their illegal cargo. Fuel was leaking from every poorly welded tank. I knew diesel was not as explosive as gas but still prayed we wouldn't be burned alive. Every man in Turkey smoked it seemed, and truck drivers were no exception. Just one carelessly tossed match or cigarette and I thought we'd be history.

Looking ahead at the long line of parked trucks, Bob decided to go around to the left of them and drive in the oncoming traffic lane. Nobody was using those lanes at this time of night, anyway. The lanes were separated by a low muddy and fuel-filled ravine, but he figured his SUV could handle it. We crept along on the wet pavement. The road was passable here but still slick as butter. The SUV began to slide around a bend. Blincoe struggled to regain control, put his Mitsubishi in four-wheel drive, and slowed to a crawl.

His three children continued singing in the backseat, oblivious of the dangers all about them. Keith, age six, was the loudest, "The Lord said to Noah, build me an arkie, arkie." The repetition was beginning to grate on my nerves. Still I was thankful that they were so happy and content. How many American children could handle the stresses and deprivations of living near Iraq just months after the Gulf War? The darkness intensified as we neared the customs buildings on the Iraqi side of the border. There were buildings located on each side of the border. One set of buildings served to secure those exiting the country and the other for entering the neighboring country.

Earlier that day we had been in Zakho visiting some of the other relief workers and we were now headed back over into Turkey to Bob's home. But we had gotten a late start. It was recommended that nobody attempt to cross the border after dark; the uncertainties and dangers were simply too great. Kurds in Turkey were assaulting government positions, particularly military and police installations. This was part of the ongoing internal battles between Turkish Kurds and the Turkish authorities. Jane and I had moved in with Bob and Jan in a lice-infested rented house in Silopi. We had moved our bed up on the flat roof because the heat inside the house was unbearable. And there were fewer bugs out in the open. We could hear gunfire and explosions throughout the night from our rooftop bed. We had grown accustomed to the sporadic gunfire, and the roosters and donkeys at the break of day.

Nighttime driving was also dangerous since Saddam's army had been fighting Iraqi Kurds. However, all Iraqi territory near the Turkish border was under the control of the (Iraqi) peshmerga, the Kurdish freedom fighters. In addition, Turkish jets would fly into Iraqi airspace from time to time at night to bomb their own Kurdish rebels, who ostensibly were hiding in Iraq. This violation of international law and of the no-fly zone went unanswered by the US or by Iraq. It was all rather unpredictable.

The last section of asphalt pavement before the Habur river/ Turkish border stretched out for a hundred yards in every direction. All the overhead lights in the vast parking lot in Iraq had been shot out, the government border buildings had been bombed and then ransacked, and coils of razor wire lay heaped across the pavement. We drove carefully through the mess. The Iraqi Kurds had set several tents up where they sold cigarettes and snacks to the many truck drivers. But we failed to notice that it was strangely deserted of the normal bustle of human activity. Our attention was drawn instead to avoiding the obstacles in the roadway.

The Habur river separates Turkey from Iraq at this point of the border. The coalition forces in the Gulf War had bombed the two large bridges spanning this river, I would guess to prevent Iraqis from fleeing into Turkey. After the conflict had ended, army engineers completed a temporary repair of one of the bridges to open it again to traffic. Gravel had been piled into the gap in the bridge up to the level of the roadway, creating room for two vehicles to carefully pass. Nobody knew how long it would hold. The swelling river from the winter rains threatened to wash it away. It was only a matter of time before it would give way, cutting off all transport into Turkey. Bob bounced his way carefully over the rocky surface, his headlights illuminating the road ahead erratically.

There were no official buildings occupied on the Iraqi side of the crossing point. Normally, there would be buildings in both countries to process people and goods exiting and entering both countries. The Kurds, however, following the collapse of Iraq, had destroyed all vestiges of Iraqi power in the north, including this crossing point.

Comparatively speaking, the Turkish side of the border was a picture of organization. Four long concrete buildings housed customs, police, postal, and telephone services. At the border itself, a small kiosk with a single desk handled incoming traffic. It was manned by a border official and armed Turkish guards. Often, they stood in the roadway itself, automatic machine guns at the ready, and directed vehicles to pull off to the side, to be inspected. It was another reminder that eastern Turkey was under martial law. My stomach was always in knots when crossing this border.

As we pulled up to the office on the Turkish side of the border crossing, it was strangely quiet. There were no officials, no guards, absolutely nobody.

I leaned forward. "This is weird, Bob. Something is up." He stopped the vehicle. Broken glass littered the pavement ahead of us. An overturned swivel chair lay in the middle of the roadway. To the left was a desk on its side. Every window in the small security building had been smashed. Stones were scattered about. Suddenly, an armed soldier appeared out of nowhere and began talking rapidly to us in Turkish. Neither of us understand Turkish. He looked terrified. His point was obvious: clear the area; do not proceed! And yet there was nowhere to go.

Bob's wife, Jan, said excitedly, "Children, be quiet. Lock your doors."

"We can't just sit here," Bob said. "Let's get out of here." He shifted into drive and drove away from the demolished shack and toward the long customs buildings. He stopped in front of the chief customs officer's office.

"I'm going to find out what's going on," I said and climbed out. A Kurdish man approached us quickly.

"What's going on?" I asked him in Kurdish. He made a half turn and pointed over toward the row of buildings.

"There was a riot by the truck drivers. The Turkish army shot five men." Together, he and I ran around the end of the first building. I stopped suddenly. Some two hundred men were mobbed in front of the police office. There were no Turkish police, no customs officials, no soldiers to be seen. Every man present had a stone in his hand, and the asphalt was littered with hundreds more. Then the familiar face of our Turkish friend Yosef appeared on the edge of the crowd. He was a UNHCR worker and spoke passable English. His job was to monitor the transport of UNHCR shipments crossing the border. He had his own office next to Turkish customs.

"Come with me!" He took my arm and led me back around the building. Several dozen men followed us.

"We have got to get out of here," I told him. "There's a woman and three children in that vehicle over there." I pointed to Bob's SUV.

Yousef replied in his halting English, "You can't leave. Nobody can get by the soldiers at the end of the customs area." He pointed to the guardhouse two hundred meters across the expanse of pavement. Several military vehicles had blocked the roadway that left the customs area and headed toward Silopi. I guess they planned to try and arrest all the rioters or maybe just prevent them from crossing illegally.

"Let's go into this office," Yosef said and led me though the mob toward the long building.

Before we had taken five steps, an ambulance screeched to a halt just feet away. Then a heavyset man came from around the end of the long one-story building and met my friend Yousef. He pushed his way into the tight mob of men, then unlocked and opened one of the tall glass doors to the customs office. As the big fellow slipped inside the front door, the crowd of desperate and angry men pressed forward. Yousef and I were still standing outside in the dark among the rioters. It was getting pretty ugly. They were shouting, cursing, and pushing. One of the rioters squeezed through the partially opened door into the customs office. The huge man inside met him squarely and with one massive punch to the face knocked him back through the opening and into the crowd of men. Yosef turned to me, grabbed my shoulder, and shouted, "Go in!"

"Are you sure?" I looked at the big man in the doorway. "How do I know this guy won't give me the same welcome?" I had never seen the man before. Yousef led me forward, careful to remain behind me. I weighed perhaps a 125 pounds and, at six feet, was as skinny as a rail. I didn't want to tangle with that big fist. I stepped into the doorway, looked the big man in the eye, and held my hands open.

"May I come in?" I was fully aware he couldn't understand English. I took a small step forward inside the doorway. He moved forward and then to my left. I felt him pull Yosef and me inside and then slam the glass doors behind us. The men outside pressed immediately against the glass.

Yosef stepped quickly across the sparse hallway and passed into the office of the chief customs inspector. I was amazed at all the communications equipment at this remote corner of the country. Except for the two-lane highway, this part of eastern Turkey did not have paved roads, light poles, guardrails, utilities for the towns and villages, and seldom had telephone service. People settled where there was a well or stream. They lived off the land with their flocks and grew their own food. Homes were built by collecting large rocks to use for flooring and walls; poplar logs were laid crossways to support a roof. The one-room homes had tiny twelve-inch windows. It was a big deal if one had concrete. Turkish Kurdistan was a primitive place.

But here in front of me were telephones, a fax machine, hand-held radios, etc., everything needed to contact the military, police, governor, or whomever. But these customs offices had been evacuated in fear of the rioters. Yousef and I were alone in the building. At least we had the big guy with the massive fists. I picked up the phone and dialed the UNHCR office twenty kilometers away in little Silopi.

"Is Lois there?" I asked. As chief field officer, she should be apprised of the situation. She had a take-charge attitude, was perhaps forty years old, Caucasian, and had no doubt seen conflicts in many countries. She was a good leader and very thorough. She also had the communications equipment to notify the UN guards stationed behind us, across the border inside Iraq. Because Iraq was a country in conflict, the blue helmets had been positioned in Zakho. The UN was not present in Turkey and consequently there were no UN guards to contact there.

"We're on our way," she assured me as she left Silopi. I went outside through the crowd of men to the Mitsubishi. Bob, Jan, and their children were inside, waiting anxiously.

"I think we should get away from this crowd," Bob announced. He drove toward the Turkish guardhouse that funnels the vehicles entering the border area from Silopi. The military trucks had all left by then, having moved closer to the unruly crowd, so we pulled out onto the highway and headed toward Silopi. There was nobody in the guardhouse at the actual border nor standing out on the pavement as we went by. The entire border was unprotected and unguarded. It was chaos. *How bizarre, and yet how typical for this region*, I thought. Minutes later, we passed the UNHCR vehicles in downtown Silopi. They were parked in front of a bakery, discussing the best course of action. The UNHCR is not a military force. They had no weapons or armor on their vehicles. The UNHCR is designed to monitor refugee or displaced persons in conflict places. It is concerned with repatriation, local integration, or resettlement of refugee peoples. Their main mission is not to diffuse crises. Lois and her team did check with us, however, to make sure we were fine, and then we headed home to our quiet place on the roof.

No report of the riot appeared in the papers. Turkish media is controlled by the government. No announcements were made about the wounded or dead. We asked our Kurdish friends what they had heard and were told one of the truckers had died from gunshot wounds. The truckers had stormed the border in exasperation after having waited ten days in a long queue in the Iraqi heat for permission to cross into Turkey. Truckers didn't have trouble leaving Iraq; there were no Iraqi border officials anymore. They were waiting in no-man's land to get into Turkey. Why did they have to wait for so long? Turkish customs officials were keeping the border closed until a sufficient bribe was offered. I was told the guards were demanding US $600 from each driver per trip, though I have no way to corroborate this. The border officials knew these truck drivers/owners were getting rich importing illegal fuel. Gas and diesel purchased in Iraq shouldn't be brought into Turkey; the international trade embargo against Saddam's regime prohibited that. However, when sufficient money was offered to the border officials, the fuel was allowed in. In vegetable trucks, of course.

Chapter 7

Bullets or Bibles?

Silopi, Turkey, Early December 1991

T he days following the border riot were a return to "normal." Mercy for All was continually changing, both in personnel and in the many projects we undertook. It all depended upon the continuing changing refugee crisis. The current team in the fall and winter of 1991 had six members: my wife and I; Dave and his wife, Dorcas; a single German woman, Irmela; and a young American, Barbara. Others came and went as they were able. Our job was to interview the refugees who had been settled in the Haj camp. It was called the Haj camp because each year the thousands of Turkish Sunni Muslims who were making the overland pilgrimage, the Haj, to Mecca in Saudi Arabia, could use this enclosed space outside Silopi to camp. Each Muslim is required by the Koran, if able, to make this pilgrimage once in their life. No one was using the camp in the fall and winter of 1991, so Turkey opened it to the refugees.

By the end of summer in 1991, most of the refugees who were going to return to Iraq had done so. There were some five thousand, however, who had decided they would never go back, and they were housed in large UNHCR tents in the Haj camp. They had suffered incredibly and wanted to leave Iraq permanently. These were not just Kurds but also Aramaic-speaking Assyrians (who also spoke Arabic—the national language of Iraq). The Assyrian kingdom dated from at least two millennia before Christ to its collapse in 612 BC. The Jews had been captive to the Assyrians at various times, as related in 2 Kings 17. Most of the Assyrians who were now in the Turkish refugee camp outside of Silopi practiced forms of eastern Christianity; they were from the Assyrian Church of the East, the Syriac Orthodox Church, and the Syriac Catholic Church. There were also Assyrian Evangelicals and Assyrian Pentecostals. Christians were feeling increasing persecution in Muslim Iraq and so many had left their homes for the last time.

Some of the tents for the 5,000 refugees in the
"Haj Camp" outside of Silopi, Turkey.

The Haj camp was perhaps a half mile by a half mile and sur-rounded by a cinder block wall and cyclone fencing with barbed wire across the top. The ground was stones and dirt, which became sticky mud in the rainy season. There were several vacant buildings and two large bathroom facilities. Of course, there was a stone mosque with a minaret. By the one entrance gate, there was a security office, where everyone coming and desiring to leave had to be checked. Mercy for All was given use of one of the buildings to conduct interviews. Each refugee family was asked a detailed list of questions which would be later used by foreign governments in deciding whether to allow them to immigrate. We bought some steel chairs to use for our interviews and occupied the vacant buildings each day. We also bought chains and padlocks so the chairs in our offices would stop disappearing.

Some young men in the Haj camp gathered for a photo. Kirk is in the center. In the background are some new apartment blocks under construction on the outskirts of Silopi.

The Mercy for All team were all unpaid staff seconded to the UNHCR. Our simple lifestyle was paid for by friends and family in our respective countries who believed what we were doing was worthwhile. In late October, Mercy for All rented and shared our own two-story concrete building outside of town, which had been recently built. There was living space upstairs for our team of six. The lower level was unfinished concrete and was not part of the living area. It might be completed someday with shops that had slide-up metal doors.

The three-bedroom home had two small bathrooms: one had a western toilet, the other a Turkish style ceramic floor commode. It was affectionately known as the squatty potty. The kitchen was tiled everywhere with white tile and had a countertop and sink. The grout had never been sponged off the tile. Irmela and Jane spent two days cleaning it to German standards. A low shelf was built where we could put a stove and place an LP gas tank. There was no heating in the house, no trash pickup, and the bathing room had a tub that leaked water through the wall into the living room. A serious case of mold developed in the living room wall. There was a showerhead that dropped water onto the bathroom floor where the water could run across the room to a drain. The water from the black plastic rooftop tank never got really hot, but the summer sun would take the chill off so one could have a decent shower.

During the winter rainstorms, water would run from the open balconies off each bedroom under the doorways and into the bedrooms. The balcony floors were slanted the wrong direction. It was not premium construction, but it seemed a palace to Jane and I, after living in tents. We did have a household shrew who came up through the Turkish floor toilet on a regular basis to look for food at night. Not so nice. We solved that problem by shoving a plastic liter water bottle in the toilet hole.

The army had abandoned a warehouse full of water bottles and toilet paper when they ended Operation Provide Comfort in the fall of 1991. So we created many uses for cutup bottles: candleholders, pots for plants, drinking glasses, doorstops, toothbrush holders, shrew stopper, etc.

We furnished our bedrooms with army cots and cardboard boxes for nightstands. A large roll of blue carpet purchased in town and laid out on the living room floor kept us from sitting directly on the concrete floor tiles. Two freestanding-room LP gas heaters helped keep the living room at a tolerable temperature. Evenings were spent sitting, talking, journaling, or reading in the living room. Nobody went to their cold bedrooms until it was time to sleep. Our bedding was the sleeping bags we each had brought. Meals were served on a plastic sheet spread on the living room carpet, while we were seated on cushions. Food consisted of military rations from Italy, Britain, France, and America, augmented by produce and bread from downtown Silopi.

There was one bank in Silopi, but it did not accept any traveler checks or credit cards and would only convert US currency to Turkish lira, if one had one-hundred-dollar bills that were not torn, marked, or damaged in any way. There were no ATMs. Sometimes, we ran out of Turkish lira and had to wait for Mercy for All visitors from Europe to bring us cash.

Mercy for All had provided us with a well-used Land Rover that had two bench seats running lengthwise in the back cab. Each day, I would drive to town and pick up our translators and then drive to the Haj camp. Every afternoon, when we were finished with our interviews in the camp, the entire team would assemble at the gate, wipe the two inches of mud from our shoes, and drive back to the office in town. Then we filed our reports, and we'd exchange any necessary briefings with the UNHCR.

I was surprised one evening to see my supervisor Lois and her assistant at the front door of our home in Silopi. I had only seen her at her office.

"We need to talk," she said. "Privately."

She had never even paid us a visit before. I wondered why we deserved the sudden attention. "Please come in," I said. "We have guests in the living room. Why don't we go into the kitchen?"

I led her and her Turkish office administrator into the narrow kitchen and pulled chairs out for them. Never one to waste words, she came straight to the point.

"What's this meeting you're having tonight?"

Over the past weeks, several of our Kurdish and Turkish colleagues had shown interest in the Bible. Our team of relief workers were all committed Christians who volunteered out of compassion and concern for the suffering refugees. However, the United Nations High Commissioner for Refugees seemed suspicious of us and of our motives for working in the region. After all, I was told that the local UNHCR officers received several hundred dollars a day, plus all expenses paid, for working in a hardship region. Why would anybody do it for free? The head field officer earned three hundred and fifty dollars, seven days a week. The refugees and nationals were also curious about these people from Mercy for All who work for free.

"Why do you do this?" they frequently asked. "How much do you get paid?"

"Our motivation comes from Christ, who has compassion for those who are suffering," we told them. "Our reward is eternal, not financial. We aren't paid anything."

Often, they continued their questions by asking us about our beliefs, about the Bible, etc. Several had been reading the New Testament and peppered us with questions each morning as we car-pooled together in the team Land Rover on our trip to the refugee camp.

It seemed fitting to invite the Kurdish and Turkish employees over for dinner in our home and focus on the Bible as part of the evening of hospitality. As I invited each of them to come for dinner, I told them we would discuss the Bible after our meal. The employees were all male; it would not have been culturally appropriate for a single woman to go out in the evening to visit, even if there had been females employed by the UNHCR in the camp. If the guys weren't interested or were offended, they could politely decline the invitation, or as is more culturally appropriate, simply not show up. I had extended the invitation to the national workers in the UNHCR office, being careful to invite everyone lest someone feel slighted.

It was now 3:30 p.m. on the day of our planned gathering, and Lois wanted to know what was up. I knew it would be of no help to point out that dinner was to begin at 5:30—after work hours—and it wasn't the first time we had hosted a large gathering for a meal. The UNHCR felt responsible for us twenty-four hours a day; none of our activities were considered personal.

"Lois," I began. "As you know, we're hosting a dinner tonight, homemade pizza, in fact. We invited quite a few of our friends and coworkers to enjoy the evening together—"

Lois cut me off.

"I understand you are having some kind of *religious* meeting. As you know, the Turkish police are nervous about any kind of political meetings."

In Turkey, which is entirely Islamic, religion and politics are one and the same. This can be best understood in the context of Islam itself. Mohammed led not just a religious conversion to Islam but a political one, building a government ruled by Islamic law.

I knew as well as Lois that the police could misconstrue any informal gathering, as somehow antigovernment, revolutionary, or even as a terrorist plot, particularly in this part of the country. It seemed absolutely ludicrous, but this was reality in eastern Turkey. The government was highly suspicious, always fearing the worst, and looked at all non-Turks as potential revolutionaries. Nevertheless, I tried to calm her fears.

"Lois, it's not a political meeting. It's a dinner party. Sure, after the meal, we'll talk about the Bible, but I assure you it isn't a religious or political meeting."

She wasn't convinced.

"'If the police come and arrest you, it'll look bad for the UNHCR. I don't want to take that risk."

If she forbade the gathering from taking place, I would comply, but I and the whole team had been looking forward to this event for weeks. I already felt the disappointment at the prospect of being forced to cancel it. I had invited fifteen young men, but even if only a few came, I knew it would be a valuable experience. As I spoke, I could see that Lois hadn't made up her mind.

"We'll keep everything low key, I assure you," I said, hoping to persuade her.

She turned to her administrative assistant (a Turk), whom I had, of course, also invited to the dinner.

"Listen, you mustn't tell others about this. People may get the wrong idea," she said.

"Oh, you can't keep something like this a secret! Nobody has ever spoken about the Bible in this town before. Everybody is curious. It's a big thing!"

Pleased as I was to hear his enthusiasm, I feared that he had just ruined it.

Surely Lois will forbid it now, I thought. I was sure she would say no.

"I guess you can go ahead with it if you keep it informal."

God had heard our prayers and had answered!

Little did I realize that the battle for the evening had just begun.

My colleague Dave parked our muddy Land Rover in front of the UNHCR office. It was 5:15 p.m., dark and cold. It had been an arduous day at the camp. We were exhausted. One by one, the team members unfolded our tired bodies from the cramped vehicle, stepped out onto the narrow dirt road, and climbed the concrete steps to the office. We greeted the office personnel and began storing the completed interview forms from the day's work. Upstairs, Dave's wife Dorcas peered out the window into the darkness. The sun was setting earlier and earlier as fall was turning to winter. The weather had turned to a biting cold. Soon there would be snow. From the second-story window, Dorcas had a fairly good view of the western half of the Turkish town of Silopi. Fifteen kilometers to the east was the Iraqi border, and a kilometer or so to the southwest lay Syria. In the distance, one could see the lights of a Syrian city.

"What are those strange red lights shooting up into the sky?" Dorcas asked.

Amman, the Turkish desk clerk, joined her at the window.

"Hey! Those are tracer bullets!" I explained to Dorcas that they are special bullets that are placed intermittently in the cartridge and they light up when fired. It allows bullets that are fired (at night) to be directed better.

Everyone leapt to the windows to get a look.

"They're over there too!" someone exclaimed.

The sound of machine-gun fire reached our ears.

"Get down! Everybody get down on the floor!"

The sound of the shooting came closer until it was on all sides of us. Directly behind the office was an elementary school. A flare went up over the school, fired probably from the nearby police station or military outpost.

Since we had been in town, there had been several attacks by Kurdish rebels on military outposts. The Kurds resented the control of the Turkish army, the daily searches of their cars, the demands for identification documents, the interrogations and arrests, and the general restraints of martial law. The only people in town of Turkish ethnicity were police officials, the military, and the mayor. The mayor traveled with a bodyguard, had his home encircled with razor wire, and had armed guards at the town hall as well as his home.

During the previous hot fall months, my wife and I had slept on the roof to catch the first breezes of the night and get a bit of respite from the incessant bugs. We were often awakened by machine-gun fire, occasionally by explosions. Most of it was unexplained—events the locals accepted as normal. But tonight was different. The intensity and duration were exceptional. It sounded as if the Kurds were shooting weapons from every home in town. And we were right in the middle of it. The only sensible thing to do was to stay put. We bolted the steel door at the bottom of the stairs, closed and covered the windows, and turned out the lights. I sat with my back against the concrete wall of the office, beneath the window. I reasoned that any bullet that passed through the window would travel over my head.

Interspersed with the firing, we could hear the high-pitched trilling of Kurdish village women. It was a sign of excitement, of victory, of joy. We had heard it before at weddings and at the New Year's celebration on March 20, the first day of spring.

"What is the date today?" I asked a colleague.

"November 12," he replied.

None of us could think of the significance of that date. Later, we realized it was the anniversary of the 1979 Kurdish uprising in Turkey. That explained the intensity and massive simultaneous shooting. The gunfire we heard was actually a celebration of sorts, a remembrance of their identity, their stubborn refusal to submit to Turkish authority. It was a demonstration of Kurdish power and feeling. But at the time, it was still a mystery to us.

As the shooting continued, it sounded like a full-scale war. The only thing missing was explosions. This perplexed us somewhat. Any attack on the military or police station would surely be accompanied by a planned bombing. Flashes of light came from the roof across the street as our Kurdish neighbor fired his weapon into the night.

I held my watch up to catch some light from the street lamp. It was already 6:30 p.m. I knew that Jane and two other teammates had gone to our house across town in the afternoon to prepare for the evening dinner. We had no news of them and no way of getting any. The rental costs for a telephone line were prohibitive, and we didn't have enough UNHCR radios to leave one at the house. The best I could do was simply entrust Jane and the others at our team home into the Lord's hands. But trusting isn't always so easy. I peered over the windowsill to look in the direction of the tracer bullets that were being fired from the field near our home. Located at the edge of town and close to the Syrian border, the house would be the first in line if Kurdish rebels were planning to overrun any buildings. With its flat roof and the low wall around it, the house would be ideal for launching an assault. I hoped Jane and Irmela had thought to lock their doors and turn out the lights.

Seated on the concrete floor around the perimeter of our office, the entire UNHCR Silopi staff as well as the hired nationals and my team members listened and waited. We decided that it wouldn't be safe for anyone to leave the relative security of the office and venture into the streets until the firing stopped for at least fifteen minutes. Although most of the people we had invited to dinner were with me in the office, we had no way to contact the others. I doubted they would be traveling anywhere tonight.

As I thought about the hindrances to our plans to simply discuss the Bible in Turkey, the phrase "spiritual warfare" took on an entirely new meaning. As the minutes ticked by, my thoughts and prayers were consumed with two things: *when will the shooting stop, and will anybody come to dinner in spite of the danger?*

It was 7:15 when the last shots were fired and 7:30 before I headed out to the Land Rover. As I opened the car door in the darkness, three strangers appeared from around the corner of a nearby building. With panic-stricken faces, they made it clear they wanted to get into our vehicle. Thoughts raced through my head: *Are they running from the military? Obviously. But why? Are they guilty? Or just scared?* Anybody found on the streets by the military would surely be immediately taken to jail, beaten, questioned, and who knows what. Perhaps they were just on their way home from work and had been stranded when the shooting started. All they wanted was a ride home. We let them climb inside the back of the Land Rover.

A moment later, a crowd of maybe fifteen adults and children appeared from a side alley. They looked both ways and then, as one body, raced by. I had never seen a Kurdish adult run; they were clearly scared to death. In a flash, the three strangers from our vehicle joined the crowd and raced up the muddy path.

I decided the best course of action was to drive slowly, stay in the light, and act normal. I turned the dome lights on as my teammates climbed in. No sooner were the doors closed than an armored Turkish military vehicle raced up the street with its gun turret turning. At the muddy path on our right, its searchlight scanned the road beyond the rear of our vehicle. It paused but a moment, apparently saw nothing, and then sped on.

We drove slowly along the deserted streets. It was eerie. Normally at this time of evening, people would be walking and passing us in the street. We drove by the bakery where we had planned to have our pizza baked. Irmela was an expert at rolling out the dough, which she purchased from the bakery. Then she would add the toppings and bring it back to the bakery to be baked. There is nothing like a bit of western cooking when far away from home. I was disappointed but not surprised to see the bakery all shuttered up. *Who in their right mind would keep their business open during all this madness?* I thought. But there were our guests to think of, after all. Several had told us earlier while we all huddled in the office that in spite of the danger they would come. It was astounding. Two of the older men, who also wanted to come, had first gone home to check on their families, but the other young men were quite interested and said they'd be coming right away, probably by foot. There were precious few cars in Silopi; if one was fortunate to own one, then it was automatically used as a taxi. No sign or meter was necessary; people would just wave, and the driver would stop and then haggle over a price. So most people walked.

I pulled up in front of our house, surprised to see the kitchen and living room lights blazing like normal. The downstairs door to the outside was closed but unlocked. I wondered what our team would find as we climbed the steps to the front door.

The three women were busy in the kitchen as we came in.

"When are you going to get this pizza baked?" they asked.

It was as if they had missed the gunfire entirely. We had been seated in the office on the floor in complete darkness for two hours, hiding behind concrete walls, and they had been standing in the kitchen, preparing supper with all the lights on!

"I guess you weren't too worried about the fighting," I said.

"Oh, we heard it all right," Jane responded. "But it seemed to be mostly in town, except for some shooting from the field out there." She pointed out the southern facing window from the living room to the pasture below our bedroom window. Across the pasture was a barbed-wire fence, the Syrian border.

Everyone was glad to see everybody safe and sound, and our attention soon turned to our expected guests. At that point, we did not understand the reason for the gunfire nor why it stopped nor why the Turkish army was racing about in armored personnel carriers. It was a strange phenomenon I can only describe as the mentality of a war zone. Life must go on. Food must be served; people must be welcomed if one is expecting guests. We loaded Irmela's prize pizzas into the Land Rover and went in search of a bakery. We did not expect to find any shop still open. But to our astonishment, there was a baker who had remained open on the other side of town. He said he had been too afraid to walk home because the firing was near his home and the Turkish army was stopping people in the streets to be "questioned." He gladly baked our pizza, and then I gave him a lift to his home. It was much safer to ride in a vehicle with a UNHCR emblem on the side than to walk the streets.

Five men (from the eighteen I'd invited) joined us for a rather late dinner and an even later discussion. Nobody was anxious to quit talking after the meal, and the questions and answers stretched late into the night. Some questions were theological: "How do you that know the 'One that Jesus promised would come' is the Holy Spirit and not Mohammed?" This is a common misunderstanding that Muslims have about the third person of the Trinity, the Holy Spirit.

And then there was the most frequent objection to the Scriptures we often heard: "We have always been taught that the Bible is full of errors and that it has been changed many times. Is that true?" This required some historical and archaeological explanations and a discussion about how the books of the Bible were formed into one book.

Other questions were more personal: "How can you know God's love?" This question was posed by a Kurd. Many Kurds are reticent to cling to Islam, since it is an Arab religion, and Turkish Kurds do not read Arabic nor identify with that culture. It is the Arabs who have oppressed Kurds in Iraq. They also do not identify closely to the Turks who have a historical animosity toward Christians (the Armenian massacre). The Love of God is a powerful motivator when their entire lives have been dictated by hatred.

Another asked, "How can one know that Jesus is the Son of God?" A major stumbling block for Muslims is to comprehend how Christians can agree that "God is One" while still maintaining the divinity of Christ, God incarnate here on earth. The concept of the Trinity is often taught in mosques as a belief in God, Mary, and Jesus. Such misconceptions prevail throughout the Islamic world.

We had grown to know these men well, considered them more than just work colleagues, knew them as friends, and it was perfectly natural to talk about spiritual things together. What in the west might be construed as religious talk, or too personal, is something in the Middle East that's common discussion. They loved talking about faith, belief, and the supernatural.

As followers of Jesus we were delighted to talk about our Lord. My purpose in life is to know God and to make Him known. It was this meeting and similar discussions that seemed the culmination of our work there.

There simply wasn't time to begin to satisfy the curiosity and searching. We parted regretfully, knowing that our project in the Silopi camp would soon be complete and our days together were limited. Winter was coming, and our detailed interviews in the Haj camp would soon be finished.

Part 2

Do not be afraid, for I am with you; I will bring your children from the east and gather you from the west.

—Isaiah 43:5

Part 2

Chapter 8

Two Starving Children

Silopi, Turkey, December 9, 1991

A short stocky man in obvious distress approached me in the refugee camp late in the afternoon as we were winding up the day's interviews. I had seen him before in the camp.

"My name is Serwan. I am alone here in the camp. I have received news that my children in Zakho are very sick." He had several days' growth of beard, and his wet black hair was combed back. He had something urgent to say. He thrust a slip of paper out at me.

"My baby was in the hospital last week. She is very sick. I am afraid she will die. Can you help me?" I wasn't sure what he wanted from me. We were living and working in Turkey at the time, not Iraq. And I had nothing to do with hospitals.

His pleas continued unabated. Great beads of sweat ran down his forehead into his bushy eyebrows. I didn't know what I could do, yet I felt compassion for his situation. I knew countless requests in the Haj camp each day went unanswered. Perhaps there was something I could do; I just needed some time to think. So I began asking him questions.

Serwan reminded me that he had two small children, girls. Jane and I had visited his children at his request some months previous in a home in Zakho. We had brought them nutritional supplements. We had suggested back then to Serwan that we bring the children from Iraq to join him in the camp in Turkey. However, he did not want his girls with him, unlike all other refugee parents with children. Serwan said he had left his girls at the home of an Arab man, Abdul Rahmann, prior to crossing the border into Turkey. He said he had knocked on the door of a random house in Zakho and begged the man living there to take his children, "For the sake of Allah." Serwan could not take care of them himself, he said. He had fled his village home near Kirkuk, Iraq, with his girls when the Kurdish uprising failed. Saddam's planes had bombed his home, killing his wife and parents. Prior to meeting me that evening, Serwan had received a message from Abdul in Zakho that the younger of Serwan's daughters, an infant, was extremely ill. We knew that letters and sometimes people were still smuggled back and forth across the border. I assumed Serwan had received this note from a surreptitious currier.

"Did you ask Ismet at the UNHCR office in Silopi for help?" I asked. Ismet was employed by the UNHCR to handle special and sometimes quite complicated situations.

"I asked them to help me. But they cannot do anything." I knew that was only a slight exaggeration.

In cases like this, the UNHCR was supposed to apply for permission for the children to be reunited with their parent, but as was often the case, things simply were not done, because of the huge caseload. Furthermore, the UNHCR was in the habit of changing personnel so frequently that their staff was either uninformed or incompetent.

But I wasn't sure I could do anything, either. Jane and I had visited Serwan's daughters in Abdul's home in September 1991. Serwan had given us small photos of them to take with us so we could identify them. They had seemed healthy at the time, though the older of the two had sat Indian-style against a wall and never looked up. Her eyes were full of tears. She had grabbed the photo from me and clutched it so tightly I decided not to attempt to retrieve it. Jane and I had returned to the Haj camp and reported our visit to Serwan. We told him his daughters needed him. They were lonely and afraid.

Serwan, however, was adamant that the girls not be brought over to join him in Turkey. He complained that conditions in the camp were not good enough. He said he didn't know how to take care of babies.

"Men don't know these things," he said. I tried to get him to look around and see all the children with their families; I even pointed out that women gave birth in the camp. But he was intransigent. He would not allow us to bring them to him. Now here he was again, waving his note in my face and desperate for help. His children were sick.

I didn't want to give Serwan any false hopes that I could solve his dilemma. But I assured him I would do what I could. He begged me personally to help him. In all honesty, I just wanted him to leave me alone; he sure was persistent! He gave me the slip of paper. It had the address of Abdul in Zakho, written in Arabic on it. This was where Serwan's sick children were living, in the home of Abdul Rahman, house number seven. I cannot read Arabic, however; so I couldn't identify Abdul's name, the street name, nor the house number. It was just a piece of paper with what looked like random scribbles on it.

I headed back across the expanse of tents in the Haj camp toward the entrance of the huge compound and spotted Bob Blincoe in his white Dodge pickup. Bob had rented a house across the border in Zakho, Iraq, with his wife and three children. But his work brought him often to Silopi, in Turkey. The market in Silopi also had more food compared to what Bob could buy in Zakho. One could even buy hamburger, ground up on the spot from a side of beef hung from a big beam in the store. Most of the shops in Zakho, Iraq, were still closed down or had been looted. Bob crossed the border almost daily. Sometimes, he came into the Haj Camp to visit the families of people he had met in Zakho, Iraq. On Sundays, he chauffeured the Orthodox priest over from the Assyrian Church in Zakho to come into the camp. Worship services were held inside a huge plastic tent that the refugees had constructed to serve as a church. It was the largest Christian gathering in Turkey, a country of seventy million people. Ironically, it was in the locked enclosure of the refugee camp.

I spotted Bob walking in the camp, ran up to him, and asked him to take me across the border. Crossing the Turkish/Iraqi border still involved a lot of uncertainty. One never knew if there would be a trucker's blockade, a strike, or even another riot. Sometimes, the Turkish guards closed the border; sometimes, they demanded we get special registration for our vehicles or come in to their office and present our passports to be stamped "exit." Other times, they waved us through. Bob crossed so often that the guards usually waved him through. I told Bob about Serwan's open-ended request for help and showed him the note. He agreed to give me a ride to Zakho that evening and to look for Abdul's house. Bob would be able to read the Arabic numerals and read the street names on the homes.

My purpose was to visit the children and check on their condition. Bob suggested we bring along Dr. Fred Pullen from one of the visiting medical teams. Teams of NGO volunteers came at regular intervals and assisted in various ways. Dr. Pullen was on a Baptist medical team from Texas. We found him in the Haj Camp, and he agreed to go.

Although Bob could read Arabic, we had considerable difficulty finding the house in the dark. Although I had been to the city of Zakho before, everything looked different at night. There were no landmarks. It was quite chilly as we drove up and down the narrow backstreets, looking for the hand-painted Arabic numbers on the concrete walls. I was grateful for my wool coat as I pulled it about my neck.

We found number seven on the correct street finally and knocked on the metal gate. Moments later, we were graciously ushered into a very simple family room, where eight children sat huddled on a bare concrete floor before a blaring TV. A young woman whisked a tiny baby girl out of the room and returned moments later, drying her off. She set the baby down on the cold concrete, close to the single kerosene heater and began drying her hair with a rag. I instantly recognized the baby and her sister from my earlier visit. I felt compassion for the tiny infant dressed in damp thin rags, shivering on the hard concrete floor. Then the woman said something in Arabic, and her six children left the room. Bob Blincoe, Dr. Pullen, and I stood there, looking down at Serwan's two children. Abdul began telling Bob in Arabic how difficult it was to feed eight children when he could not find work. He had been collecting furniture and reselling it. When people abandoned their homes and fled for their lives, they usually returned to find all their belongings gone.

Abdul's wife looked like she was twenty. She had a large belly. It is not uncommon for Kurdish girls to marry at age fourteen and begin having children right away. Abdul explained that this was his second wife; his first wife had died. I could not imagine what it would be like for a twenty-year-old pregnant mother to care for eight children under the age of seven.

Dr. Pullen took a careful look at the baby's tiny limbs and its distended belly and gave his diagnosis.

"Marasmus.[1] The baby has a severe form of malnutrition called marasmus. And the older one," he said, examining the baby's older sister, "her face and limbs are swollen, which is a symptom of a protein deficiency called kwashiorkor. It's also a kind of malnourishment." He continued to examine them, listening with his stethoscope and taking vital signs.

He turned to speak to us privately. "They must get out of here if they are going to live." Dr. Pullen continued, "The baby will die within a few days if she is not removed from this home." He concluded his examination of her by adding, "She also has an ear infection. And the toddler has a respiratory infection." My heart went out to them. I knew how debilitating a chronic respiratory infection could be. The baby was so weak and her muscles so deteriorated that she had difficulty holding her head erect. When I picked the little girl up from the concrete, she remained bent at the waist, her skinny legs parallel with the floor. She was as light as a feather. Serwan had

---

[1.] "Morasmus is a form of severe malnutrition characterized by protein deficiency. A child with marasmus looks emaciated. Body weight is reduced to less than 62% of the normal expected body weight for the age. Marasmus occurrence increases prior to age 1, whereas kwashiorkor occurrence increases after 18 months. Kwashiorkor is protein deficiency with adequate energy intake, whereas marasmus is inadequate energy intake in all forms, including protein." (https://en.wikipedia.org/wiki/Marasmus)

said the baby's real name was Payman and that the Arab foster family had given her the Arab name Nuha. I looked at little Payman. She had the biggest brown eyes I'd ever seen, with long brown eyelashes. She was clothed in just a thin and worn light-blue pajama and had no diaper.

Payman's brown hair was thin and falling out. Her belly was severely distended, and her arms and legs were mere bones with skin hanging loosely in folds. She had a bad burn on her foot, which was not healing due to the malnutrition, Dr. Pullen explained. It was likely she had been placed next to the kerosene heater to dry off and had been burned. Her fingernails were very long, an obvious sign of neglect.

The toddler's Arab name was Suha. Her sad eyes were also dark brown and her dark-brown hair a tangled mess. A big tear ran down a dirty cheek. She avoided us; we were strangers in her home. Her eye was infected and her swollen legs and feet in obvious pain when standing. She wore yellow baggy sweatpants and a very worn white top. Neither child had socks or shoes to protect from the cold concrete floor. I was wearing wool socks and a heavy coat.

Dr. Pullen knew better than Bob or me how urgent the situation was. Dr. Pullen turned to speak to Abdul Rahman, but Abdul spoke first. Abdul's English was passable, and he explained that the baby Nuha had been too weak to eat, so they had taken her to the little hospital in Zakho. Nuha was too weak to take milk from a bottle. So the doctors there had given Nuha two blood transfusions to keep her alive. Dr. Pullen then explained to Abdul his diagnosis of malnourishment. He turned to us and said we should go to Silopi and get a supply of Milupa, which is a powdered milk supplement, as well as liquid vitamins for both children. Although it was getting late, we decided to go and come right back; they needed food that night. Dr. Pullen had access to the meds.

We returned thirty minutes later and explained to Abdul and his wife how to prepare the milk powder and how to administer the vitamin drops. They wanted to give it to their own six healthy children as well, which Dr. Pullen wisely permitted; but he emphasized, "It is the two sick children who really need it. They mustn't miss a feeding no matter what."

As Bob and I drove the doctor to his home, we discussed the situation. The couple was obviously poor. They had six children of their own, plus the young mother was pregnant, making the care of Serwan's babies even more difficult. With little food in the house, it was clear who was getting it. Even though they meant well, we knew they were overextended.

Dr. Pullen realized that, even if we did supply the family with supplements, the two who needed it the most probably wouldn't get it. He was convinced that, given the present living conditions, the infant probably would not survive more than a day or so. The children needed a drastic and immediate change. As we paused at Dr. Pullen's house in Zakho, the three of us prayed together for wisdom and a solution. God was capable of the impossible. Surely, he would not have led us this far to fail us now. My heart was deeply stirred.

On the return drive to Silopi, it seemed utterly hopeless to me. Among the relief organizations, none were looking after orphans. We needed someone who would do what Mercy for All had done in the Zakho transit camp of the previous summer: look after the "vulnerable" people. But that camp was gone, as were its supporting structures. Mercy for All now had a new assignment. We were tasked by the UNHCR to interview, document, and register the five thousand refugees currently in Silopi who were waiting resettlement abroad.

Bob and I were aware that all the NGOs in the current relief effort in Iraq had special assignments, which could not simply be abandoned to look after two starving children. There were no more camps within Iraq, like there had been the previous spring and summer. We also knew that all the NGO workers in the region were preparing to leave Iraq for the Christmas holidays. (Even crises workers needed a break.)

"Who could stay and take care of two orphans?" we asked one another. "And where would they live?" Even more significant, "What would happen in the long term? When would the children be healthy enough to join their father in the refugee camp in Silopi? Would Turkey grant them permission to join their only living relative?" There were so many questions and no obvious answers.

"There is only one certainty," I said to Bob. "If the children stay where they are, they won't survive." Still alive in my memory was the death of the infant Baqtiar, who, according to UNHCR policy, had been placed with a refugee family in a tent…and died a week later. Our request to take care of him had been denied. He lay buried just a few blocks away in the Zakho cemetery where Jane and I had brought his tiny body.

"I will not sit back and watch these children perish," I told Bob. We both knew we would be having some serious discussions with our wives when we got home. Jane would still be awake when I got back to our flat on the outskirts of Silopi. She didn't usually sleep well when I wasn't home, and that was especially true when she had to listen to gunfire.

"If it is of any help," suggested Bob, "there is a house for rent around the corner from my place in Zakho."

"But we would have to find someone to live in it," I said. "That seems to be the more difficult problem. Who is going to take care of these girls?"

My heart was moved. Quietly, I pondered things over. *If Jane and I were to take care of the children, it would mean moving over the border into Iraq. The children could not be brought into Turkey: they had no birth certificates, no passports, not even identification cards! They had been born in a mountain village and were never registered with any civilian authority. Without papers of identification, they would have to obtain permission from the Turkish Ministry of Foreign Affairs to enter Turkey.*

"We need a short-term as well as a long-term solution," Bob summarized as he dropped me off at my house. "Something must be done tomorrow."

I slipped into our bedroom in the team house that night and got ready for bed. Sitting on the edge of the army cot, I nudged Jane. "Honey, we need to talk." She was still awake and wanted to know every detail of my visit. As I got ready for bed, I filled her in as best I could. The situation was so critical that my mind was racing. Jane's brown eyes filled with emotion as I described the condition of the little girls. Her dark-brunette hair flowed smoothly over the top of her flannel nightgown, her collar barely showing beneath several army blankets piled atop our sleeping bag.

Just a few days prior, she had said she was glad we were living in Turkey, where things were a bit safer than in Iraq.

"But, Kirk," she had said with a serious tone, "I never want to go back to Iraq again." I had told her that was fine; there was plenty of work for us to do in Turkey. But now I was considering asking her to move to Iraq. I posed the big question.

"To save these children, would you be willing to move to Zakho?" I asked. She felt the gravity of the situation and needed a bit of time to decide. There was a long silence.

Then I added, "I wouldn't be able to be with you continually. I will have to travel back and forth to Turkey to wind things up with the interviews. I still have to lead the work in the Haj Camp." I needed to be there most days, but there were other team members who were conducting the interviews. Dave, Dorcas, Barbara, and Irmela worked tirelessly.

"I don't know how often I could come across the border to be with you, but I'll come as often as I can."

"Where would we live?" she asked.

"I don't know yet," I responded. "Bob mentioned he knew of a place near his home that's for rent."

"What about clothes for the children? What about food? What about sheets, diapers...?" I appreciated her practical approach to things. Both of us knew that everything was scarce.

Then she reminded me, "Kirk, you know I said I never want to go back there."

"I know." I felt bad for having asked her. But I knew I would feel worse if I hadn't asked her.

"Let's pray about it now," I suggested. "Let's ask God to make it clear what we should do." We knelt on our army cots, under the warm two-person sleeping bag, held each other's hands, and poured our hearts out to our caring Lord.

"Lord, you are the Father of the fatherless. You call your children to serve the poor and needy. You said to us, 'True and undefiled religion is this, to care for the widow and orphan in their distress, and to keep oneself unspotted by the world." The words from James 1 that I had memorized when I was a teenager flowed from my lips. Surely, the plight of these little ones was of even greater concern to Him than to us; He would make a way if we would trust Him.

Turkish/Iraq Border, December 10, 1991

The next morning at 8:00 a.m., the Mercy for All team piled into our Land Rover, and I drove them to the Haj camp. They set themselves up in their cold empty rooms and then allowed families to come in one at a time to conduct comprehensive interviews. On the drive into the camp, I told the team about my visit the previous night, about Serwan's children and the need to find help for them before it was too late. I then returned to town. Silopi was just a few kilometers from the Haj Camp.

I drove the Land Rover up the main thoroughfare of town, avoiding the crowd of private taxis, which gathered at the main intersection with the highway, and paused to let a donkey and cart cross the roadway. I turned left onto a muddy side road, slid around the corner in the mud behind Silopi's only gas station, and drove up the street to stop behind the elementary school. Across the street was the UNHCR Silopi field office. The rented rooms had been well equipped with the latest technological gadgets. These would allow me to make some inquiries in other towns both in Turkey and Iraq on behalf of Suha and Nuha.

I climbed the stairs and met Lois and the other employees in the long open office area. I updated them on the situation; they knew about Serwan from previous appeals he had made. Some refugees were very persistent and pestered the UNHCR with pleas whenever the official vehicles entered the camp. Serwan was one of the familiar ones. Lois suggested to me that I try and locate an orphanage.

There was no telephone line connecting Silopi with Zakho, so I used a UNHCR radio. The first call was to the UNHCR office in Zakho, Iraq, to find out if there were any orphanages where the children could receive care. The midsize city of Dahok, Iraq, had an orphanage, I was told. However, due to the war, it was poorly equipped and was certainly unable to cope with a seriously ill child.

"It was out of the question," they told me.

Then I telephoned the UNHCR field office in Diyarbakir to ask their advice. We often had to try for thirty minutes before a call was connected. Kurds often cut the solitary power lines that ran from Silopi westward, we were told. The Diyarbakir office had authority over the Silopi office. The chain of command within the UNHCR traveled all the way up to Geneva, Switzerland. There were extraordinary resources spent sustaining the huge bureaucracy. I often wished more money was spent down where the needs existed.

The office in Diyarbakir advised me about changes in border travel. The UNHCR in Turkey was separate from the UNHCR in Iraq. It was becoming increasingly difficult for UNHCR vehicles, registered in Silopi, to cross into Iraq. Lois, the UNHCR officer in charge in Silopi, had made exceptions for emergencies. In special cases, her officials were granted permission to cross into Iraq to trace lost individuals. The UNHCR in Turkey had been issued a document from the Turkish government to expedite crossing border. We had a copy affixed to the window of the Mercy for All Land Rover, since we were contracted (unpaid) with the UNHCR. It smoothed over many border crossings. Turkish border guards would take a cursory look at the sticker in the window, then wave our vehicle through.

Bob Blincoe seemed to cross from Iraq quite frequently without problem; I envied him. Bob did not work for the UNHCR in Turkey but for Northwest Medical Teams,[1] which was contracted with the UNHCR in Iraq. The Iraqi UNHCR followed different rules. Besides, Bob had a great smile, a hearty laugh, three little kids, all of which endeared the guards to him. In Middle Eastern culture, relationships usually trump rules.

In my phone call to Diyarbakir, I asked the UNHCR protection officer what resources he could offer to help the two abandoned children in Iraq, who were surely going to perish.

[1.] Now called Medical Teams International

He replied with a question, "Isn't there some NGO down there that can take care of it?"

I told him, "I checked with everyone here. No organization is equipped to provide long-term care to sick babies. There is no orphanage that can take them in." In Iraq, there was no foster care system; most often an orphaned child was taken in by family members. I was told that adoption was considered unethical.

He continued, "What about Christian Outreach?" It was an NGO tasked with the distribution of providing nutritional supplements for babies and giving feeding and parenting instruction to young mothers. It seemed like a good suggestion. But I had already asked them.

"Their feeding teams are busy visiting villages all day long and can't remain at a solitary home to care for two sick infants," I explained.

We could think of no other possibilities.

Finally, he replied in exasperation, "Can't Mercy for All do something about them?" *It occurred to me that these two small people were merely irritants in this man's busy schedule.*

For a man whose job title was protection officer, it didn't seem like he was doing his job. I stifled the temptation to share my opinion with him.

I said instead, "Mercy for All will take care of it." I wasn't sure just how that would happen, but I was determined Suha and Nuha would not die just because the UNHCR was unprepared to deal with them.

"Fine," he said and hung up.

That's fine with me too, I thought. In the UNHCR chain of command, the decision of the Diyarbakir office trumped the Silopi office. I informed Lois that the protection officer in Diyarbakir had asked Mercy for All to handle Serwan's two children.

I left the Silopi office around 11:00 a.m. and drove to the Mercy for All team house on the outskirts of town. Jane had stayed home from interviewing that day; team members were allowed time off as they felt necessary. She'd struggled constantly with illness, sometimes respiratory, sometimes digestive, sometimes both at once. As I fidgeted with the downstairs entry door lock, which never seemed to open the same way twice, I wondered what her response would be when she heard about all my futile efforts. I pushed the door open and saw two cardboard boxes on the cement tile floor by the doorway. I knew she had made up her mind on a solution.

Her first words were, "These are some things I thought we might need," giving me a hug. I looked through the boxes: apple juice, biscuits, drinking water, candles, matches, toilet paper, cereal, army rations from various nations, and a bag with some of our clothes. We didn't have many possessions, so there wasn't much to bring. Besides, she didn't know where we would be spending the night anyway. *Now that is faith*, I thought, and smiled. She was prepared to leave one country, go to another, take but a few boxes, move into an undisclosed location, and begin to nurse someone else's children back to life. She was a real giver of life, and my greatest hero.

I loaded the things into the Land Rover, and we left for Zakho. It was now noon; I would have to be back to the Haj camp to transport the team back to our team house at 5:00 p.m. The Land Rover was the team's solitary vehicle.

In Zakho, we proceeded to Bob's home and then, at his suggestion, to the home of a couple who worked with another NGO in Iraq. Anja and Jon Van Denberg were providing medical services to surrounding villages in Iraq and were hosting traveling team members in their house. I explained our dilemma to Anja and appealed to her for help. She immediately invited us to stay with them and said that if her supervisor approved, we could continue to live in the house when Anja and Jon left for Christmas. In fact, they had paid the rent through March, and we could stay until mid-January when their new team members would arrive. And at no cost! *Dear God, you are indeed wonderful. Bless your holy name!* What an answer to prayer! Jane looked around the simple home and began to put away our few belongings.

At 4:30 p.m., I had to drive back to Turkey to transport the team from the Haj Camp to the team house, so I kissed Jane goodbye and left Jane with Bob Blincoe and Anja in Anja's home. Anja and her husband had rented half of a large house from an Assyrian family.

Most homes in Zakho were built, and added on to, so multiple generations and extended family could all reside on the same property. There was a door that connected Anja's living room with the rooms of the Assyrian family. Each had its own kitchen and bedrooms and bathroom. The backyard was shared, as was the flat rooftop.

Jane and Bob would collect Suha and Nuha from across town around six that evening and take them to Anja's home, which was on the other side of Zakho. There were separate communities in Zakho: the Sunni Kurds lived in one neighborhood, the Assyrian and Chaldean Christians lived in another neighborhood, and the Arabs lived in theirs. Each had its own market *(suk)* and schools. People could move freely between the neighborhoods, and the citizens of Zakho prided themselves on their peaceful coexistence.

I wondered as I left my wife in Iraq in the early afternoon, and crossed the border into Turkey, if I'd have trouble returning to the Van Denberg's in Zakho...

God, what am I doing leaving my wife in Iraq? I prayed silently. *Never in my wildest imaginations did I ever think I would do such a thing. Lord, you must be in this, or I would not feel this unexplainable peace inside. Protect her, I pray.* We knew unmistakably that we were doing the right thing. Of course there were dangers involved, but being fully confident of what was right made choosing anything else out of the question. We could not sit back impassively and watch two children die.

Once I was in Turkey, I drove to the Haj camp to pick up the Mercy for All team and bring them back to the team house in Silopi. At the same time, Bob and Jane were driving to Dr. Pullen's home in Zakho. Fortunately, the three residences—Bob's, Dr. Pullen's, and the Van den Berg's—were all rented from Kurdish or Assyrian families and were conveniently located within a block of each other. Dr. Pullen was in Iraq for December on a short-term outreach.

Together, the three drove across Zakho back to Abdul Rahman's home. They were warmly received; Abdul and his wife were a young couple, and they were greatly relieved that someone was taking the little ones. Serwan had told Abdul six months previously that he would be back in a couple of days to get them. But he never came back. He abandoned them there. Now Serwan wanted us to intervene and help his girls. He gave us a letter to give to Abdul giving us permission to take over their care.

Jane told me later how the first few moments with the girls transpired. Jane held baby Nuha in her arms. Her heart was stirred. She was a precious infant. She was hungry and sick but lovely. Jane opened her beige wool coat and placed Nuha inside against the warmth of her sweater. The temperatures were freezing cold outside. She looked down at the baby's frail figure. A pair of giant brown eyes with long dark eyelashes stared up at her from a beautiful olive skin face. Her body was skin and bones.

"Her name is Nuha," said Abdul Rahman. Nuha seemed unaware of what was happening.

"And this is Suha." A very weak and frail two-and-half-year-old cuddled up quietly in Dr. Pullen's coat. He carried her out to Bob's SUV.

Serwan had said Abdul was an Arab and that he had changed the children's names to Arabic names. Payman had become Nuha. Firmesk had become Suha. We were't sure which names to use.

Fifteen minutes later, they were each carried upstairs in the home of the Van den Bergs. There was no heater in the bedroom; the tile floor was covered with a cheap woven mat called a *kilim*. A large steel crib would serve as their bed for the first night. Later, Suha would sleep on her own low cot, left to us by the Italian Army.

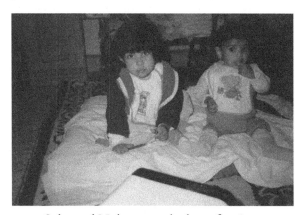

Suha and Nuha a couple days after Jane
began taking care of them.

Jane set about bathing the girls. She gently began to remove their clothing, but Suha began to cry. When confronted with a bathtub and water, Suha began screaming. When baby Nuha saw how upset her sister was, she started crying too. Anja assisted by heating water in the downstairs kitchen and carrying it upstairs to the bathing room. There was a water spigot and drain in the small square room, and Anja had brought a small plastic bathtub from Holland for her own nine-month-old son. This experience was just one more heart-wrenching and frightful transition in Suha's young life. Jane and Anja did their best to comfort and clean them.

Dr. Pullen had given Jane a bottle of special shampoo to de-louse their long dark-brown hair. When the water was poured over Suha's head, she launched into a full-throated scream. Nuha chimed in to voice her concern. The concrete walls seem to amplify the wailing. Jane's head was about to burst.

In a moment of divine inspiration, she asked Anja to slice an apple. The yearning for food was far greater than that to scream. Behold, it was instantly silent as each began chewing away. For Nuha, it was more like sucking; she only had a couple of bottom teeth barely showing. Her apple slice lasted the whole evening.

With each of them bathed and hopefully de-loused, Jane clothed them in things borrowed from Anja and the landlord's wife, Suheyla, whose family lived in adjacent quarters. As long as that apple stayed handy, things went smoothly. With diapers from Anja's supply and old sheets from the Haj Camp that had been cut up to form cloth diapers, they were all set for bed.

As Jane tucked them into the crib that night, she bowed her head in prayer. Her husband was miles away in another country. Outside, she could hear sporadic gunfire. Through a broken windowpane poured the freezing night air. At the end of her queen-size bed lay two very sick girls in a crude steel crib. But in her heart, Jane knew that God was very near, and yes, all things would work together for good. Humanly speaking, there were no answers for these little ones. She surrendered them to Him.

Back in the team house in Silopi, I lay awake for hours. The US Army cot beside me was empty. *So much is happening,* I prayed. *We*

*have just taken custody of two children. And here I am in Turkey, and
Jane is in Iraq. I'm glad you are Lord of all, Jesus! This is unbelievable!*

December 11, 1991

Five thirty in the morning came sooner than usual for Jane.
This was the first day she began taking care of the two girls. The
smell from the crib at the foot of her bed reached her nose before
the light of day. Both girls had serious stomach agony, which meant
changing lots of diapers and cleaning up their clothes and the bed.
The unpleasant cleanup job would become routine; each of them
filled their diapers and whatever they were wearing at least five times
a day.

Once the girls had clean clothes on, ragged as they were, Jane
decided this would be a good time to teach Suha how to brush her
teeth. She gathered her brush and toothpaste and led Suha into the
bathroom. Suha followed despondently and watched in silence as
Jane tried to explain how to brush teeth. Suha wanted no part in it.

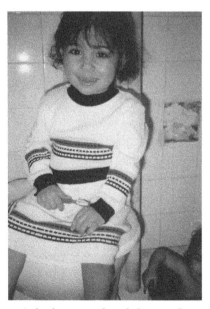

Suha learns to brush her teeth.
(The bathroom upstairs in the home in Zakho.)

Nuha demonstrates her flexibility
(after several weeks of nutrition). The water had to be heated
downstairs on the gas burner, then carried upstairs.

The beds had to be stripped and the sheets cleaned. The house was equipped with a miniature washing machine, but there was no dryer. The washer was "like a Suzie homemaker washer," Jane told me. It operated with cold water only and had to be filled with a bucket. It did not adequately spin.

After the first couple of loads, she decided to wash the rest of the laundry by hand in the tiled bathroom. It at least had a spigot and drain. Squatting on the floor, she worked with large plastic pans and buckets to do load after load. Jane went downstairs to heat water in a pot on the LP gas burner in the kitchen. Then she hauled it up to the bathroom. But within a few days, LP gas availability from the city ceased. Jane had to rely on sporadic deliveries of LP gas tanks that I would bring from Turkey. Soap was scarce, both for the washing machine and for personal hygiene.

The infrastructure in Iraq was dependent upon Baghdad. Oil revenue from the country's wells provided all the energy for the cities. During the Gulf War, Saddam set fire to over six hundred oil wells, depriving the country of energy and income. Over five billion barrels of oil were lost each day until the fires were extinguished.[1] Putting the fires out was difficult, because Saddam had mined the areas around the wells. Most cities received subsidized electricity. When the Kurds rebelled, much of that was cut off. Water was available in the house, but it was not safe to drink.

Everything edible that Suha and Nuha laid eyes on they wanted to eat. The second night I was able to stay the night in Iraq. Jane made a delicious dinner, including a pan of fried potatoes, but we had a small disaster. Suha caught sight of the serving platter covered with sliced potatoes, and as Jane set it down on the table, Suha grabbed wildly for the dish. I stopped her, and she threw a fit. She wouldn't let anybody near her. With one mighty swipe of her arm, she sent her cup of chocolate milk into orbit, followed by her plate and silverware. That made Nuha cry, too, which added to the chaos.

Jane carried a screaming Suha up the stone steps in the house to the bedroom, while Suha furiously beat on Jane with a metal spoon. I followed Jane up to the bedroom so Suha could calm down. I sat down beside Suha on her low cot, and she promptly sunk her teeth into my leg. I decided a couple of thick quilts between us might be a good idea. Her tantrum carried on and on. Screaming for hours on end was one thing both of the girls seemed adept at.

One day, Jane cut a cucumber in half and gave it to Suha. She grasped it in her fist and carried it with her everywhere she went in the house the whole day, nibbling on it sporadically at will.

Most of the days were spent feeding, cleaning, and giving medicine. The girls cried and cried unless they were eating or sleeping. They were experiencing the pain of illness, the discomfort of being constantly cleaned with cold water, and the pain of separation. When morning came, they were crying not just because they were dirty; they were both hungry for breakfast. They had experience hunger for six months. Now was their chance to eat!

Since the Van den Bergs had a little boy, they were equipped to handle a baby. Anja gave Jane a bottle for Nuha and a child's cup

---

[1] https://en.wikipedia.org/wiki/Kuwaiti_oil_fires

for Suha. Anja had a rubber mat for the baby to sit on and a supply of diapers that she'd purchased in Turkey at about one dollar apiece.

Anja had given us one of the upstairs bedrooms to share with Suha and Nuha. The kitchen and living room were used by both Jane and the Van den Bergs. December was really cold; it would begin to snow any day.

On December 12, I brought Jane a large gas heater from Silopi. It was designed to accommodate a five-gallon propane tank. The problem was that when used indoors without ventilation, a person could get carbon monoxide poisoning. Several army blankets kept Jane and the girls somewhat warm through the night. A piece of cardboard and a rag jammed against the broken window frame prevented some of the cold air from streaming in. It was shoddy at best.

In the ensuing days, we were challenged to establish the girls' ages. Serwan had been very vague at this point, giving us different birth dates on two different occasions. Dr. Pullen guessed that Nuha was about a year old, judging from the two baby teeth that had appeared. During the week of December 11 through 18, she cut four more. She weighed a mere 11.6 pounds. She was unable to even roll over. Her muscles were so atrophied that standing, or even crawling, was out of the question.

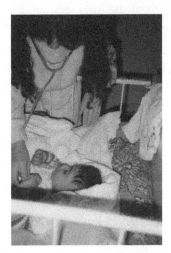

Jane found her nursing training invaluable. Nuha was
over one year old and weighed 11.6 pounds.

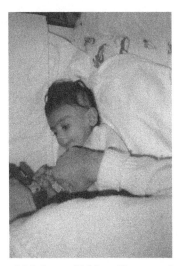

Kirk and Nuha in Zakho. She was alert and
responsive, just very, very hungry.

Suha looked like she was perhaps two and a half years old, judging by her size. I'd never seen a little girl so depressed. Nothing could make her smile. She didn't even want to make eye contact. I thought, *Lord Jesus, can we somehow bring joy into this sad little face?* They were both so vulnerable, so in need of love.

Suha's days were filled with long periods of crying, interrupted by occasional fits of rage. *Lord, what tragedies has this poor creature endured?* we wondered. Serwan said that, nine months previously, which would have been around the time of the suppression of the Kurdish uprising, Suha's mother and grandparents had died when Saddam's forces had attacked Kirkuk. *But what did Suha remember from that awful time?* I pondered. *And then fleeing and living in Zakho with Abdul's family?* It was deeply troubling.

I thought back to the night we had met with Abdul Rahman. I asked if he knew Serwan personally before taking his children in.

"I only did it for Allah," said Abdul. "The man said he needed work and was going to come back in two or three days and get them." He continued, "I didn't know the man who brought me these children. He just arrived at my door and pleaded with me to take care of them. I didn't do it for him. I did it for Allah," he repeated.

I tried to return from Silopi to be with Jane and help her every night from December 11 to 22. But most evenings, when I finished traveling from the Haj Camp in Turkey to the city of Zakho in Iraq, I was exhausted. And Jane was also *kaputt*, as we said in German. It was important that I regularly bring her drinking water, toilet paper, diapers, groceries, and the five-gallon tanks of gas. From the *suk* (market) in Zakho, I purchased some simple clothing and shoes. Suha delighted in a pair of plastic green boots and tromped around the house in them. A plastic black and white rubber ball gave her a bit of momentary pleasure. But most of the time, the precious little girl sat in my arms and cried her heart out.

I spent hours at night lying in bed in Zakho beside Jane, thinking of possible ways to get the children across into Turkey where medical care was available and where, hopefully, Serwan would assume care of them. During the summer of 1991, Kurds frequently crossed the border to get into and out of the Haj camp. Turkey allowed families to be reunited. But in December 1991 that was no longer possible.

I wondered if Serwan would agree to come to Iraq and resume care for them. But he said he was unwilling to leave the Haj camp. We discussed every option. Perhaps the Kurds in Zakho had some kind of authority that would help. We realized we needed some kind of proof that they were Serwan's children; then we could present them to the Turkish authorities.

Neither of the girls had any forms of identification. They had no birth certificates, Iraqi ID cards, nothing. Without proper papers and permission from the Turkish authorities, the border was impenetrable. *Only you can make this happen, Lord Jesus*, I prayed.

On December 16, while the team in the Haj camp had a day off, I left Jane with Suha and Nuha and went to downtown Zakho to visit a group of Kurdish men. They had set up a public affairs office in lieu of a provisional Kurdish government for the region. At 10:00 a.m., I walked into the otherwise empty public schoolroom where they were gathered and presented my case.

The Kurdish men listened carefully. I wondered what they would think of an American taking care of two abandoned Kurdish children.

With a warm smile, an elderly Kurd stood up and said to me, "What you are doing is wonderful." He walked up to me and gave me a hug. "If these two girls were sent to live with a relative, they would become a slave to the family. And then when they reached the age of thirteen, they would be married off to an old man to get a dowry. You are doing a great thing!"

Feeling encouraged, I then asked if they could help.

"I'm sorry," was the reply. "We have no official documents. We don't even have a government stamp. None of the children in the north have been registered, if they were born after the uprising and the sudden departure of all government officials. Thousands of people are without any identification here in the north. We have no way to register them." His final statement was most disheartening: "Anyway, in Iraq, you can only be registered in the town where your father was born."

I knew what he was saying about the Baghdad government evacuation of employees was true. I had driven by the police station; it was thoroughly trashed and torched. All prisoners had been freed from Iraqi prisons in the north of Iraq during the uprising. Most likely, they were all living in the Haj camp. Many of them were political dissidents. I knew that the schools were closed, since teachers had been paid by Baghdad. None of the Arab government employees dared return to Zakho for fear of their lives. Without a government, there could be no documents prepared for anyone; there was no way they could assist me. I thanked the fine Kurdish elders and left them, feeling discouraged.

Lord, where do I go next? I prayed as I stood outside the schoolroom on a busy street in Zakho. There were simply no Iraqi officials in Zakho. And even if there were, the birth father was registered in Kirkuk, and thus his children would have to be registered in Kirkuk.

Civilian registration in a totalitarian state like Iraq was a foreign concept to me as an American. The central government of Baghdad wanted to know where they could find any citizen at any given time. They had developed a simple system so that families would be all connected to the birthplace of their ancestors. A baby had to be registered where his father had been registered. A person's given name was followed by his or her father's given name, followed by his or her grandfather's given name. The registration card showed the family tree, the place of birth, the birthdate, a photo, and the baby's religion, which was of course the religion of the family. In their world view, to convert from one's given religion meant the person was absolving themselves of their family and its history.

But how was I to get Suha and Nuha registered in Kirkuk? Serwan would not return to Zakho in Iraq, much less the oil-rich city of Kirkuk, where Saddam's army was still fighting Kurds. Serwan told me he could be hanged as a collaborator immediately if found by the Iraqis. Serwan had served seven years in the Iraqi army during the Iran/Iraq war in the 1980s. Now he had fled with the Kurds.

In fact, his children could be imprisoned as an incentive to get him to turn himself in. I had heard many such accounts during interviews in the Haj camp. Wives, mothers, even babies were arrested and tortured because their spouses, fathers, or sons had deserted from the army. We found it hard to understand how a government could arrest and torture a baby. But the evil genius of Saddam knew that people would divulge any secret, indeed say anything, to spare the life of their child. Mothers had reported to the UNHCR that their baby had had electrodes hooked up to it while the mother was forced to watch so she would tell the whereabouts of the father, who had deserted from the Iraqi army.

Then it got even more complex. If Serwan did return to Kirkuk, the offices were closed due to the war.

"There is no chance of obtaining ID for the children," I was told repeatedly. And without proof of their relationship to Serwan, the Turkish government would not allow them entry into Turkey to be reunited.

I crossed the street at 3:00 p.m. and rang the bell at the offices of the multiforce Military Command Center (MCC) in Zakho. I had been told that under special circumstances the US Army would fly sick people to Ankara for treatment. *Why not ask?* I thought. *The worst thing that can happen is they will say no.* And that is exactly what I was told.

"Without written permission from the Turkish government, we cannot bring anybody to Ankara. Sorry, I can't help you," the commander said flatly. I returned to the Van den Bergs' house hopelessly frustrated.

Then I had an idea. *I will create an unofficial identification document.*

It was after 4:00 p.m. when I entered the UNHCR offices in Zakho. I made my way to the room where the laptop, printer, and copy machine were hooked up. I had been to this office once before with Bob Blincoe, but curiously, nobody was present when I entered. As the Mercy for All Project leader, I had permission to use UNHCR office equipment, telephones, etc. I opened a new document on the computer.

At the top of the page, I typed out the words PERSONAL IDENTIFICATION. I entered the basic biographical data for each of the children, leaving room to attach small ID-type pictures. In a short statement at the bottom of the page, I explained the death of their mother and the flight of their father to Turkey. Serwan had given me the mother's name and the estimated dates of his hurried departure from his small village in the province of Kirkuk. I typed all the information Serwan had given me onto the single sheet and hit Print.

The following morning, December 17, I met with the new UNHCR Zakho Head of Office, a Mr. Stein. I had never met the previous officer who held that position. The personnel were constantly changing. Mr. Stein was a tall stern-looking German and was new to the Iraqi office, and he questioned me thoroughly about Suha and Nuha's case. Then he radioed the UNHCR in Turkey to verify my story with Lois and request further instructions. Silently, I thanked God that I had gone through all of the appropriate channels before taking the kids into our custody. Mr. Stein asked me why I was involved. I explained that the UNHCR protection officer in Diyarbakir had asked Mercy for All to help with the sick orphans.

Lois then said over the radio to Mr. Stein, "Go ahead and write a letter on UNHCR stationary. Ask the mayor of Silopi to allow the children to enter Turkey and remain in the care of Mercy for All, with the intent of eventually reuniting them with the father." Mr.

Stein then typed up the letter and then certified that the attached ID information was accurate. I thanked him for his assistance and left his office.

With the letter in hand, I headed into the business center of Zakho to the local copy shop. I knew the shop had a laminating machine, because several organizations had made ID cards there. I glued the letter from Mr. Stein, back-to-back to the personal ID page I'd created. I attached two pictures of the girls, which Serwan had given me to the ID page. Serwan had had the photos taken in Zakho many months prior, before going to Abdul's house.

Then I had the whole page laminated. It was not an official government identification; it was "secondary identification." I felt great. This might be the first step in getting Suha and Nuha reunited with Serwan.

It was reassuring, after all the hurdles, to know that we'd done everything with UNHCR approval. The Zakho UNHCR office had written the letter of request to the mayor of Silopi, the Silopi UNHCR office had permitted Jane and me to travel to Iraq, and the Diyarbakir office had asked Mercy for All to save the two girls.

I showed Juan Carlos, the UNHCR protection officer in Silopi, the laminated document the next day.

He smiled broadly and said, "This is great! I'll have to send a copy of this to Ankara to show them how it should be done!"

I continued driving back and forth between Zakho, where I slept, and Silopi, where I worked. I accomplished errands in Silopi or in Zakho while the Mercy for All team was on assignment in the Haj Camp conducting interviews.

Jane continued to stay in the Van den Bergs home in December, though the Van den Bergs left on December 17 and headed back to Holland to celebrate Christmas with their family. They kindly left the children's items for Suha and Nuha to use. Jane could not leave the house to buy anything or to even walk around town. Besides, it was nearing zero degree celsius. She had to stay inside with Suha and Nuha at all times.

The Assyrian Christian family next door were very kind and brought Jane food from time to time, as well as invited Jane, Suha, and Nuha into their living room for tea. Suha was making a quick recovery. She was mobile and conversant, yet both she and Nuha were having constant digestive issues. Dr. Pullen had treated both girls for worms, for parasites, and for giardia. Still they were sick.

Suha was right at home with the little tea glasses and sugar cubes. Jane would speak Kurmanji Kurdish with Suha, and she understood some, although her Kurdish mother tongue was actually Sorani. Bob Blincoe, his wife Jan, and their oldest daughter Heather stopped by to encourage Jane when they could, knowing she was isolated and working 24/7 caring for the children.

In spite of the laminated secondary identification document, it still was unclear if the Silopi mayor would grant the request for Suha and Nuha to cross the border. We knew that if Suha and Nuha were allowed to cross into Turkey, they would be legal refugees and must go to the Haj camp. We were concerned what would happen to Suha and Nuha once they were reunited with Serwan. We did not know how Serwan would react.

He had asked us to intervene and save them from dying, and I had given him regular reports about their health when I saw him in the camp. I was easy to find because I worked from one of the offices on site. And I knew in which row of tents I could go to find him. Serwan had written a kind letter (in Arabic) to Abdul, thanking him for his help and reassuring him he wanted Suha and Nuha to be cared for by Jane and myself. But we all wondered, *Would he take them into his tent and care for them?*

How would they survive, in the middle of winter, in the Haj camp? They needed intensive medical attention. The conditions in the Haj camp in December were terrible for healthy people and unthinkable for sick babies. The UNHCR had not yet obtained any heaters for the tents. There was a sea of perpetual mud and filth everywhere. The bathing and toilet facilities seemed inadequate. We knew they would perish if they did not have intensive medical attention. Since such care was not available through any organization in either Zakho or Silopi, the UNHCR stated specifically that the children were to remain in our care.

Winter rains made life in the camp miserable.

Trying to wash dishes. December in the Haj Camp (1991)

Children's art, in the Haj Camp, reflect the
trauma of their flight.

It seemed that the only way the children were going to survive
was if Jane and I had sufficient time to nurse them back to health.
But what then? Put them in the Haj Camp? As difficult as it would
be to place those two compromised children in that environment,
it seemed like that was the only option. However, in our best judgment, as well as the judgment of everyone we talked with, Serwan
was incapable of raising them. He had even said this himself.

There were so many unanswered questions. *Who has legal jurisdiction to help us in this case?* we asked ourselves. *Is it the UNHCR? The
Turkish government? The Iraqi government? Kurdish officials? Nobody?
God, help us find the answer.* The only foreseeable option was to try
and get them placed in the Haj Camp. *God, help us find the answer,*
we prayed. *Show us what to do once (Lord willing) we have brought the
kids into Turkey. But for now, help us through one more day!*

Chapter 9

"Please Adopt Them."

I prayed for this child and the Lord has
granted me what I asked of Him.

—1 Samuel 1:27

Haj Camp, Silopi, Turkey, December 22, 1991

I removed my black boots and placed them next to the mud-en-
crusted tennis shoes at the tent entrance. I stepped onto the
blanket that served as a floor to Serwan's simple abode in the Haj
camp in Silopi. The other single men with whom he had shared his
abode had moved out of the chilly tent and into a vacant building.
However, he preferred solitude, he said, and so remained there alone.
I greeted him with the customary Kurdish greetings, kissing him on
both cheeks, and sat down near the gas burner that served as stove
and heater. He lit it to provide some warmth.

Although it was past 10:00 a.m., he was just rising. The inac-
tivity of refugee life encouraged late sleeping. He splashed cold water
onto his unshaven face and ran a wet comb through his black hair. At
five and a half feet tall, he could stand comfortably without brushing
his head on the canvas tent ceiling.

"*Te çay dixwazî* (Would you like tea)?" he asked. I knew it was no easy task in those conditions to prepare anything and politely declined his generous offer. In spite of my protestations, however, he insisted in typical Kurdish fashion and prepared tea. Hospitality and generosity are fundamental aspects in the culture to a degree that astonishes westerners. If, for example, one makes the mistake of expressing polite admiration for an object in a Kurdish home (or tent for that matter), the object is joyfully presented to the guest. No amount of protestations can stop the item from being received.

We experienced this the previous April in Hakkari. Jane and I were visiting a Kurdish family in a simple mud home. I made the error of admiring a Kurdish key chain, which a colleague showed me made with a tiny pair of woolen handwoven socks. A moment later, our hostess appeared with a man's pair of the beautiful black-and-white socks. No amount of argument could stop her from giving them to me. I still have and cherish them.

After some preliminary small talk with Serwan, I came around to the purpose of my visit.

"I came to talk to you about Firmesk and Payman." I used the Kurdish names Serwan had given his daughters at birth. I did not want to offend Serwan by using their Arabic names. As a Kurd, he would prefer their Kurdish names. Furthermore, I was told that in Arabic, Nuha can mean "enough" and was given to Payman presumably because Abdul already had six children. I didn't think Serwan would appreciate that very much. However, it can also mean "mind," or "wisdom."[1] Suha in Arabic is the name of a bright star. The meaning of names is very important in the Middle East.

I reported on their improved condition. In the twelve days since we started caring for them, both girls had gained some weight and were more active. They still had severe digestive problems, however, a serious condition at that age. They required continuous care, which Jane was lovingly providing. The various infections had been treated, but healing was slow in their emaciated state.

---

[1] http://www.behindthename.com/name/nuha

Serwan spoke passable English. He also spoke German, Greek, Sorani, Kurmanji, Arabic, and Turkish, he said. He preferred to talk to me in German. He said he was concerned others would over-hear him. This perplexed me, but I was quite comfortable speaking German with him. He had traveled widely, mostly illegally, and had worked in many places in Europe. Most Iraqis spoke some English because it was taught to them in public schools. Iraq's primary school attendance rate was reportedly 100 percent, and illiteracy was below 10 percent.[1]

"What is your plan for Firmesk and Payman?" I asked even-tually. "My wife and I have to leave Iraq soon." Our home was in Berlin, and I personally required regular medical attention due to being born with cystic fibrosis (CF).[2] Serwan could see I was having difficulty breathing and he knew of my illness.

I continued, "In fact, our plane tickets are for five days from now, December 27. What do you want Jane and me to do? We can-not live in Iraq indefinitely." There was a long silence. I waited for Serwan to speak. This was his decision to make. I knew making a firm commitment was difficult for him, but they were his children, and something had to be done.

We discussed the alternatives. Since Turkish officials would not permit Suha and Nuha to cross into Turkey without special permis-sion, they could not immediately come into the Haj Camp, to join Serwan or to be cared for by other women refugees living there. Lois and I had suggested that he locate some other refugees to help him, as an alternative. He was unwilling.

---

[1]. https://en.wikipedia.org/wiki/Education_in_Iraq
[2]. https://www.cff.org/What-is-CF/About-Cystic-Fibrosis/

There were thousands of children in the camp.
Pictured here are some preschoolers in a portable
school building, donated by Israel.

The girls had to remain in Iraq for now, and someone in Iraq would have to be found to care for them when Jane and I left. I explained that I was working hard to obtain permits for them to enter Turkey. If the permits were granted, what then?

"I have prayed about this," he began in English. "And God has given me a peace to ask you to adopt them. Would you and Jane be willing to adopt them? Could you love them as your own?" This was a surprise to me. There was a long silence.

Jane and I had grown attached to them in the twelve days during which we'd cared for them. We knew we could love them as our own but had tried to remain as emotionally detached as possible, thinking of ourselves as temporary foster care givers. We assumed they would be reunited with Serwan. So adoption didn't seem like a real option. But we were willing to pursue that if it were a possibility. We had prayed for years about adopting.

"Yes, Serwan," I said slowly. "We could love them as our own." My heart was jumping up and down. "In fact, we have grown very fond of them as we have taken care of them each day. We have a love for them already. If you truly want us to adopt them, then I know we would be very happy to become their parents." Jane and I had privately talked about this possibility. There was a long pause. However, Serwan needed a reality check. "I don't know if it's possible, Serwan, but we are willing to try. Firmesk and Payman are in Iraq without papers. You are in a Turkish refugee camp. Jane and I reside in Germany, and we are American citizens. It is probably impossible." There were a few hurdles to cross.

"That is most important to me," he said, "that you love them." I wasn't sure he'd heard me mention the hurdles.

"Of course we love them. And if we adopt them, they will be to us just like biological children. They will have every right of natural children, become our heirs—"

"What matters to me is that you love them," he interrupted.

We would always remember this day as a turning point in our lives (along with December 10, when we began to take care of the children). On this day, December 22, Serwan said he wanted us to adopt his children! Wow! What an answer to nights of prayer. The longing in our hearts to give these two precious girls the health care, love, and home they need had been growing daily. We rejoiced that we could now begin to think of these children as perhaps someday ours.

During the past twelve days, we had been completely committed to returning them to their father. Emotionally, we had to force ourselves to maintain a certain distance from them. We talked about our feelings and prayed about it a lot. It had been extremely difficult to do so. *Maybe they would end up in an orphanage*, we thought. We reminded each other that we were only taking care of them. Yet we had sacrificed greatly to help them. Jane had been working tirelessly to save Suha and Nuha from death. We had extended our stay with Mercy for All beyond what was healthy for me. I had developed one of my recurring lung infections, that I repeatedly got as a person with cystic fibrosis. We were taking great risks ourselves to see the girls survive.

There was a strange transformation that happened, when we, who wanted to have children but couldn't, suddenly were faced with the remote chance of parenthood. Something undefined stirred within our hearts.

When Jane and I became married in 1984, we had no anticipation of having children. In fact, when I was diagnosed with cystic fibrosis, it was expected that I would only live to be twenty. Jane accepted that her new husband, who was now twenty-six, would probably only live five years or so. When God saw fit to extend my life, she began to want to adopt children. We prayed about it, and eventually, I was also wanting children. We knew that men with CF are born sterile.

In 1989, Jane and I had prepared all the documents and home studies to adopt a child from Romania. The corrupt Nicolae Ceausescu had been deposed, and as Romania opened up to the world, the orphanages were found to be deplorable. Over a thousand Americans adopted children from those orphanages.[1] We thought that might be possible for us. We had completed the paperwork in California, as well as in Berlin. We were prepared to adopt a little Romanian boy, Daniel Budisan, one of twelve children, whose parents were both alcoholics. We made preparations to drive from Germany to Romania when the time was right.

But in 1991, Romania temporarily halted all their adoptions so they could rewrite their laws. There had been increasing abuse of the system, and their government wanted to fix their adoption system. We understood from God that He was closing that door. We would never meet little Daniel. Then quite suddenly, God took us out of Berlin and led us to complete involvement with Kurdish refugees in the middle east. First, we were in Çukurca, then in Zakho, then in Begova, then in Silopi, and then back in Zakho. During this time, we hadn't thought seriously about adoption.

We were willing, if it became necessary, to open our lives to the little baby boy George (Baqtiar). That didn't happen; we had stood beside his open grave in the Zakho cemetery as he was buried.

[1.] http://www.npr.org/2012/08/19/158924764/for-romanias-orphans-adoption-is-still-a-rarity

So our hearts had been willing to adopt. When Jane and I held baby Nuha in our arms on December 10 and held the hand of Suha as she hobbled along, it was natural to be drawn to them and to want to fulfill their need for love (and food!) We are both compassionate by nature and drawn to those with great need. That was part of the driving force that led us to minister to Kurds, a people without a country, without a church, without the gospel. Was there any greater physical need than to rescue two dying children?

But we knew adopting would not be easy. I feared that the UNHCR might be against us adopting because of their general policies.

"Suha and Nuha are not presently refugees, and thus don't fall within the UNHCR's jurisdiction," I said to Jane. I also knew that my employer, Mercy for All, did not want us to do anything that would upset the UNHCR. Mercy for All operated with a Memo of Understanding with the UNHCR, which had been approved by Turkey. The UNHCR did not want to upset Turkey; it did not want to be kicked out of the country. Turkey was never happy about having the international agency operating within its borders.

I took a taxi back to the Van den Bergs' home as the sun was setting. I realized if Jane and I were to pursue an adoption, at Serwan's request, I needed to discuss it with my bosses. Yet that afternoon passed, and I was unable to communicate Serwan's change of mind to neither Lois, the Silopi UNHCR field chief, nor to my supervisor Julyan, from my agency, Mercy for All. Lois had left for Christmas to vacation in Diyarbakir. It was at least a four-hour drive from Silopi. There were no telephone communications possible between Zakho and Diyarbakir. And there was no telephone in the Van Den Bergs' rented residence.

I tried to organize my thoughts. *Where do I begin?*

My first priority was to find a notary or attorney who could legally document Serwan's decision to give his children up for adoption. My brother had adopted children, and I knew from his experience that the birth parents, or the father, in this case, had to declare he was giving up his children for adoption.

Then I would need to arrange travel permission through Turkey to Ankara. That meant somehow getting Suha and Nuha into Turkey. But they mustn't be put temporarily in the Haj camp, for that would make them refugees. I also must find out from the US embassy the requirements for us to adopt them. We had very little knowledge how it should work.

I thought over our unique situation: We were Americans, adopting Iraqi children, traveling through Turkey, and continuing on to Germany where we resided. That meant there were at least four languages involved: English, Arabic, Turkish, and German. Serwan spoke all four languages, so he would understand any documents he had to sign. Kurmanji Kurdish, spoken in Turkey, was not yet written in the Latin script, because the language was illegal in Turkey. Sorani Kurdish, spoken in Iraq, had been written in the Arabic script. That language was permitted by Saddam in Iraq and was written and used by Kurds in northern Iraq. However, there were no officials or governments that might be involved in an adoption that used those languages. Because northern Iraq had no official government.

The night of December 22, I wrote in my journal, "We've a long road ahead of us. But we are on it. We praise God with all our beings for His affirmations of our decisions and answers to prayer." In our minds and in our hearts, we felt this was a miracle God was going to do. We had to be faithful and work diligently to jump over every hurdle, but we believed He would make it happen. We had a secure sense that we would adopt them. Serwan wanted us to adopt them, and we were going to do everything possible so that these two precious children would live and have a future in our home.

Like any parents anticipating children, we discussed various names. God gave His people a name, and it had a powerful meaning behind it. We believed the two girls deserved names full of meaning and hope. Suha understood her name when it was used. She did not respond to the Kurdish name 'Firmesk'. And the baby was too small to respond to either the Kurdish name 'Payman' or the Arabic name Nuha.

Jane made a list of names and put a lot of thought into it. The one-year-old would be called Jessica Ruth. She had always loved the name Jessica, and it is pronounceable for Germans, as well as Americans. We gave her the name Ruth as a middle name. We wanted to give her a biblical name and were reminded of Ruth's statement, "Where you go, I will go, and where you lodge, I will lodge. Your people shall be my people, and your God, my God" (Ruth 1:16b). We also had a very dear friend in Berlin whose name is Ruth. We had been part of a weekly Bible study in her home, and they were among our closest German friends.

The toddler Firmesk or Suha would be called Delal Esther. We liked the name Delal because it means "sweetheart" in Kurdish. We both like Esther as a name, not just because of its biblical significance but because we were studying that book of the Bible when we met in the spring of 1981. The biblical woman Esther was a remarkable lady, for she trusted God in a foreign land, under a foreign people, and under great pressure. She determined to obey God, regardless of the consequence, saying, "If I perish, I perish." And because of her obedience, her people were rescued from destruction.

Delal said her first words in English on December 23.

"Bye, bye," she said cheerfully as I went out the door. How ironic. Soon, Lord willing, she will say, "Bye, bye," to the miserable suffering in Iraq and begin a new life. Then we can find a cure for the perpetual stomach troubles. Then she will fall asleep to the normal sounds of a city, instead of the *rat-a-tat-tat* of machine-gun fire. Bye-bye to Iraq. She and her sister had been caught between Iraq and Turkey for far too long.

As I prepared to leave the house, I checked my wallet. I could see Jane and I were going to soon be short on cash. We had money, just not the right kind. There was no way to cash our travelers checks, use a visa card, or our euro checks—all of which I carried in case of emergency. American Express may be "accepted around the world,"[1] but southeast Turkey operates solely on cash, as does northern Iraq. The bank in Silopi would hold your money for you in their vaults but offered no other services. And the Zakho banks…? There were none. Over 120,000 people and no financial institutions. Those, too,

---

[1.] https://www.americanexpress.com/uk/tc/faqs.shtml#9

were controlled by Baghdad. There were just some empty shops with various currencies taped to their dirty front window panes, advertising that they exchanged money.

I took an Iraqi taxi from the Van den Bergs' home to the Iraqi border, walked across the decaying bridge, then took a Turkish taxi into town. I ran into Clarke, the Mercy for All coordinator. He held the team finances. I told him my situation. He sympathized with me, he said, but he could only afford to give me 40,000 Turkish lira, which was about ten dollars.

"I am leaving Silopi today to spend Christmas in Diyarbakir," he said. "I'd like to help you more, but our whole team is short on cash right now." It was common knowledge that we operated on a shoestring budget, but ten dollars to support my wife and me for the next two to three weeks was laughable. In addition to the lira, I had the equivalent of $4.50 in Iraqi dinars, plus $150 in US dollars that I carried for use only in emergencies. *I guess this qualifies as an emergency*, I thought.

Travel was going to be a problem too. There was no bus service to the Iraqi border nor from the Iraqi border into the town of Zakho. Our team had just one vehicle, the Land Rover, and it had been decimated in an accident on December 13. One Mercy for All member, whom I shall not name to spare her the embarrassment, had taken the Land Rover out at night to show the Iraqi border to some visiting friends from Istanbul. The right front wheel slipped off the five inch thick tarmac; she overcorrected, and it spun off the elevated highway, rolling over and over down a twenty-foot embankment into a field. Two of her friends had been taken by a US helicopter to the hospital in Diyarbakir. The driver had minor injuries. The top of the vehicle was flattened right down to the height of the dashboard. I had hired a local farmer to chain his tractor to the Rover and drag it back up on the road. I put it in neutral, and he towed me to Silopi, mud from the tractor tires splattering me in the face the whole way. Clarke had it transported to Diyarbakir, the nearest repair facility.

Our faithful Land Rover before being
ferried to Diyarbakir for repair.

Since then, I'd been relying on friends, favors, and taxis to get
back and forth from Zakho to Silopi. Taxis could not cross the actual
border; that's why I had to walk and hire another one on the other
side. After dark, there were no more taxis, and sometimes, the border
closed unexpectedly. It was generally open each morning after 8:00
a.m. The Turkish police and gendarme were worried about the daily
attacks by Kurdish separatists, the Kurdish Worker's Party (PKK),[1]
so they controlled the border tightly. The number of relief vehicles
traveling to and from Silopi had decreased dramatically, since most
of the foreigners had left the country to celebrate Christmas. And
that meant fewer opportunities to hitch a ride from Silopi back to
the house in Zakho.

I found that negotiating for a price in advance on a taxi, as was
the custom, actually worked to my disfavor. (There were no meters in
these taxis since the cars were private vehicles whose owner was earn-
ing a bit of extra cash.) Instead, I just chatted with the driver as we

---

[1.] http://www.pkkonline.com/en/

drove. They were so astonished and overjoyed that I, an American, could speak some of their language, Kurmanji, that they insisted on giving me the ride for free. They were seriously offended when I tried to leave money on the seat or stuff it in their pocket. One fellow insisted on carrying my boxes of bottled water and groceries all the way up the dirt hill to the house. I was especially thankful for that, since I was developing pneumonia, and was having difficulty breathing, even when I wasn't carrying anything. Recurring pneumonias were something I had learned to live with, since age fourteen. They meant hospital intravenous antibiotics, every three months or so. My new Kurdish friend would take no money for the twenty-minute taxi ride and said he would gladly drive me anywhere I needed to go anytime.

In the same way, I was invited for so many meals; I could not count them.

"*Wêrê, wêrê*" [*WUH ruh, WUH ruh*], I heard again and again as I visited from tent to tent in the refugee camp. "Come, come!" they shouted, pulling me into their humble abodes and seating me at the place of honor (furthest from the door). I was invited to eat with Kurds, as well as the Assyrian Christians in the refugee camp. We had rice, bread, and vegetable soups with chunks of lamb, tomato, and beans. From their simple possessions, they gave and shared. We laughed, cried, and talked together. They were honored, they said, that I had come to be their guest in their tent. I was humbled at their great kindness, and when we parted, we were both blessed.

I was often invited to share a simple meal
with refugees in the camp: bread, potatoes,
yogurt, tomatoes and, of course, tea.

Returning to the Zakho house on December 23, I gave Jane a big hug and began to share about my day. She led me into the kitchen—the only room which was a tiny bit warm. It had our solitary gas heater. The gas bottles were scarce and difficult to get refilled. Jessica lay on the tiled floor, on an insulated mat, bundled up and gnawing on a carrot. Delal was content with an army biscuit. "*Biskêt, biskêt,*" she repeated over and over until she received one of the tasteless crackers. The Kurdish word *biskêt* means "cookie" in English.

We were fortunate to have the leftover army rations to eat. They were intended for Desert Storm, the invasion of Iraq to liberate Kuwait. Then they were used during Provide Comfort, the humanitarian relief effort for the Kurds. Finally, they were given to the NGOs, who had agreed to stay in Iraq and in Turkey and work with the refugees. It wasn't gourmet food, but it was food. And it was free. Our rent was free, too, since the Van den Bergs were taking a three-week or more Christmas break.

As I bowed in prayer over our simple meal, I thanked God for all his provisions. It was amazing to see our daily needs met when we were truly in need.

"How was your day, honey?" I asked as she served my plate.

"It seems like all of the NGOs have gone home for Christmas," she began. "Most of the organizations have left just a skeleton crew, if any at all." We both knew that meant fewer people to turn to for help in the event of a crisis. I was pleased to see Suha not throw her food anymore; she had learned that, although the plate had been passed momentarily to someone else, she was still going to get some.

"Even the UNHCR in Silopi has left, leaving just the Turkish nationals to keep the offices open," I said.

"Bob and Jan Blincoe with their three kids have stayed, of course. Iraq is their home. Heather Blincoe is coming over tomorrow to help me around the house," Jane said.

"Well, she is twelve. I'm sure she can help you with all the diapers you're changing. Her little sister ought to come too. She is a very capable young lady."

"It would be great to get some help with the laundry!" Jane added. *This is what young couples with kids talk about at the end of the day*, I thought.

That night, the Blincoes came over for popcorn and played with Suha and Nuha. It was great; both girls were very social and loved visitors. Suha and Nuha craved the attention. We decided to spend Christmas with the Assyrian family from whom the Van den Bergs rented. After all, the landlords lived right behind the living room door and had invited us to visit them many times. Then we would go to the Blincoes for a two-o'clock gathering. The next day, December 24, would be my last chance before Christmas to contact the US embassy in Ankara and perhaps find an attorney.

As I closed my tired eyes after a very long day, I spoke my heart out to God, *Lord, bless these efforts. Guide me, I pray. Help us save these children.* We trusted God to guide us each step of every day; We relied upon Him for courage and direction. We certainly had no idea how to adopt undocumented Iraqi children! *"Trust in the Lord with all your heart; lean not on your own understanding. In all your ways submit to him, and He will make your paths straight."*[1] It was a verse I'd memorized at age twelve. It meant more to me now than ever.

---

[1] Proverbs 3:5–6

Chapter 10

A Crazy Christmas Eve

Zakho, Iraq, December 24, 1991

C hristmas is not celebrated in Turkey. So for Turks, December
24 and 25 are days just like any other workdays. On
December 24, I sat down at my Toshiba laptop in the office
of the Silopi UNHCR and composed what seemed to me to be a
statement signifying Serwan's decision to release his children to be
adopted. It made sense to me that this should be the first legal step
if, indeed, Serwan intended for Jane and me to adopt his daughters. I called the document *Relinquishment of Rights*. The language
sounded official to me, and it seemed to communicate the essence of
his decision. He was giving up his rights as a father of his daughters.
In the document, I specified that Serwan's wife had died, as Serwan
had affirmed, and that Serwan specifically wanted Jane and me to
adopt his daughters. It was a simple document, not more than three
paragraphs long.

The next step, it seemed, was to get the document translated
into Turkish so the Turkish official could understand it and notarize
it. The translation would have to be by an official translator. Then,
I hoped, I would be able to sit down in private with Serwan and
explain the document to him and then, in the presence of an attor-

ney, have him sign it. It was a bold agenda for a backward little town like Silopi, where going to the bank might take a person half a day. I needed a translator for Turkish and it had to be discreet.

Although Serwan, Jane and I were in agreement about pursuing adoption, I knew we would still be facing huge obstacles. The UNHCR might be the first. So I tried to be as discreet as possible, even avoiding UNHCR personnel in town so I wouldn't be asked what I was doing. It was not normal for me to be looking for translators or seeking out an attorney. That wasn't what they expected of me in my role with Mercy for All.

I had a radio the UNHCR had provided our team. I could radio Bob Blincoe across in Iraq or national employees of the UNHCR in Silopi as needed for my job. The radio had a good range, but everyone communicated on the same channel. I had a question for Bob.

But if I had radioed and asked, "Hey, Bob, are any of your staff fluent in English and can translate into Turkish? I need to get a form translated," all the UNHCR staff in the Silopi would wonder why I needed a translator. One has to have lived in a small town to understand the way news traveled around. I might be in the market buying vegetables, and when I got to the UNHCR office, I would be asked what I bought. There was no privacy. That meant I couldn't reach Bob on the radio. So where else could I go to find a translator?

Mercy for All had translators who worked in the Haj Camp with Dave, Dorcas, Irmela, and Barbara. The translators were fluent in Arabic or in Sorani Kurdish and of course in English. The refugees in the Haj camp would sit down with a Mercy for All volunteer, and the Mercy for All volunteer would ask them questions.

"Were you ever imprisoned in Iraq?" Then the translator would ask the question of the refugee. Nobody needed Turkish translation. None of the refuges spoke Turkish as a mother language. So the UNHCR would naturally wonder, why would I need a Turkish translator? I needed to be careful how I conducted my search.

Bob and Jan knew that Serwan had asked Jane and me to adopt Suha and Nuha. They lived in Zakho and visited Jane often. I had tremendous respect for Bob. *If it were possible for me to have a son, I would name him Bob,* I thought; he had made a huge difference in our lives. We relied on Bob and Jan for feedback, advice, and companionship. We shared the same faith in Christ, whereas none of the staff at the UNHCR were believers in Jesus. During their off hours, they would party, drink, and carouse. This was confusing to Kurdish and Turkish nationals, who assumed that all Americans and westerners were Christians. *How could Christians behave in such ways? Such behavior is forbidden in Islam. Christians must not love God. They sure don't obey Him.*

The absolute highlight of my day came as I stepped through the front door for lunch. Suha came running up to me from down the hall, a big grin on her face, and gave me a long, warm, happy hug. Her simple expressions of affection were absolutely wonderful. They were strength to my bones and food for my soul.

I traveled with Bob to Silopi later, did some errands, and then set out on my own to find someone who spoke English. I was carrying the type written *Relinquishment of Rights* document with me that I had written. I needed someone to read it and put it into Turkish so the attorney could read it. Serwan understood both languages, but there is a huge difference between understanding a language and the proficiency of translation. I stepped into a vegetable shop just as a UNHCR vehicle drove by. I worried how they would respond once they heard Serwan wanted us to adopt his daughters. *Would they try to prevent it from going forward?* The thought troubled me. I knew I would let their office know in a day or two if Serwan, indeed, signed the necessary papers. But I didn't want to be premature in making an announcement. I decided it would be best to wait until Serwan had completed the proper documents. Then I would tell my boss Lois how Serwan had decided he no longer wanted his children to be reunited with him.

I walked up the middle of "main street" in Silopi, wondering where on earth I would find legal assistance in this remote town. There were more donkeys than cars. An attorney, in Silopi? It would be far easier to find a blacksmith, shoe repairman, or vendor of plastic pots. But legal assistance? There was only one shop in town that even had paper for sale. I doubted there would be anything as sophisticated as a lawyer. There were big mud holes, piles of construction debris, large sections without pavement, children at play, and everybody's farm animals roaming about. Nobody used the narrow sidewalk; they walked in the street. What seemed like chaos, I actually found enjoyable. I liked unpredictability, surprises, variety.

Standing in front of the solitary bank, I was accosted by a Silopi high school student. He had a familiar face; Galip was his name. The student was always desperate to practice his limited English and would follow me everywhere saying memorized lines.

"How are you doing, señorita? My, you have nice legs!" he declared to me. (I guess the selection of English language videos was pretty sparse.) I knew his English was very limited, so I decided to ask *him* a question this time.

"Where can I find an attorney?" I asked.

"A what?"

"An attorney, a lawyer, you know someone who makes legal papers, works with laws…" I groped for words I thought he might understand.

"Why do you want him?" Like many people in the Middle East, this kid was curious, even nosey. Suspicion was a part of his life. There was the additional fascination with the West; he had not met many Americans in his life. Life in a rustic town can be pretty boring. I was something out of the ordinary. It appeared he would gladly help me for the price of learning something personal.

I realized I resented his prying questions. After living day after day with people always asking me questions about everything in my life, I had built up a shell around me.

"How long have you been married? Do you have any kids? Why not? Don't you want kids? How much money do you make? Where do you get your money?" It was wearing me down. I never realized how much I valued my privacy and my own personal space. Here, in this part of the world, Jane and I enjoyed neither.

"Never mind," I said. "I will just take a walk and look around." I stepped off the curb and he followed close behind me.

Galip kept talking. "In Diyarbakir, or even Mardin." He paused. "Those are big places. You find everything you need there." I liked his accent. It was British English, learned in school, with a Turkish accent. All schools in Turkey teach some level of English, and the language of instruction is Turkish. Children who speak Kurdish in school are punished. Corporal punishment is common, even for a five-year-old who had only heard Kurdish at home growing up. He must only speak Turkish in the classroom, or he will be struck by the teacher.

"I can't go to Diyarbakir," I said. "I need someone closer than that." I passed the hardware store, where shovels, wire, crude tools, and anything made of metal were on sale. Beyond that was the plastic shop. Bright colored pots, washing tubs, pitchers, and buckets were displayed out on the sidewalk. Beyond that was the furniture store where we'd purchased our metal chairs. I passed the gas store, construction supply with its rebar and concrete, the paint store, the tailor, the barber, and the feed store. Then the appliance store—with its small water heaters, room heaters, and for the very wealthy, simple washing machines. Galip continued to chatter.

I turned up a side street, being careful to watch the ground with each step. Here there were no sidewalks; a person had to look down to place each step on the uneven ground.

"Oh, I know someone. I will take you there. It's no problem," Galip finally said. I was surprised but skeptical. By far, the most common sentence I heard in Turkey was, "No problem." It usually meant there really was a problem, a big problem, but I should trust the person to take care of it.

"Don't worry," would have been more accurate. *Right.* If Galip did lead me somewhere, I could just imagine him hovering near the office door, listening to my personal business.

"That's okay, Galip. I can find him. Just tell me where his office is." I seldom walked more than one hundred feet without meeting some shopkeeper, tea salesman, or person with whom I'd done business. Everybody recognized me. The only non-Kurds or non-Turks in town were Lois with the UNHCR and the Mercy for All members. The UNHCR staff traveled incognito in their big new Toyota SUVs. They could remain anonymous behind their tinted glass, whereas I was usually on foot. I decided any merchant could give me directions as I passed. Even when asking a complete stranger for directions, I would always get an answer. It might be totally erroneous, but they would point me to go somewhere. That was polite.

"Thanks, Galip, I will find him." I turned again and crossed the street behind a horse-drawn cart.

He could see that I was going on without him, so he loudly said, "His office is right behind that building there. Go around the corner." Galip finished with, "There is a sign. It says, 'NOTER.'" He turned abruptly and headed back toward the bank. I felt foolish. The kid really was trying to help me. I was too consumed with being secretive and also fearful I'd be conned.

"Thank you very much, Galip," I hollered as he disappeared down the street. This time, I really meant it. Perhaps I had found the office of a lawyer. The sign above the door said, "*Noter*," which sounded to me like a person who authenticates signatures with a stamp and a thumbprint. I was doubtful this *noter* would be the legal representation Serwan and I needed. Anyway, the office was closed. I decided I first needed to find somebody who understood English well enough to translate my document, the *Rights of Relinquishment*.

The US Consulate in Adana, in south central Turkey, had, at my request, faxed me a list of attorneys. Adana had a consulate because it is a large Turkish city next to the large US military base in Inçirlik. Turkey was the second largest recipient of US military aid in the world, second only to Israel. Turkey allowed the US military to maintain this huge base, giving the US a constant military presence in the Middle East. With so many US citizens in Inçirlik, it made sense to have a consulate there. And since Americans from time to time needed an attorney, the consulate kept a list of them. The attorneys on the list were scattered all over Turkey. I didn't recognize the names of the cities, and I had no idea if any of them were close to Silopi.

Holding the list of attorneys in my hand, I stepped inside a shop and began asking a stranger (in rudimentary Kurdish) the distances to some of the cities on the list. Then I needed to figure out which attorneys spoke English and which I should telephone. They were listed according to city.

A Turkish soldier suddenly piped up and said in flawless German, "I speak English. What do you need?" My eyes lit up.

"Come, let's go drink some tea together," I said.

More Turks speak German than English. There were two million Turks living in Germany as guest workers or refugees, and most of them go back to Turkey to visit family. When a Turk saw a Caucasian non-Turk in his homeland, he assumed he was German. Turkey is a major tourist destination for Germans. In any case, the soldier addressed me in German.

Every Turkish male was required by law to do military service at age eighteen. Turkish men living in Germany did not wish to become Germans; they proudly remained Turks. The youth, therefore, came back to Turkey to do their eighteen months of military service. Hence, this Turk spoke fluent German and wore a Turkish military uniform.

In my mind, I tried to envision this soldier translating the *Relinquishment of Rights* from English into Turkish, in order that a local Turkish attorney could understand it. I led him down the street a few shops to a teahouse. It was a narrow shop, with low tables and stools. A television was blaring in one corner, and several youths seem to be watching it until we came in. They all turned to watch us instead. Teahouses in Silopi are frequented by the same repeat guests. They are places to hang out and talk with friends. Hours and hours are spent playing backgammon. I am sure many Kurdish and Turkish wives sit at home wondering when their husbands will finally come home from the local teahouse. They are the Turkish equivalent to the American bar or the British pub.

The table was covered with the residue of a thousand glasses of sugary tea and black soot from the coal stove; I wiped it off with some tissue. The tissue was black. I laid my neatly typed document on the table as I shared my problem with him. He seemed genuinely interested. *This is a miracle*, I thought. As far as I knew, the only person in Silopi who was fluent in Turkish/English was working in the Haj Camp for the UNHCR. His name was Erdoğan, and he worked nonstop. I couldn't ask him to translate the *Relinquishment of Rights*. If I did, the entire office would immediately know Serwan had asked

Jane and me to adopt his girls. I wasn't ready for that. Erdoğan was a fantastic translator, however.

The soldier was not from Silopi; he was visiting. His German was pretty good, but it was his command of English I was concerned about, so I began speaking English and then showed him the document.

After twenty minutes and four glasses of tea, we both realized it was too much for him. "My English is not good enough for this," he said as he handed me the document back. I was crestfallen. We finished our tea and left the shop.

I turned up the street to a little shop with a telephone. There were no telephone booths on the street. Rather, the national telephone system (PTT) placed yellow telephones inside of businesses. The phones required coins. As I stood in the shop I glanced through my list of attorneys. There were seven pages. Fortunately, the embassy had noted in its list if the attorney spoke English. The ones who spoke English were too far away, and the Mercy for All Land Rover was getting repaired in Diyarbakir so I couldn't drive anywhere. I was on foot.

Finally, in exasperation, I asked aloud (in Kurdish), "Doesn't anybody in this town speak good English?"

"Erdoğan," two men said in unison. Then another one suggested someone named Sami.

"Who's Sami?" I inquired.

"Oh, he has a clothing store across the street," came the reply.

Two minutes later, I was seated before Sami's desk drinking tea. The lights were out in the store. Electricity in Silopi was unpredictable, so we sat in semidarkness, making small talk. I wasn't interested in buying cheap clothes. Finally, I told him what I needed. He looked at the document. "My English isn't good enough," he said.

"Sure it is," I said, hopeful. "Just come with me to the noter and tell him what it says so he can notarize it." He looked uninterested. "Look," I pleaded. "This is really important to me. I would give you ten bucks for your time and effort." That was a lot of money in Silopi. He didn't want to accept money, but he finally agreed to accompany me to the noter.

The shopkeeper's brother said he'd look after the store. There were no customers anyway. We headed off together for the noter's office in the next block. Halfway there, Sami stopped. He had changed his mind.

"Listen," he began, "I'd really like to help you, but there simply isn't any way I can translate those words. They're too complicated. I'm sorry." I was slowly realizing that people wanted to help; they were generous at heart. But my request was more than the average person could handle.

We parted in front of his shop, and I headed off down a small dirt side street. I had been so full of hope. I really thought God had led me to the right person; but in the end, I'd received no help whatsoever. *Perhaps I will just go to Erdoğan's house after all*, I thought. *I'll ask around till I find his home and then wait for him to return from the UNHCR office.* I had heard that he lived very close to the office, but to visit him at the office would raise suspicion. Everyone would want to know what my business was.

I heard whistling from behind me in the narrow street. *That's strange. Turks don't whistle*, I thought. *It must be a foreigner, and the only foreigners in town are my colleagues at the UNHCR.* I ignored the sound and continued my pace without turning or pausing.

"*Hevalo* (Hey, friend), I heard, and Sami trotted up. But what could he want? He just said goodbye; he said he couldn't help me. His words in Kurdish came quickly. "Come back to my shop. I've a friend who I think can help you."

"God, I praise your name!" I said out loud in English.

"Sami," I said, "I was just praying that God would hear my prayer and send someone to help. Thanks for coming!"

His friend turned out to be a lieutenant in the Turkish military. We found him in a nearby store buying several cartons of cigarettes. We exchanged pleasantries. He agreed to help me.

"Where did you learn such excellent English?" I asked him as we walked toward the office of the noter. "I lived two years in Florida," he told me.

Before entering the notary's office, I told him the story of how we had found the children and explained that the birth father wished to give them up for adoption. We stood outside, and the lieutenant read the short *Relinquishment of Rights*. We went inside.

Mr. Ahmet,[1] the notary, was a short, balding, stocky man in his late forties. He looked at me with a look somewhere between disdain and disgust. I wasn't sure, however, if the expression wasn't permanently etched on his face. I never saw him appear otherwise. His clothes didn't fit well, and like most men in eastern Turkey, he was unshaven. His desk was piled high with books, binders, and scattered with documents. A manual typewriter and black telephone were half buried in the disarray. Several cheap vinyl chairs were placed on the bare concrete floor for his clients. Behind him was a wall of bookshelves, made from various pieces of rough-cut lumber.

I soon realized the source of his sour expression. He was offended that I couldn't speak Turkish. I had tried to express myself to him in English, German, and finally Kurdish. But he understood none of it and was obviously offended when I spoke Kurdish. He was perhaps the only ethnic Turk besides the mayor and the military police who lived at this outpost, Silopi. I could speak Kurdish at the local bank, and they understood me just fine. Silopi is located in the middle of greater Kurdistan. Kurds have lived for millennium in the region. The lands of the Kurds are comprised of eastern Turkey, northern Syria, northern Iraq, western Iran, and southwest Armenia. The citizens of Silopi all speak Kurdish. But Mr. Ahmet was not from the Kurdish part of Turkey and certainly not from Silopi.

Mr. Ahmet listened to the lieutenant give an oral translation of the affidavit. He got the general idea. He then gave me some instructions, which the lieutenant translated for me.

"Bring the birth father's identification tomorrow, and I will have his identification translated from Arabic into Turkish," Mr. Ahmet said. Serwan's own identification papers were all in Arabic, the national language of Iraq. The lieutenant continued to translate Ahmet's instructions to me. "Also bring identification for the children so Serwan may attest that they are his children." Finally, he said, "I will prepare a document (in Turkish) for the birth father to

---

[1.] Name changed

sign. Then we can go together to the refugee camp, talk to the birth father, and bring him the relinquishment of rights document (in Turkish), which he will then sign. We will return to the office, and I will notarize it. It will cost a hundred and seventy thousand liras." That equaled thirty-five US dollars.

He knew his business, even if he didn't charge much for it! I thought.

I agreed to meet Mr. Ahmet the following morning, Christmas Day. It was a workday as usual in Silopi. We would have no Christmas lights, no evergreen tree, and no holiday music. There would be no bright decorations or an exchange of gifts. But for Jane and me, it was going to be a Christmas never to forget! After all, we were celebrating the Baby who came into the Middle East in a miraculous way. We too were going to need another miracle.

Jane was in bed trying to get warm when I finally came into the Van den Bergs' rented home that night. Suha and Nuha were in bed, too, although Nuha had been put in her own room with a little electric heater. Her screaming had become unbearable. Nothing would satisfy her, not even a carrot to suck on. She had been fed plenty and had been given lots of affection, but she was clearly miserable. We didn't know why.

I related the day's events to Jane. We had plenty to think and pray about as we fell asleep.

Chapter 11

Christmas Day

Silopi, Turkey, December 25, 1991

At 9:00 a.m., I stood outside the small side street in Silopi, looking at the rusty sign hanging above the iron door. "Noter." I had borrowed an old white Dodge pickup truck (also donated from US Army surplus) from Bob Blincoe to drive to Silopi that day. It was used by some of his team members with his NGO. I entered Mr. Ahmet's office, a single small musty room that was perhaps fifteen feet by fifteen feet. The office had three chairs besides the mammoth desk behind which sat the overweight notary. The lights were not on, but some sunlight filtered through the partially closed blinds. I hoped he'd remember what we were going to do. Naturally, I couldn't communicate with him, but I wished him a Merry Christmas, anyway. He scowled when I handed him a large gift-wrapped bar of chocolate that I'd bought in Germany. I thought of all my friends living in Turkey who were dying for European chocolate.

"It's chocolate," I said, hoping to cheer him up. He tossed it onto his desk amid his papers and grunted. *I wonder if this guy knows who the scrooge is?* I asked myself and sat down.

His intentional failure to offer me tea expressed his feelings toward me; I just sat in silence on the dusty chair by the front door as he began to type. *Click, click, click,* his fingers worked slowly on the ancient machine. I figured he knew why I'd come, and sooner or later, he'd get tired of my presence and help me. Perhaps he thought I'd get bored and leave; he made no effort to appear helpful. I was determined to stay, however; Mr. Ahmet was integral to beginning the adoption process. Living in a third world country had increased my ability to be patient. I waited for buses. I waited in long lines at the bank. I waited for security guards to examine my papers. I waited and waited. It was part of life in Turkey.

After thirty minutes, an elderly man entered the room and sat across from Mr. Ahmet. They greeted one another as friends and began discussing something. Then the stranger addressed me in Kurdish. I learned his name was Mehmet and that he worked for the notary as a translator for Arabic/Turkish transactions. He was also overweight, had a bushy beard, and seemed short of breath. He was going to translate Serwan's Arabic identification card into Turkish. Mehmet was the Silopi mullah, and his main work was in the nearby mosque, a large impressive domed building under construction. I explained my story to him as best I could using Kurdish.

Mullah Mehmet began translating the Arabic identification card. Serwan had made a copy of his identification card in the Mercy for All interview office in the Haj camp. We had a copy machine because we were generating so many crucial documents for the resettlement of refugees. Serwan had given me the copy. One line of the photocopied document was illegible. Mehmet wanted me to go to the Haj camp and ask Serwan what the line said. This meant at least an hour's delay. I would have to drive to the Haj camp, find Serwan, and somehow avoid the curious UNHCR workers who worked there. I went outside the *Noter's* office to the Dodge pickup. Then I had an idea.

"This is Kirk, calling Bob," I said into my handheld radio. It was a long way to Bob's home in Iraq, but there was the slight chance he might hear me if the reception was good. It depended on the weather and terrain. I had given Bob a copy of Serwan's identification so he could have it translated into English.

I heard Bob's garbled voice. "I read you poorly. Please try another location. Over." I moved out into the middle of the dirt street and said a silent prayer.

Into the radio, I said, "Can you hear me better now, Bob? Over." After a moment of silence, he said he could. "Would you please read line five of the identification card, Bob? Over."

Bob could read his copy, and he quoted line five to me. I stepped back into the office. The mullah was a bit surprised to see me so quickly. Nevertheless, he translated it for Mr. Ahmet, who slowly typed it up and then notarized it. With that complete, I put my own version of the *Relinquishment of Rights* (written in English) on Mr. Ahmet's desk. Neither he nor Mullah Mehmet could read English. Mr. Ahmet began to type out a new document. It was entirely in Turkish, so I could not understand its contents. The mullah asked me several questions (in Kurdish) before he could finish it.

It was like the old puzzle with the guy and a small boat. He has to get across a river, but he can only take one item at a time. He has a fox, a chicken, and a sack of corn. If the fox and chicken are together, the fox will eat the chicken. If the chicken and the corn are left together, the chicken will eat the corn. How does he get every-thing across the river?[1]

In my case, I had a notary who spoke only Turkish and Arabic. The mullah spoke Kurdish, Turkish, and Arabic. The *Relinquishment of Rights* document was written in English. Serwan spoke and under-stood all the languages, but he was in the Haj camp, and the Haj camp Turkish security would not let him leave. *How do I get this document notarized in Turkish in the office in Silopi by the notary?* I wondered.

Finally, Mehmet stood up and said we would go to the refugee camp to get Serwan's signature. The Turkish police at the Haj camp knew me well; but I was driving a truck, not the Land Rover, and had a passenger, the mullah. Still they waved me through. I made an immediate left turn down a dirty mud path to avoid driving across the expanse of tarmac, where all the men hung out all day. The area

---

[1.] http://www.mathsisfun.com/chicken_crossing_solution.html

by the security office was always crowded with men roaming about in search of anything interesting to do. A long line of people stretched across from the Turkish security office; people were hoping for a permit to go into Silopi to buy produce. I wanted to remain inconspicuous, but the white Dodge was the only motorized vehicle in camp, and my visit might be the most exciting thing that happened all day for the five thousand refugees. It is difficult to fathom the boredom of life in a refugee camp. I was told of another camp in Turkey who had people who'd lived there ten years with nothing to do. Children grew up as refugees and knew no other life.

As always, crowds of small children, some barely old enough to walk, chased the truck and tried to jump on. It was a deadly game they played, and no matter how harsh one admonished them, they continued.

"Hello, mister! Hello, mister!" they shouted. The refugee tents from the UNHCR were, a drab olive or tan, and were supplemented sometimes with bright plastic where someone had tried to keep out the rain and cold. The ground was muddy and slippery. I switched into four-wheel drive to maintain traction. Walking was a nightmare; my feet sunk into the mud and stuck with each step. Sometimes, my shoe remained firmly cemented in the mud while my foot slipped out. Then I hovered precariously, hoping I found my shoe with my foot before losing balance. There were no proper ditches; rainwater just sat atop the clay surface or flowed into the tents.

I stopped the truck in front of row number twenty, where Serwan lived. As we approached his tent, he came outside. It was almost noon. His hair was not yet combed, and like many refugees, he had slept late and hadn't yet shaved. In spite of being awakened, he was congenial.

"Please come in," he offered. I stooped low, went under the canvas flap, and began removing my shoes. Mehmet, however, refused the invitation to accept hospitality and looked on disdainfully. He wouldn't accept Serwan's offer of a warm beverage despite the cold, frosty morning air. He was clearly above such humble circumstances and wouldn't stoop or degrade himself by partaking of refugee life. Mullahs don't stoop to such levels.

I thought back to our experience with another Muslim leader. One of the refugees had come to Mercy for All interview offices in the camp for his interview.

"I am an imam," he said as we began the interview. I knew that meant he was a teacher and gave the sermon each Friday in a mosque. "I am a Muslim religious leader. I'm not like the other people in this camp. I am a holy man. I should not be treated just like the common refugee. I deserve better." Clearly, Mehmet felt he was not to be dirtied by association with the refugees. He stood outside the tent in the mud, looking very uncomfortable.

Serwan carefully read through the Turkish translation of the *Relinquishment of Rights* document. Fortunately, he could read quite a bit of Turkish.

"They spelled my name wrong," he said. I took a closer look at the Turkish words, even though I don't read or speak Turkish. I noted the misspelling of his name. Further on, I saw the children's names, followed by the words "Haj Camp" in Turkish.

"Does this say that the children are residing in the Haj camp?" I asked him. He confirmed my suspicion. We handed the document back to Mehmet and explained why it was unacceptable. If the Turkish government believed that the children were residing in the Haj camp inside of Turkey, they would wonder why I was requesting permission to bring them from Iraq. After all, according to the document, they were in Turkey. Furthermore, they would require papers issued by the local police, granting permission to leave a refugee camp.

"It just won't do," I explained to Mehmet. It would have to be redone. He wasn't too pleased and tried in vain to convince us to accept it, anyway.

"Bring him with us to Mr. Ahmet's office," Mehmet said to me. *Easier said than done*, I thought. I knew how difficult it was for refugees to leave the camp; sometimes, they stood in line for hours to receive one of the limited permission slips to go into town to shop. Mehmet insisted we go into Silopi. It was the only way to ensure the document was correctly prepared. Perhaps the guards at the front gate would allow us to exit without a permit for Serwan.

We pulled up to the guardhouse and stopped. Mehmet was sitting on the passenger side, and Serwan was seated in between us. Mehmet exchanged some words with the guards on duty. Apparently, Mehmet was well-known to them since he led the Muslim prayers in the small mosque. They waved us through.

When we reached the notary's office, Serwan spoke Turkish and explained the necessary changes directly to Mr. Ahmet. The notary had a pile of other work on his desk and was obviously unhappy about the added work. He slowly went over the facts again. When he got to the point of asking Serwan's wife's name, Serwan replied, "Kurdistané." Mr. Ahmet gave a look of surprise, shock, and disbelief.

"What?" he asked incredulously.

"Kurdistanê," Serwan repeated. "The mother's name was Kurdistanê." To even utter the word *Kurd* had been forbidden in Turkey. An irrational fear of these people and their dream of autonomy had led to decades of repression and persecution. And certainly nobody ever dared utter the word *Kurdistan* in public. To do so could get one a prison sentence. It was tantamount to sedition. It is standard practice for the Turkish military police to beat and torture those accused of aspiring for Kurdish autonomy. Their villages are burned to the ground if they are suspected of supporting the Kurdish underground separatist movement.

It was also forbidden to give Kurdish names to children in Turkey. Mr. Ahmet was clearly astounded to learn that someone had had the audacity to name his daughter Kurdistanê. It seemed to pain him greatly to type the name on the *Relinquishment of Rights* document.

Once Mr. Ahmet and Serwan were satisfied, Serwan and I left the notary office and took the completed, stamped and notarized *Relinquishment of Rights* to a copy shop down the street and made a copy for Serwan. I drove him back to the refugee camp, grateful once again for the provision that day of the Dodge pickup. Serwan went into his tent and came out with two gifts for his daughters. His love for them was very evident; it was an extreme act of love to put them up for adoption, when he could not care for them himself. He had thought and prayed about his decision for weeks. I gave him a third-party address for Jane and me so that we could stay in touch. I would send him reports and pictures when he wanted, and he would pass on his future address when he moved from the camp, so I could always stay in touch with him.

As we sat and talked together in his tent, he told me that he had decided to become a follower of Jesus.

"Islam has never made sense to me. It is inconsistent," he said. I knew he was thinking of the endless atrocities he had witnessed and experienced in the name of Islam. He continued, "I want to learn more about following Jesus. I have been so happy since you Christians have come to the Haj camp." Serwan wanted to find fellowship in the camp itself but was reluctant to approach the Assyrian Christians, many for whom Christianity was just a set of traditions. "I asked to be registered a Christian when I did my interview for the UNHCR," he said. "Although my Iraqi identification card says that I am a Muslim, in my heart I am a Christian. And that is what matters."

"I have written a poem," he said. "I would like for you to have it." It seemed remarkable to me that he could write poetic verse in a second language, but even more amazing was the transformation he spoke of in the poem. He gave me what he'd written.

In his composition he spoke of being born anew, of freedom he had found, of Jesus calling him to himself. It was deeply encouraging to see the impact of the witness of the team.

Chapter 12

Affidavit of Abandonment

Zakho, Iraq, December 25, 1991

I returned to the house in Zakho, after first stopping at the grocery store in Silopi to pick up groceries: bread, bananas, and diapers, all which were unavailable in Iraq. I was eager to share the day's news with Jane. But I still had an unanswered question in the back of my mind.

Mr. Ahmet had completed the *Relinquishment of Rights* document in the Turkish language, and Serwan had signed it. But I wasn't positive of the contents of that document, since I can't read Turkish. I had explained what I wanted to the translator, Mehmet, who spoke Kurdish.

I had said in simple Kurdish, "Serwan's children will become my children. My wife and I and the children will go to Germany. I will become their father." It seemed clear enough. But I still had an uneasy feeling.

"It would be a lot better if I knew exactly what this document said," I told Jane as we prepared for another cold night. What I needed was a "back translation." I was familiar with this from my friendships and experience with friends who do Bible translation. In order to be certain that what was translated from the Greek into

Inaru, for example (a tribal language in Papua New Guinea), the finished translation had to be translated back into Greek, but by a different person. This was then compared to the original Greek to be certain of accuracy. It had to match perfectly.

But where could I find someone who could translate the Turkish *Relinquishment of Rights* document back into English? Everyone I knew who was fluent in Turkish and English had left town for the Christmas holidays.

Christmas day, I stopped by to see Bob Blincoe and shared my problem. He suggested I ask one of his employees, a Turk who spoke fluent English, if he would back-translate it.

"Great! I didn't even know you had anybody here who spoke Turkish," I said. Bob explained that while most of his transactions required Arabic (or Kurdish), he still had supplies of medicines that came through Turkey. So he needed a Turkish employee. Due to the embargo, there was no other route possible for his supplies. He introduced me to Aydin. Aydin read carefully through the Turkish translation of the *Relinquishment of Rights* document.

"This is a certificate of consent," he told me. "It gives you the right to take Serwan's children across borders and do any kind of legal transactions involving them."

"But does it specify that I can adopt them?" I asked. I held my breath. He read over the document again.

"Let's see... No..., the word *adoption* doesn't actually appear here," he said.

"Does it communicate that concept?" I asked. "Can you say that this certificate of consent gives me the right to adopt Serwan's children?" I waited hopefully, knowing that Aydin was not a legal expert, but I still wished he would say yes.

"You know", he said slowly, "I can't say for sure, but if I were you, I wouldn't count on this document to grant you the right to adopt. It doesn't specify adoption. And if the word isn't on here, then, well, there is just no way of knowing for sure." As much as I hated to admit it, I knew he was probably right. If it didn't specify adoption, then I was likely going to have problems. I would have to do it all over again. My heart sank. *Why would Mullah Mehmet create a document that didn't specify adoption?* I wondered. It was perplexing.

I waited for Bob to finish his business in his office, and then I told him Aydin's assessment. He didn't know what to say. Clearly, I needed to communicate more clearly to the notary Mr. Ahmet. Bob wanted to help me, but he didn't have anyone who could go to Silopi with me to be a translator. He needed Ahdin in Zakho.

"You know," I said, "my wife and I read several journals of people who had adopted children in Romania. In the cases where mothers had placed their babies in orphanages, the adoptive parents still had to get written proof that the mother was abandoning the child and consenting for it to be adopted. If the father was alive, his written consent was also needed. I don't know exactly what it will take to adopt these girls, but it seems to me that something similar would be required here."

"You are free to use my Macintosh computer if you want, Kirk," Bob said. "You can write whatever is needed and print it. Wait just a few minutes, and I'll be done here. We can go to my house together." This was an incredible luxury in that time and place. Nobody in northern Iraq even had telephones, and electricity was very sporadic and uncertain. To have a computer set up in a private home in 1991 with a printer, in that remote corner of the world, was almost too good to be true.

Later that day, as I sat down before his computer keyboard, I tried to think of the key ingredients to include in the statement. I decided to call it an affidavit of abandonment. There were three key ingredients. Number one was that Serwan was giving up all of his parental rights and giving the children up for adoption. Second was that his wife had died. Finally, the document should specify that Jane and I were to be the adoptive parents.

The only drawback to the document was that it was only in English. Serwan spoke fluent English and would understand it perfectly, but I would have to find a translator who could explain it to the notary. This was the text:

Affidavit of Abandonment

I, Serwan Mohammad Abadi,[1] the father of Firmesk Serwan Mohammad (female, age two) and Payman Serwan Mohammad (female, age one) do hereby declare my intent and desire to place my two children up for adoption. I relinquish all of my legal rights to the children and request that Mr. Kirk Legacy and Mrs. Jane Legacy be permitted to adopt them.

They agree to keep me informed of the children's progress upon my request.

The mother of my children, Kurdistanê Hemin Sura, died as a result of the bombing of my village in Kirkuk, Iraq, March 1991.

date signature

The following morning, I stood nervously at the copy machine in the UNHCR office in Silopi. Laid out before me were all the documents pertaining to the children's case. I had letters from everyone who had been involved in Iraq and had assisted in one way or another. These included the Iraqi doctor's summary of Jessica's hospitalization, when she had received the blood transfusions. I had letters from a relief agency and from Medical Aid International (Dr. Pullen) confirming the condition of the girls in the "foster home" (Abdul's house). Then there was the identification documents for Serwan in Arabic and their certified Turkish translations. Finally, I had the *Relinquishment of Rights*, which the notary had produced. However, I did not have the secondary identification card that I had made and laminated. It was still in the possession of the UNHCR office in Silopi. I had given it to them when the they were trying to bring the

---

[1.] Name changed

girls into Turkey. I wasn't sure where they had put it. I would have to go to the UNHCR office in Silopi and find it.

Nobody was in the office that morning, and I worked quickly making photocopies. A vehicle pulled up outside. I looked out the window just as Ismet, a UNHCR employee, climbed out of a Suzuki. Ismet had dark hair and a broad smile; he was a Kurd from Diyarbakir. He had been hired as a translator of Kurdish-English-Turkish but had been given many more responsibilities to match his skills. He was in charge of all of the "questionable cases" at the refugee camp, such as late arrivals, relatives who had sneaked into the camp illegally and wanted to stay, and other special problems. He was familiar with Serwan's case, as I had briefed him regularly. Serwan had been to his office in the camp repeatedly, asking for help for his two daughters across the border, but Ismet had been unable to help him.

Ismet faced an additional problem, as did all the relief workers helping in the crises. The UNHCR had an unfortunate habit of regularly transferring their staff to different locations, sometimes as often as every week. The result was that, oftentimes, nobody knew what was going on. The impression was that they spent most of their time learning their new jobs and precious little helping the refugees. This added to the burden on the Turkish staff, especially on the translators. Ismet and the two other locally hired staff were told to continue working through the Christmas holiday in order that the expatriate staff could take holidays in Ankara or western Turkey. Ismet was alone in the office except for me.

As we talked, I expressed my concern about the girl's identification card.

"If anyone were to challenge me in Iraq about my caring for these two infants, I wouldn't have any way to prove that I have legal custody," I explained to him. "Do you know where their ID card is?" I asked him. This was the secondary ID card which I had created. I had brought it to the office several days previous. He looked through several binders and stacks of papers and found it.

"Here," he said. "Our office has photocopies of it. You can take this with you." I rejoiced inwardly and thanked him very much. That single item was invaluable as we proceeded on the road to adoption.

With the photocopies finished and the precious identification card, I drove joyfully back to Iraq, stopping only to buy more diapers in Silopi. All along the highway, I sang praises to God. It was too much to believe the way things were going. Without the necessary papers, we were stuck. But one by one, God was seeing that we got what was necessary. We still weren't sure what would happen or how it would happen, but we were confident that our Lord, who watched over even the sparrows, would take care of us.

Arriving in Zakho around 2:30 p.m., I drove straight to the Blincoe's home. Several friends had gathered to celebrate Christmas with Bob, Jan, and their three kids. Jane, Suha, and Nuha were already there; and it was all I could do to contain my excitement. It had been a productive day.

We had agreed not to talk about the potential adoption with anyone except the Blincoes, so I had to wait until the guests were gone to relate the day's victories. Bob was always exuberant. Both he and his wife Jan were tremendously supportive throughout this time of stress.

"This is better than a Steven Spielberg adventure," Bob joked.

"Let's just hope it has a happy ending!" I responded.

Suha was showing signs of greater independence when we returned to our Zakho home. She managed to walk down three steps on her own. Her swollen legs and feet were slowly improving as she got the necessary protein in her diet. She bent over and looked her little sister in the face.

"Be happy!" she said cheerfully in English. Neither of us use that expression, so we were a bit surprised. We conversed with her exclusively in Kurdish but expected she'd begin to pick up some English as she heard us talk. Still it was a surprise and special joy when she came up to Jane that afternoon and looked up into her face.

"I love you, Mommy," she said. That was a Christmas gift Mommy will not soon forget.

Still there were challenges in discipline. We had to be sensitive to what we expected from them. Some outbursts by Suha or Nuha were certainly a result of the changes that had come upon them. But some of it was simply childhood, and knowing the difference was not always easy. Nuha was being pretty ornery at night, even when she was clean and fed. She whined and cried. After a steady hour of yelling and tears, we, again, put her in the next room with the small heater by herself. Within minutes, she fell fast asleep.

Realizing Serwan was serious about the adoption taking place, we began inserting their new names into some of our daily routines. Instead of Suha, we used Delal.

Delal stayed with us in our bedroom; it was the only other room in the house that was currently heated. She was quite content to curl up on her cot on the floor near the heater. We were grateful for the used sheets that had been donated; they served every purpose from sheets to cleanup cloths. Delal wasn't used to having a sheet over her; she preferred to pull the wool blanket over her head and sleep. We wondered how she could breathe like that but then realized that in her previous home, she had to contend with the freezing cold and seven other kids, several of them must have been crying at any given time. Indeed, she slept through Nuha's screams as well as the machine-gun fire we heard each night. We also began calling Nuha, Jessica.

As the sun came up the day after Christmas, we began cleaning the girls and getting them ready to be fed. They both still had stomach issues, and although we put double diapers on them their clothes were still soiled. They didn't have pajamas, and since it was so cold, they slept in their winter clothing. Once again, God knew our needs; that little semiautomatic washing machine was a little help. It would have been impossible to wash all that very dirty laundry by hand every day and still have dry clothes for them.

When Delal awoke that morning, her first words were, "Biscuit, biscuit." And when she was downstairs in the kitchen, she wanted food immediately. She knew it was the place where we ate. She didn't want to wait for someone to cook. She wanted food, and she wanted it *now*! This was of course understandable, considering that she had been starving; we knew it would take extra patience and work for her to adjust.

We started her on a bowl of Rice Krispies (left by the US army after Operation Provide Comfort), and Jane began preparing eggs and some leftover meat. The doctor told us not to give heavy foods to her because of the fifteen days of digestive chaos, so we didn't serve her any of the eggs or meat. She was furious about this, even when the reason was clearly explained to her in Kurdish. She refused to eat her cereal. She wanted what I was eating.

We insisted she eat her food. Her response was a tantrum of epic proportions. We both tried our absolute best to ignore it, even dramatically shrugging our shoulders. That had the effect of turning the volume up. She took a swipe at her glass of chocolate milk whereby I responded with a tap on her offending hand. She burst forth with what must have been Kurdish epithets and then more screaming. After twenty minutes of furious screaming, she tapered to a steady whine and then quieted down. Jane hugged her, and she sat down and ate her cereal.

"Ah," I said gently to Jane, "a hard-won victory."

Delal slowly began to exchange looks with me, and even looked directly into my eyes and smiled. It was a tremendous step forward. The first week we had been together, she avoided all eye contact and frowned when smiled at. We had told her countless times in both Kurdish and English that we loved her, but most of all, we tried to demonstrate that love by meeting her needs and gently disciplining her when appropriate.

When it warmed up a bit in the afternoon, Jane took the girls outside into the little backyard. Both girls loved to sit on the metal swing and be gently pushed. The sun came out in the daytime, although it did not warm up much. Jessica couldn't sit up unaided, so we tied her in to the swing with an army jacket. She loved swinging back and forth in the afternoon sunshine.

The Assyrian family was terrific company and support for the children as well. They spoke Kurdish with Delal, and their little girls enjoyed her company. We ate dinner with them, enjoying the Jesus film in Arabic afterward. They had a firm grasp of the Bible and showed genuine hospitality and kindness.

Chapter 13

An Infant Dies. Strike in Silopi.

Silopi, Turkey, December 28, 1991

"Silopi, Silopi, this is Emer. Come in please." I turned my radio up to hear Emer's reply. Emer worked for the UNHCR; she had just arrived and joined the other Turks who worked with the Haj camp refugees. Lois and the Europeans were still gone for the holidays. Both the UNHCR and Mercy for All operated on one radio channel to simplify communications. I was driving from Zakho where I had spent the night with Jane and the girls. I was on the two lane highway in Bob Blincoe's Dodge pickup, and I could hear Emer talking clearly to somebody else on my radio.

"Silopi, Silopi, this is Emer. Come in please. Do you read me? Over." She was trying to reach the office in town. She was evidently inside the Haj Camp, and her office was perhaps a mile away. She tried again, "Sam, Sam, come in please. Do you read me, Silopi? Over." Sam was a timid man in his forties. It seemed he had a difficult time making decisions and developing plans. I continued to listen to the interchange.

Finally, the response crackled back, "This is Sam. Go ahead."

"Sam, this is Emer. I'm at the Haj Camp. Listen, Sam. A ten-month-old baby died in the camp last night. It had gastroenteritis. Do you read me, over?"

170

"Yes, I read you. Over."

"The family is here with the baby. They are upset because there are no heaters in the tents. A sick baby cannot survive in this cold, Sam. A lot of people are angry about this. They are here by the security gate, and they want to know what we will do. Over."

I could imagine Emer's situation. She was compassionate and hardworking. Fluent in Arabic, she coordinated a health education program among the women in the camp. She gave everything she had to serve the refugees. Even when she broke her leg in a car accident, she returned on crutches and continued to help. Unlike most of the UNHCR employees, she spent her days visiting tent to tent, rather than sitting in the relative comfort of the office in town. I admired her stamina and determination. But now she was faced with a most difficult situation.

For months, the refugees had been asking what would be done to prepare the camp for winter. Their tents were summer tents; it was frequently over 100 degrees Fahrenheit, reaching even 125 degrees in July and August. But the winters in Kurdistan are just as extreme, with months of icy rain and snow. Beginning in September, they had daily asked for winter tents, for heaters, and for more blankets. But no winterized tents had been distributed. Officials and bureaucrats discussed the cost and feasibility of various heaters in the warmth of their offices. But not one heater had been delivered to the camp, except to the offices of the Turkish security. And the UNHCR warehouse in Diyarbakir, full of blankets, remained locked.

The refugees were justifiably angered. And Emer had to deal with their wrath. She was by no means responsible for the decisions that had kept them freezing at night, but she was the only one present to whom they could express their outrage. As they crowded around her holding the dead child, some were crying, and others shouting. She pleaded over her radio for assistance.

"Sam, Sam, they are angry. What should I tell them?" Surely Sam would act now. He was the acting head of office while Lois was in Diyarbakir. The only problem was he was new and inexperienced.

"What do you want *me* to do about it?" he asked as if he were powerless.

"The people want to know when the heaters are coming," she continued. "They have been told so many times they're coming, and still there are no heaters. They are angry because the baby died in the cold."

"Look, do you want me to come out there and talk to them myself?" he said in frustration. I could not believe his insensitivity. It was matched only by his level of incompetence.

There was a pause as Emer struggled for words. "I will talk to them Sam. What do you want me to say? Over."

"Tell them the heaters are coming," he lied. "Over."

"Okay, Sam. Over and Out."

But I knew as well as she did that the heaters were not coming. The subgovernor of Silopi was using his political power to gain status and prestige. He was demanding that bottled gas heaters be purchased for the tents. He insisted that the UNHCR pay for heaters, but of course, when the refugees would receive them, they'd be given as if the Turkish government was the donor. Cards would be issued to the refugees for gas refills, and they would be stamped with the governor's stamp. But the UNHCR would pay for the gas. That was his position. Unless the UNHCR complied with the governor, there would be no heaters. The camp was in Turkey, and if the foreigners wanted to help, they would do it on his terms. So there were no heaters.

To further delay things, UNHCR policy required three bids before major purchases (like heaters for five thousand people) could be approved. They were finding it difficult to even find three suppliers to provide bids.

"Silopi, Silopi. Come in please. This is Emer. Over."

"This is Sam. I read you. Over."

"Listen, Sam, the family of the dead baby has a request. They want to bury their child in a village cemetery near Silopi. They would like us to arrange for transport for the family and dead baby. Over."

"What do they want, Emer? Over."

"They would like us to provide transport, Sam. One of the Suzukis and the Land Cruiser would be enough, Sam. Over."

"Please stand by, Emir." There was a lengthy pause of a couple of minutes.

"Emir, do you read me? This is Sam. Over."

"I read you, Sam. Go ahead."

After a few moments Sam answered, "I telephoned Lois, and apparently, the Turkish authorities have some arrangements for taking care of the dead in the camp. Over." He must have called Lois in Diyarbakir to receive help. Lois was spending Christmas there. I continued driving and listening.

"Do you know what those arrangements are, Sam?"

"No, but I don't want to set a precedent. We won't provide any transport for the family. Over."

"Sam, can you inform the *kaymakam* (Turkish for *subgovernor*) that a baby has died because of the cold and that we really need heaters out here? Over."

"I will mention it in my meeting with him today. Over and out."

As I drove by the camp, the tears streamed down my face. Tears of sadness for the child and the family. Tears of anger and frustration at the godlessness, the injustice, and the heartlessness of those who were supposed to be helping. It was a shame. The UNHCR was an embarrassment. They were invested with experience, money, and every available resource. But the refugees felt they had invested it in themselves, their fancy cars, and the advancement of their careers at the expense of those they were sent to help.

A Haj camp refugee told me later, "When the UNHCR came, we were filled with hope." They have such a big important-sounding name: the United Nations High Commission for Refugees. And they have those big shiny vehicles and worldwide status. But they have done nothing to relieve our suffering."

The unmuffled roar of the white Dodge drowned the sound of my crying. *God, oh God*, I prayed in desperation. *That ten-month-old baby could have been Nuha, had we not insisted on taking care of her. She too has gastroenteritis. She couldn't face this terribly cold weather unprotected. How many more babies are there like her that continue to suffer?"*

Earlier in December, the subgovernor had refused entry into Turkey for Suha and Nuha. He did not want any more refugees. I thought, *If he had permitted their entry into Turkey in early December, they would have been placed in the Haj camp. They would have met a similar fate. Oh God, protect the children.*

My thoughts were interrupted by engine noises. Cough. Sputter. Cough. I tapped the accelerator lightly. Nothing. "Oh no," I said aloud, "Not again!" The fuel indicator was on empty that morning, but since there was no gasoline to purchase in Zakho, I had no choice but to attempt the twenty-six-kilometer drive. Saddam had put his own embargo on all goods going to the Kurdish north to discourage and weaken the Kurdish resolve for autonomy. I had already run out of gas once on my way from Zakho to the Turkish border. I had been fortunate, however, to run out in front of an NGO warehouse, a group called Medical Aid. I went inside to get shelter and warmth, and after drinking tea with a couple of Kurdish guards, they appeared with two plastic water bottles full of gasoline. Their generosity and hospitality knew no end!

I put the truck in neutral, straightened the wheels out, and tried to will the truck over the next rise in the road.

Perhaps I can coast down to the abandoned US Army post, affectionately named the White House. When the US Army left Turkey after Operation Provide Comfort, they left an enormous amount of supplies and equipment. This building was kind of white if one ignored the mud, hence the name. The old Dodge wasn't going to clear the slight incline, however, so I coasted off onto the shoulder. An icy-cold drizzle greeted me as I climbed down from the Dodge and started my walk westward on the highway in search of civilization. I hadn't walked fifteen steps when a truck driver pulled over and offered me a lift.

He dropped me at a truck stop, the last one for Turkish drivers headed in the opposite direction toward Iraq. But my mind was not on the dozens of trucks waiting in the dirt lot, nor on the piles of odd-shaped tanks and the men welding them into big rectangular boxes. I was hoping to find a couple liters of gasoline to help me make it to the single gas station in Silopi. I found an empty two-liter

Pepsi bottle in the dirt, and several friendly Kurdish men siphoned it full from a fifty-five-gallon drum.

I began to wait for another truck to come to take me back down the highway to my stranded vehicle. There was very little traffic now since the border was closed to civilians. The US Army had left, and the relief workers were all away. The drizzle had turned to rain, and it was getting down my neck as I stood hoping for any vehicle to stop. After several minutes, I could see a new Toyota Land Cruiser heading my way. I waved vigorously. As it passed me, it began to slow. I ran to catch it in what was now a steady rain. It was Sam, the acting UNHCR office head.

"What are you doing out on the highway?" he asked accusingly. I didn't appreciate getting the third degree. What did he think, anyway?

I wanted to say something sarcastic, like, "I thought it'd be fun to take a stroll in the freezing rain out here in the middle of nowhere," but I answered, "Thanks for picking me up. I just need to get back up the road to the white pickup truck. I ran out of gas." He took me to my disabled vehicle. After pouring the precious two liters into the gas-guzzling pickup, I pulled onto the highway and continued my drive west into Silopi.

As I pulled in to town, it looked eerily deserted. For the third day straight, all the shops had been closed. This was the Kurdish version of the intifada. Only nobody was throwing any stones. Everyone had gone on strike because of the mistreatment of civilians by soldiers, gendarme, and police. Ankara, the capitol of Turkey, had sent military reinforcements to discourage any uprisings. They had beefed-up checkpoints around the city where they searched all private vehicles and had placed armed patrol throughout the town.

Armored personnel carriers, antiterrorist vehicles, military trucks, and dark-green Land Rovers were continuously making patrols throughout the area. Civilians were stopped on the street, harassed, and hauled off to jail if they didn't have an identification card. Refugees who went into town to shop were at special risk. They had no Turkish identification; they had to rely on a paper permission slip issued by the Haj security police. Then they were dependent upon the mood of the policeman or soldier. The increased pressure had made the Kurdish citizens of Silopi furious. They had unanimously decided to close all businesses for three days. The streets were deserted.

I still needed to buy more gas, and Silopi's only gas station was all shuttered up. There was nowhere else to go but the Mercy for All residence, so I drove there. Then a bus pulled up across the street from the house. Adjacent to the Mercy for All home were a couple of dilapidated shacks set back from the road. From their grimy sheet-metal shacks, they sold black-market fuel. These shacks were all shuttered up in compliance with the strike. I watched with interest to see what this bus was up to. These shops had fifty-five-gallon oil drums lined up in front of them containing fuel from Iraq.

Since the gas station was closed, perhaps I could buy some gas from one of these roadside gas dealers, I thought hopefully. I watched as the shop owner carefully raised the shutter a few feet, ducked under, and came out with a pump and hose. He looked up and down the deserted street, then quickly pumped diesel into the bus's reserve tanks. I approached him slowly. I guessed he was violating the strike to make a little money.

"*Roj bas! Gas heya*" (Good day! Have you got any gas)? I said in Kurdish. He appreciated my Kurdish greeting and answered that, yes, he had gasoline. We chatted briefly as he hurriedly pumped forty liters into my truck. I paid him ninety-thousand Turkish lira and thanked him. He smiled, glanced both ways, and ducked into the garage, pulling the shutter down behind him.

It was like Moses in the desert. He struck a rock, and water came forth. I drove into a shuttered town and gas flowed into my truck. God was indeed providing in miraculous ways.

Chapter 14

The Confrontation

Silopi, Turkey, December 28, 1991

The time to notify Lois had come. I was excited but also anxious; I don't like confrontations. As the head of the UNHCR Office (Sam had been a temporary replacement), she needed to know of all that had happened during her week away. I expected her to make the four-hour trip from Diyarbakir to Silopi and arrive in the afternoon, and I needed to report to her the progress in the Haj Camp. I wanted to also talk to her about Suha and Nuha. She needed to know that Serwan had changed his mind and that he wanted us to adopt his girls. Lois had expected Serwan would want to be reunified with his daughters. Thinking back to her comments of the week before, I was particularly nervous.

"You know you will have to put the girls in the refugee camp with their father," Lois had said.

"Of course, they are his children," I had responded. At the time, we all thought that reunification was Serwan's wish. As soon as they were healthy enough to tolerate the camp environment, we would bring them there, I had assured her.

It was obvious that could be several weeks' time, considering their desperate physical situation. Lois did not want us to become too attached to the girls. But now the father wanted us to adopt them, and I was not at all certain how she would react. *Will this upset the UNHCR?* I wondered.

My heart was beating rapidly as I drove to the office. The consequences of our personal involvement with Suha and Nuha would soon be apparent. I did not want to jeopardize the contract between Mercy for All and the UNHCR. If I continued to be affiliated with Mercy for All, I reasoned, and Lois was angry with me, it would affect the way they treated everyone from our organization. I considered that I might have to resign from Mercy for All, which would sever my ties with the UNHCR in Turkey. I weighed the cost and decided that if it were necessary, I would resign.

When I pulled up to the Silopi office, Lois was not in the building. I climbed the concrete stairs to the upstairs office and began to make some photocopies. I would have much preferred to use the copy machine at the bookstore in town, but it was closed like all the other shops due to the strike. I was copying documents relating to the potential adoption.

The suspicion and curiosity of the locals employed in our office was a real nuisance at times. Nothing was private. I heard footsteps on the stairs and quickly turned the documents over. I knew it would be inappropriate for Lois to learn of the adoption from an office employee. I could just imagine the confrontation, *Why wasn't I informed first?* I preferred to break the news to Lois face-to-face. Secondhand or thirdhand messages are invariably miscommunicated.

Sabre—a young blonde woman from the States, who, with her husband, had begun working with the UNHCR—entered the room. She had worked diligently at every assignment given her, but she told me she'd become disillusioned and disappointed at the inefficiency, the bureaucracy, and the petty politicking that was keeping the refugees in their misery.

"Lois and Sam are at the mayor's office here in Silopi," she informed me as she walked in.

I had gone to the Silopi mayor's office the day before with a letter I'd written, requesting his assistance. I had asked specifically that he would give permission to the children to transit through

Turkey, not just to enter Turkey. The purpose of a transit permit was to bring Suha and Nuha to Europe. He was very kind and said he really wanted to help but that he couldn't.

"My advice to you," he had said as he leaned over his huge mahogany desk, "is to ask the US embassy to help you get the permission from the Turkish Ministry of Foreign Affairs. You see"—he continued kindly—"the girls have no official identification cards or passports from Iraq. I don't have the authority to allow such people to enter the country. Only the Ministry of Foreign Affairs Office can give that. I wish I could help you, but it's impossible. Go to the US embassy in Ankara. They can help you."

Go to the US embassy, I thought. He said it so simply as if it were a trip to the market. But it was eighteen hours by bus to the US embassy in Ankara, each way. I had thanked the mayor and left his office feeling a bit disappointed. However, I thought, *Now I know the next step in this confusing process.* Somehow, I would have to contact the US embassy and get all the documents to them for their review. I surely hoped I wouldn't have to make a thirty-six-hour bus journey for a simple permission slip, but I knew others had done that, and more, to get Turkish officials to give visas or visa extensions. I also knew many of them had had their requests denied.

"It's one of the most difficult borders in the world," a friend had told me. I was beginning to understand what he meant. I decided to first fax the US embassy all the paperwork I had assembled. That is what I was needing to do when Sabre entered the office.

Sabre sat down and began to organize some cards for gas bottle exchanges for the refugees. I headed into the room where the fax machine was located. It was also Lois's office. I wondered if the mayor was at that very moment talking with Lois about my request of the previous day. It would be embarrassing to me if she learned from the mayor about my transit request. Mercy for All had agreed with the UNHCR not to initiate high-level interaction with the Turkish government. I had made my inquiry solely as a US citizen and not as an employee of Mercy for All. And the mayor, although the highest local official, did not have that much power. My concern was that Lois, if she were upset, could challenge me about having talked to him, even on a personal basis. I felt I'd been a bit sneaky, and I didn't like the feeling at all.

I sat down at the fax machine and began typing in all the digits to fax the documents to the US embassy. Telephone connections were a very uncertain thing in Silopi. There were very few telephone lines reaching the tiny town; and as with most things in eastern Turkey, the phone system was underdeveloped, poorly managed, and sorely in need of repair. The central government purposefully allowed the east to remain underdeveloped. Some villages still had no electricity, and many had no school or medical facility. For a resident of Silopi, who needed a simple X-ray, for example, an eight-hour trip on the bus was required.

I assembled the pages together and counted them. It wasn't uncommon to spend an hour or two trying to send a single page. I had sixteen pages! *Lord*, I prayed, *only you can make this happen.* Over and over, I dialed the numbers but never got a connection. At last, I heard the fax signal connection. *Oh, what a happy tone!* Eagerly, I fed the first three pages into the machine.

The confirmation report stated, "No result." I kept trying. Minutes crept by. Any moment, Lois was going to walk into her office. I wondered what she'd say when she saw me faxing sixteen pages.

Finally, after over half an hour, I got a good connection and began slowly feeding documents into the machine. There were long pauses of thirty seconds for each page, as the line tried to send the data. The stress of waiting for transmission was killing me. My back began to ache.

A vehicle pulled up outside. I looked down from the window. It wasn't Lois. *Lord, let this fax go*, I prayed. The sixteen pages provided a complete explanation of who we were, how we had found the children, their condition, the permissions from the birth father, and our intentions to adopt them. My primary request of the US embassy, stated in a cover letter, was for aid in obtaining permission from the Turkish Ministry of Foreign Affairs so Suha and Nuha could travel through Turkey to Germany.

Another vehicle drove up. This time, it was Lois. There were still several pages left to send. I had full permission to use the fax machine, as well as the other office equipment, and I would pay for the phone time. That wasn't an issue. My main thought was to share the news of Serwan's decision at an appropriate moment. Lois came into the outer office area, followed by Sam. She seemed to be preoccupied and hardly recognized my presence. There were still two pages to fax.

Then Lois walked straight up to me and commanded, "It's urgent that I see you right away." My heart leapt into my throat. I swallowed hard.

Lois had addressed me with these exact words (and tone of voice) when we'd met accidentally in the appliance store prior to her departure to Diyarbakir for her vacation. She had a forceful personality. But in the appliance store, she had been distracted by a sudden radio call, and an emergency. She had had to hurry away before speaking to me. I had stood there in the appliance store with heightened interest. *What was on her mind? She sure seems intense today*, I'd thought. But after the radio call she had left abruptly and then departed to spend Christmas in Diyarbakir. I hadn't seen her since.

During her absence, Serwan and I had returned a second time to see Mr. Ahmet to have the second document—the affidavit of abandonment drawn up. This accurately reflected Serwan's intention that Jane and I adopt the girls. It was the most critical piece of paper in the process of adoption. Erdoğan, the UNHCR translator, accompanied us on that trip. The office had shut down much of their work in the camp during the holiday, so Erdoğan had had extra time. Erdoğan's translation was critical; he spoke fluent Arabic, Turkish, Kurdish, and English. The affidavit was fully understood by Erdoğan, Serwan, Mr. Ahmet, and me. The affidavit of abandonment was one of the documents on its way to the US embassy in Ankara via the fax.

Lois wanted to talk. Her facial expression and tone of voice conveyed the urgency. There was no courteous greeting or small talk about vacations. Lois had something to say.

"We are calling a staff meeting immediately," she announced loudly, and then turning to me, she said, "You and I need to talk, Kirk." The tension was palpable.

She held the staff meetings in the adjoining room to her office. Her office door remained ajar due to cables running across the concrete floor through the doorway. Several people crowded into the tiny outer room. The fax machine was right next to the open door to her office, and it continued to click away as everyone found a chair to sit on. I sat next to the partially open office door, and the table with the fax machine. Suha and Nuha's identification papers lay faceup as they slowly crept into the machine. Their pictures were plainly visible.

It was uncommon for all the staff to be present at the same time; people were usually out in the field.

I was sure somebody would ask, "What is that huge fax you're sending, Kirk?" But nobody did. *Thank you, Jesus*, I prayed. I did not want to brief the entire staff regarding Serwan when Lois had yet to be informed.

The last page was finally in. The transmission time seemed to take an eternity. There were knots in my stomach from the anxiety. At last, the confirmation report rolled out. I tore the thin thermal page off the fax machine.

I read the single line: "Result okay." I could have whooped out loud with joy, but a sigh of relief had to suffice. As I sorted the papers back into order, the electricity went out. The fax machine went dead. One minute sooner, I would not have known if it had been received or not. But now I knew that the US embassy in Ankara had all the documents. Work could begin on getting the girls out of Iraq at the highest levels. I didn't have to take buses for thirty-six hours.

I pulled a chair up and joined the meeting. They were debating a distribution system for gas so that no one would get too much gas and be wasteful. It dragged on and on, giving me adequate time to collect my thoughts for the coming discussion. From the binder of documents I'd put together, I retrieved the letter I'd written to Lois. It explained Serwan's change of mind, our willingness to adopt the children, and my visit to the subgovernor to arrange travel permission. I attached a copy of the affidavit of abandonment as legal evidence of my actions. I took a deep breath. I was ready.

"Come into my office," she said, and then she shoved a big rock in front of the door to prop it closed. Sam sat down at his desk to her right. He had little to say.

"There are two problems," she began to say. As I listened, I realized that she still had no idea about the adoption. Although I was thankful, I found it a bit amusing. Many of the residents in Silopi knew; people at the refugee camp knew, but thankfully, she had been preoccupied with internal supervision and management and had yet to find out.

"Number one," she said, "who gave you permission to travel across the border into Iraq? You say the field officer in Diyarbakir did, but he denies this." I reviewed the circumstances of the previous three weeks for her, realizing that she had been away much of the time. There had been four different people in charge of her office during that time.

"Everyone knew about the two babies in Iraq, including the people in this office, in the Diyarbakir office, and in the Zakho office. But nobody was doing anything about the dying girls," I said, "nor could they suggest any solutions. I radioed Zakho, and they could only suggest a possible orphanage in Dahok. But they were too sick to go there. The Diyarbakir officer had only one comment, 'Can't Mercy for All take care of it?' Their office was too far away, and they had no time to help them.

"And the field officer here knew that I was going into Iraq. It was discussed at the staff meeting. He, too, could recommend no other alternative. He did not prevent me from going. It was clearly an emergency situation. It is true that I had no written permission from the UNHCR, but in this situation, relying on the bureaucracy would have been fatal for that child. A sick baby cannot survive under such conditions." She had no argument about the bureaucracy. She, too, was fed up with the endless delays required of her. Decisions had to be processed first through the Diyarbakir office, then passed through the Ankara office, and if finances were involved, through the office in

Geneva Switzerland. Indeed, the red tape was the reason the refugees continued to sleep in the wet and cold.

My remark about the baby not tolerating the harsh environment was designed to remind them not so subtly of the death of the ten-month-old that very morning. They didn't know I knew about it, since they were unaware I had a radio and had listened to their entire conversation. However, she did not contest my decision to cross the border.

"The second problem is that you are now living in Iraq," she said. "This is unacceptable. Mercy for All personnel working under the UNHCR in Turkey must live in Turkey. You and your wife must come back. We have asked the Zakho office to find a family in Zakho to look after the children. You and Jane must return." I had anticipated this problem during one of many sleepless nights in Zakho. I had worked through every possible scenario as I lay in bed, much as a chess player tries to anticipate future moves. I knew immediately what my next move would be. I had a big knot in my stomach.

"Then it is necessary that I leave Mercy for All," I said as evenly as I could. "I am prepared to telephone my director and make this effective immediately." We both knew that once I left Mercy for All, I was no longer subject to its contract with the UNHCR. I was free to act as any independent US citizen. "Lois," I continued, "I will telephone our coordinator in Diyarbakir after our discussion and resign. The proper care of these children is simply more important than my job."

"Don't forget you are living in Iraq without a visa," she snapped. "You will have to see our Zakho officer and obtain the necessary permission from Baghdad." All the nongovernmental organizations working in northern Iraq had entered the country during the short occupation of the coalition forces. Those that stayed after the foreign military's June departure were issued Iraqi visas in Mosul. A few had gone as far as Baghdad for visas if they intended to travel much in the country. I knew all of this already and told her I would of course comply... "Americans are forbidden to live in Iraq unless working with a recognized aid agency," Lois said.

She was frustrated and played by the rules. She may have been receiving pressure from her bosses who were uncomfortable about my living over the border. I was glad Bob, from Medical Aid International, had thought ahead and offered me a job working for him in Iraq should I ever need to remain there. I told her of his job offer and that I would accept it.

"Henceforth, I will live and work in Iraq." She seemed relieved to be letting me go.

"There is something else you need to know," I added. "The birth father, Serwan, has changed his mind." I didn't need to explain his situation; both Sam and Lois were very aware of it. I continued, "He does not want the children reunited with him in the camp. He wants Jane and me to adopt them. I told Serwan it was a very big decision. He said he had been thinking about it for weeks. I explained to him that we would have to have such a decision written down and notarized by an attorney. So I went with him on Christmas day to town and an attorney drew up a document." I handed her the affidavit of abandonment, written in both English and Turkish. Lois and Sam looked the document over.

There was little for them to say. I was a bit surprised they didn't react; I had become accustomed to their antagonism.

"You had better get a good lawyer," Lois said. "You are in for a big challenge. It may be impossible. I heard of a US sergeant who fell in love with an abandoned baby and tried unsuccessfully to adopt it." She was silent for a moment and said, "I wish you luck." I looked at Sam. He said nothing.

Then I handed her a prepared letter.

"I anticipated this discussion, so I wrote down what has transpired during your absence." She took it from me and began reading it. It would help her report to her superiors in Diyarbakir.

I felt uneasy conducting my final business in the office. I shared the news with my colleagues, said my goodbyes, and descended the stairs to where the Kurdish staff congregated. The drivers, the cook, and the guard were watching a Kurdish program broadcast from Syria. The Turks forbade any Kurdish programming on their stations, but they couldn't stop the airwaves from the neighboring countries. I sat down and shared about the potential adoption with the Kurds seated in the tiny room. They were thrilled. They had followed the developments and had frequently asked about the girls' condition. They offered me their remaining stuffed eggplant, rice, and flatbread. I enjoyed their company.

These are my friends here, I mused. *The local Kurds. The taxi and truck drivers, the gas station attendants, the tea salesman, the baker, the small businessman, the butcher. I am at home with them, and they seem to enjoy me. I really do love Kurdistan. Never have I experienced such hospitality, kindness, and generosity from strangers as I have here. It will be sad to leave.*

Little did I realize it might be impossible to leave.

Chapter 15

Kirk in Berlin. Jane in Iraq.

Zakho, Iraq, December 30, 1991

It was with mixed emotion that we looked toward the new year. We had planned to be back in Berlin on December 27. A friend traveling to Diyarbakir agreed to try to change our plane tickets. Realistically, though, we had no idea how long it would take for permission to come from the Turkish Foreign Ministry. There was simply no way to predict when we could leave Iraq. To complicate matters, I began feeling weak and short of breath. I was coughing much more than usual and found it difficult to move the heavy gas bottles for heating. Jane needed them upstairs in the bedroom. How could I assist her in the major travels ahead of us if I was too weak to even manage my own luggage?

I knew I had an advanced lung infection, a result of cystic fibrosis. Roughly every three months, it was necessary for me to be hospitalized to combat lung infections with powerful intravenous antibiotics. The bacteria never went away entirely. Since the disease affects primarily Caucasians, there were simply no facilities in the Middle East that specialized in treatment. I had planned to return to Berlin for treatment at the end of December, but the children couldn't travel yet. What were we to do?

It seemed the only solution was for me to leave Jane with the girls in Iraq and travel alone to Berlin. It wasn't a very desirous choice, but we could see no alternative. I was reluctant to leave her in Zakho; it was not safe. There were frequent explosions, and we could hear machine-gun fire at night. The Iraqi army was fighting the Kurds in Kirkuk and in Erbil, and we never knew if or when they would advance as far north as the city of Zakho.

There was also the added problem of supplies. How could Jane leave the house to buy food or fuel? She had to stay and nurse the babies back to health. And we knew she would be lonely too. There was no telephone system functioning in Zakho or mail service. The nearest fax machine was across the border in Silopi, at Bob's office. I went to see Bob and shared my problem.

He knew I was getting weak and would need to go to the hospital. Fortunately, his home in Zakho was only two blocks away from where Jane and I were staying, and he agreed to look in on her regularly. Our Assyrian landlord assured me he would look after Jane as if she were his own daughter. I knew I could trust him and that he would do his very best. His wife, children, and deceased brother's family lived in the house too. With the teenagers and small children around, it seemed there would be sufficient company for Jane. God gave us both the peace that it was the right decision, and so I packed my bags.

The trip to Berlin involved first a five-hour drive to Diyarbakir, then a two-hour flight to Ankara, and finally a four-hour flight to Berlin. Bob was very gracious and offered to drive me on the long drive to Diyarbakir; he needed to go to his bank there soon, anyway. It was the closest bank that could receive money wired internationally. Imagine having to drive five hours to get to your bank! I flew from there to Ankara and decided to lay over for a couple of days and make some connections at the US and the German embassies. It might help speed things up if I asked about the travel permission in person. And I could apply for immigration visas for the girls for Germany.

I arrived in Ankara late at night the day before New Year's Eve. As the taxi pulled up the steep hill toward my friend's apartment block, I noticed something peculiar. All the lights in the neighborhood appeared to be out. I had no idea where my friend's apartment was, and the taxi driver had a confused look on his face. Sometimes, that is just a game they play to justify the "grand tour," but this fellow looked genuinely lost. It was well below freezing, and the roads were covered with a thick layer of ice. There was no way the taxi could climb the steep hill to the rows of tall dark apartment buildings. He stopped the car and indicated we'd arrived. I looked out the windows at the blackness and wondered where on earth I was to go.

I paid him and stepped out onto the icy pavement. The moment my bags were out of the vehicle, he backed up. His side-view mirror caught me on the hip, spun me around, and sent me sprawling on the ice.

Welcome to Ankara, I thought as I struggled up and rubbed my tailbone. "At least it isn't snowing right now," I said to myself as I made my way gingerly in the darkness toward the nearest building. It is not atypical to have a power outage in Turkey, particularly eastern Turkey, but this was the nation's capital. I expected better.

The apartment buildings were painted an identical beige color, each looked to be about fifteen stories high, and had no visible address markings on them. I was searching for building B, where the Garcias lived. I stopped the first man that came through the door.

"B?" I asked and pointed to the doorway. He shook his head, said something in Turkish, and indicated an apartment fifty meters away. I began hauling my duffle bags through the snow in that direction. Minutes later, I paused to catch my breath in the utter darkness of the first landing. Between my lung infection, chronic shortness of breath, heavy congestion, the freezing cold, and the heavy bags, I was exhausted. I scribbled the number 52 on a scrap of paper and showed it to a passing tenant using the light of a match. He pointed up the stairs. I cursed the still and silent elevators and prayed the electricity would come back on. It didn't.

After an interminable struggle, I reached door number 52 and knocked. A kindly woman opened the door, held a lantern up, and looked me in the face. She greeted me in Turkish. I showed her the address and asked where the Garcias lived. Her response was very disappointing; I was in building J, not B.

Were it not for a nice man who carried my duffle bag up the stairs in building B, I never would have made it. I tipped him and began knocking vigorously on the Garcias' door. There was no answer. Again and again, I banged, hoping in vain someone might be on the toilet, the phone, or even asleep. It was nearly midnight, but nobody was home. I sat down in the darkness in the concrete hallway.

God, I prayed, *I am tired, have a fever from my lung infection, and it's miserably cold here in this dark hallway. If I didn't feel so awful, this would be pretty funny. What should I do?* I remembered suddenly that another colleague lived in one of the other buildings in the same development. I descended the stairs, and by another lighted match and another kind stranger, I located the address. Fortunately, they were home. They welcomed me in, and soon I was fast asleep.

Jane began facing the reality that her husband was gone for an undetermined length of time. She had no idea when the permission would come for her to take the girls across the border into Turkey and no idea when she would hear from me. Her only line of communication was through the kindness and generosity of Bob. He allowed her to send and receive faxes at his office in Silopi, Turkey. She couldn't go herself to Silopi, since that would mean leaving her home in Iraq and crossing the border into Turkey. There was no one to care for the children if she left the house. So she wrote out faxes to me, Bob picked them up, and then he brought them to his office over in Silopi and faxed them. Her main focus was on caring for Delal and Jessica.

The biggest concern was their need for nutrition. Their digestion just wasn't working like it should. In spite of double layers of diapers their clothes continued to get soiled, and their meager supply of outfits were quickly wearing out with the daily laundering. To wash clothes or to get water to bathe the girls, she had to go outside in the cold, break the ice on the top of a fifty-gallon drum full of water, fill a pot with ice water, and then heat it on the gas stove. It was tedious and exhausting. She decided to dig out the suitcase of clothes the foster family had given.

"Serwan left these when he dropped the children off," Abdul Rahmann had said. "We haven't used them, but maybe you will need them."

Jane untied the string that held the suitcase closed. *Perhaps these will be useful, or maybe there will be some special outfit that will be a keepsake*, she thought as she removed the broken lid. A very unfriendly odor greeted her. It was full of filthy rags. There wasn't anything useful or repairable in the entire bundle. *How like our own condition*, she reflected.

"You, Lord, have adopted us into your family through Jesus Christ. And what did we have to offer you? Nothing but filthy rags. Useless, stain ridden, smelly, decaying rags. There is absolutely nothing from our old selves that is useful in your kingdom. And you give us an entirely new life. You purify us, renew us, and let us start afresh."

Chapter 16

US Embassy. Departure
for Germany.

Berlin, Germany, January 4, 1992

As Jane continued to care for two hungry and sick babies, I sought care at the *Kinderklinik* (children's hospital) in Zehlendorf, Berlin. (CF is a childhood disease. It was uncommon for someone with CF to live to adulthood, hence many hospitals only had care facilities set up in children's hospitals.) The hospital is located in a lovely quiet suburb on the outskirts of West Berlin. I had to complete a full two weeks of antibiotic and respiratory therapy before I was strong enough to plan my return. As soon as I was healthy enough, I obtained a hospital pass and went to the German office for immigration in the center of West Berlin. I waited half a day in line, which was typical. After completing an application to bring Delal and Jessica into the country, I was told that since an application was already in process originating from the German embassy in Ankara, they could not consider my request. I had initiated the application process while in Ankara but hoped a little nudging in Berlin would help. Furthermore, they could not inform me of their response to the application, since it was an "internal request."

"Ich kann Ihnen leider nicht helfen" (Unfortunately I can't help you), was repeated to me in every office I went to. Disappointed and more than a little bit frustrated, I left the Immigration office, returned to the hospital and then prepared for my return to Ankara.

Zakho, Iraq, Early January 1992

Meanwhile, Jane continued her struggle against the cold and the girl's illnesses. Each day, she hoped permission would come from the Turkish Minister of the Interior granting her papers to bring the girls through Turkey. Eventually, Bob went to the local governor's office in Silopi and asked if a fax had come through regarding our case.

"Oh, our fax machine has been broken for several weeks," said the receptionist. There was no indication that it would be repaired anytime soon. Bob then suggested that his fax number be given to the minister of the Interior, which they gladly agreed to do. A couple of days later, the permission came through!

With great expectation and a grand sense of relief, Jane loaded up the girls into Bob's Mitsubishi SUV, and Bob ferried them to the Iraqi border. They were stopped outside the customs building in Turkey just inside the Habur border crossing. A large contingent of men had assembled inside the building, and they were quite pleased to be witnesses of this unusual event. I am not sure what the primary purpose was for their meeting. They were the mayors from all the surrounding towns. Of course, they had Jane bring the girls inside for a moment, and she sat and drank a glass of tea with them, but then they sent her back out to wait in the SUV while the men talked to Bob. Decisions and business were, after all, affairs for the men to handle. Without the approval of these men, the girls would not be permitted to enter Turkey. For the next couple of hours, the men drank tea and told stories and then dismissed Bob with formal and cordial goodbyes. He returned out to his car, where Jane sat anxiously trying to entertain two fidgety girls.

The men had said, "Yes!" Bob then drove them back to spend their final night in Zakho.

The following day, with written permission in hand, Bob drove Jane and the girls out of Iraq and safely into Turkey. It was an immensely emotional experience for all of them. Their journey was just beginning, however. Bob then drove them four hours to Diyarbakir, where Jane purchased plane tickets to fly to Ankara, Turkey's capital. Delal was quite shocked when she climbed the stairs and entered the door to the plane. They were the final passengers to board. Jane had her hands full with Jessica on one arm, and her carry-on luggage in the other, so she was counting on Delal to climb the metal stairs from the tarmac and walk by herself onto the plane. She was after all two and a half years old. But airplanes were something totally new. And that huge crowd of strangers all looking right at her when she stepped aboard was too much. She immediately threw herself on the floor and began screaming. Jane was at a loss. A thoughtful woman, however, offered Delal some pretzels, which was all the distraction she needed. Her tears disappeared miraculously, and she bounded down the aisle.

Ankara, Turkey, January 1992

Nuha and Suha in the home of friends in Ankara,
Turkey (Jan 1992). They had each gained
about ten pounds in one month.

Upon arrival in Ankara, Jane was met by members of Operation Mobilization and driven to the home of friends. The following week, I arrived from Berlin, regrettably without the permission we sought to enter Germany. We wanted to adopt the children in Germany, according to their laws. But after repeated phone calls to the German embassy, I was informed that our request had been formally denied. No reason could be given. I could only surmise that they were afraid we might not qualify under their laws to adopt, in which case the children would become wards of the state and a burden to the economy. That meant that we couldn't go home to Berlin and complete our adoption in Germany. Then we wondered about completing the adoption during our temporary stay in Turkey, according to Turkish laws. So I then asked the German officials if we could enter Germany with our girls, if the adoption process were completed in Turkey.

"Sometimes, we do not recognize Turkish adoptions," I was told.

"And what are the conditions for accepting or rejecting the adoptions?" I asked.

"We cannot say. It depends upon each case."

"You mean we could potentially fulfill all the requirements here in Turkey to adopt, complete the process, and then still face the uncertainty of entering Germany?"

"That is correct." Well, that seemed like far too iffy. So we axed that idea.

After much prayer and deliberation, we decided to go to the US to adopt the girls. We had after all already completed the INS regulations to adopt foreign-born orphans, and so getting permission should be a relatively smooth process. When we had prepared to adopt a child in Romania the previous year, we had completed the required home study, background check, financial evaluation, fingerprinting, etc. in order to qualify to bring the child into the US. After we had finished all that preparation, the adoption laws in Romania changed (they put all pending adoptions on hold for one year), and we were unable to adopt. The government office in Bonn, Germany, had our completed papers on file. And so it was simply a matter of the US embassy in Ankara calling them and requesting that the letter of approval be faxed to the US embassy in Ankara. That official document granted us the right to immigrate with foreign-born orphans with the intent to adopt them. We proceeded with this plan and the embassy obtained the valued permission.

Ankara, Turkey, Thursday, January 30, 1992

There are some days where everything seems to go wrong. Then there are days when suddenly everything just falls into place. Today was a little of both. And it was incredible! The Lord performed miracles today that left me spellbound.

Bureaucracy can move at a snail's pace. Having agreed to issue the immigration visas, the US embassy explained the requirements to me. There was a four-page application, a two-page medical form with an examination, specific types of passport-type photos needed, and fees of $200 each. This had to be submitted before they could begin processing the visas. I was eager to get the visas as quickly as possible and decided to take the pictures myself and have them developed at a twenty-four-hour lab. It would have been an enormous undertaking to get the girls and transport them into the city to a passport studio. The apartment where we were staying was a long bus ride from downtown Ankara, and traveling with two tired and sick kids would have been a nightmare. And just for a couple pictures! I completed the paper application after the kids were in bed on Wednesday night. But before putting the girls to bed, I hung a sheet from the dining room table and had the kids sit on the floor, and then I took fifteen pictures of them. I had to estimate how large their heads would appear in a standard picture that the photo kiosk would be printing. I hoped to have at least one decent photo for each child that was suitable for their visas.

That evening, I also got the doctor's appointments. The Turkish doctor told me on the phone that lung X-rays and blood work were also necessary. These were performed at different locations from his office. I got the necessary addresses and opening hours and plotted a course through the city, figuring out which minibuses and taxis we would need to take. Then Thursday morning at 9:00 a.m., Jane, the girls, and I set off across Ankara to get the X-rays. Delal could walk; Jessica was carried in a baby backpack. First, we walked from the high-rise apartment to the taxi stand, being careful of the black ice on the sloping asphalt. The taxi couldn't bring us right to the lab, because it was on a one-way street, so we climbed a long uphill street to reach the office.

"Chest X-rays are not necessary for children under fifteen years," they informed us. But they did an X-ray of Jessica's hand to prove she did not have rickets. Infants lacking vitamin D are prone to it. Her test was clear.

"Ugh," we thought, "after all that work to get these kids ready and then drag them through the snow, those other tests were not even necessary! Oh, well, let's just get moving and get the blood work done."

This time the taxi took us right to the clinic doors. There was quite a crowd in the tiny office. Delal was fascinated with the man sitting there with a tourniquet on his arm.

"Stay with Daddy," I reminded her again. We waited as patiently as possible in the line at the small desk. Our turn came.

"No, sir," the doctor's said, "blood work is not necessary for children under fifteen years of age." I smiled and thanked him; and we began putting the kids' heavy coats, hats, and gloves back on, grateful that we'd been spared the screams and tears of children giving blood. We only hoped the physicians knew what they were talking about.

The doctor's office for the general examination was located up ahead on the same street, a busy thoroughfare of five and sometimes seven lanes, depending how aggressive the drivers were feeling. Unfortunately for us, the office was six long blocks away, and the street was one-way, coming in our direction. There would be no taxis this time. We'd have to walk. Occasionally, little snow flurries would come swirling down. We pulled the hood over Jessica's little head. She was riding on my back, but eventually, Delal became too tired from the climb on the steep streets, and so I put her on my shoulders instead, and Jane carried Jessica in her special back carrier. We found the office after about half an hour. We were early, but we figured we'd just wait in the reception room. No such luck. We had to remain outside in the cold. It was all locked up. Other patients began arriving for their appointments, too, but still there was no sign of the doctor. Finally, after having waited in the stairwell for an hour and a quarter, he arrived.

He examined them quickly and completed the forms, and within an hour, we were on our way to find a *dolmush*, a minibus. Things would be a bit tricky here. I planned to send Jane and the girls home on the little bus and say goodbye, since I still had lots of business to do in the city. We didn't want the kids to make a big scene when they realized I wasn't accompanying them. Jane got on first. Then I handed her Jessica and finally Delal. They were so tired from our four hours of trekking through downtown Ankara that they plopped down and were soon asleep. I was able to move much quicker now. I had carried Delal on my shoulders for the last six blocks and now felt light as a feather. I headed first for the film kiosk, where I had dropped off the film for processing.

"Here is my claim check," I said as I reached down in my pocket for my wallet. It wasn't there.

"It must be in my coat," I thought as I searched its pockets. Then I became frantic. It wasn't anywhere. The travel bag, pants pockets, coat pockets inside and out...

"This is terrible," I told the salesman.

"You don't need the claim check," he said. "I have your prints right here."

"But it's my wallet that I'm searching for," I said in desperation. It contained my driver's license, credit card, euro check card, car registration, euro checks, $500 in US currency, 300 Deutschemarks, and 200,000 Turkish lira. I had loaded up on money while in Berlin; I didn't want to be stranded again like when we'd lived in Zakho. But now it was all lost!

I raced out of the shop and ran back to the dolmush bus stop. People were walking everywhere. Surely, if it had fallen out of my pocket while I was putting the kids in the vehicle, somebody would have seen it and picked it up. They'd be instantly $1,000 richer without even using the checks. I walked back to the photo shop, following the route I'd taken. No luck.

"May I use your telephone?" I asked the same salesman in the kiosk.

"Certainly," he said. I called the doctor's office. That was the last time I had used my wallet. I dialed the doctor's clinic.

"Hello, I was just in your office with two small children for examinations. I have lost my wallet. Could you check to see if it is lying about in the waiting room, please?" I said a silent prayer. My greatest fear was that it had been picked from my pocket by a thief when my hands were occupied carrying Delal.

"Sir," the receptionist replied, "we can't find a wallet here." Her words felt like bullets.

Oh God, I prayed desperately. *Let it be under the coffee table or chairs somewhere.*

"Could you please look again?" I pleaded. "Perhaps it lies under the chairs in the first waiting room." My embarrassment at asking a second time was nothing compared to the disaster of losing my wallet. She came back to the phone a few moments later.

"You may come to the office," she said simply.

"Have you found it?" I inquired, almost beyond belief.

"It is here," she said. I nearly shouted alleluia!

"Thank you, thank you, thank you very much!" I said and hung up.

"Praise the Lord," I said to the kiosk salesman as I returned the phone.

"My wallet is at the doctor's office!" He smiled and seemed pleased to see my relief.

Ten minutes later, I was in the doctor's office and in possession of my wallet. I opened it to see if the money was gone. To my surprise and delight, the money was there. I still had all our family finances. It would have been a huge delay, not to mention inconvenience and expense, had I truly lost it. I thanked the receptionist repeatedly. This honest Turk meant that I was a happy American.

Before heading to the US embassy, which was a bit north of the city center, I decided to stop at the translator's office on Ataturk Boulevard and retrieve the English translations of the Turkish travel permission. The original document that I'd received from the Turkish

Ministry of the Interior was in Turkish. The US embassy required a certified translation of the document as proof that the girls were in Turkey legally. The Turkish translator accepted my last lira as payment, leaving me the equivalent of seventy-five cents in the local currency.

Without sufficient lira for a taxi, I had to walk to the embassy. I couldn't exchange my German Deutschemarks for lira as the banks were closed for lunch.

I'll do that after I get their visas, I thought.

Three and a half hours later, I was still sitting in the waiting area at the embassy. *At least I'm not outside in the snow*, I thought, remembering the many refugees still without proper shelter.

"Mr. Legacy," I heard over the intercom. I approached the bulletproof glass and greeted a short man with black hair. His name tag said Mr. Fraser. He reviewed all the materials I had brought. Everything seemed to be in order.

"Did you take these pictures yourself?" he asked. I swallowed hard.

"Yes," I answered, fearful of what was coming next.

"They are correct in every way but one," he said.

"The head size is one inch, and they are in color, with a plain white background. The profiles to their heads are three-quarter frontal, but this one of the baby is reversed. She should be looking to the left instead of the right. That way, the right side of her face will be showing. You will need to have her picture retaken." He could see that I was not happy to hear this.

He continued, "If you can bring a correct photo before noon tomorrow (Friday), we will process the visas before four thirty." I was mortified. I knew we had nonrefundable tickets to fly to Berlin for Saturday and tickets to fly to the US four days after that. I begged and pled but to no avail. He simply would not accept Jessica's picture. It was now 5:00 p.m., and the embassy was closing, as were the banks.

There was simply no way I could get to the apartment, get Jessica, and bring her to a studio in time to get the correct picture. As I left the embassy, I realized I didn't even have sufficient lira to get a taxi back to the apartment. It looked for certain that we'd be delayed in Ankara for another week. The planes flew direct from Ankara to Berlin weekly on Fridays or Saturdays. It was already Thursday, and I couldn't see how I'd get another picture of Jessica before noon on Friday. And then I had an idea.

I caught the regular bus (twenty-two cents) and got off at the film kiosk. This was my third visit to the shop, and the clerk recognized me instantly. I was glad he spoke English.

"Could you do me a big favor?" I asked him. "I need another print from this negative of my daughter for her immigration visa. The problem is she is facing the wrong way." Then I flipped the negative over. I knew from a photography class I'd taken in California that you could print a photo from either side of a negative.

"Can you please print a flop of this negative?" I asked. He said he could and, better yet, agreed to have it ready at eleven thirty the next day. I climbed aboard the dolmush with renewed hope that I might get the visas after all. I paid the fare and gave my last 500 liras to a beggar. It was enough for him to buy bread.

Climbing the icy hill to the apartment that evening in the dark, I was reminded how far the Lord had brought us. Surely, he had not led us through all these difficulties, only to leave us stranded in Ankara. I knew he was going to continue to do great things. Only I had no idea just how great they were going to be!

Friday, January 31, 1992

Friday began cold and dark. Our neighborhood, a suburb by the name of Dikmen, was buried in fog. A light snow was falling. I walked down the steep hill from our apartment to a friend's home and sent a fax off to my father. My dad had sent us a fax to that flat in Ankara, saying he needed copies of several documents to work on health insurance for the children. A dolmush brought me down to Kizilay, the city center. The photo shop was open, and better yet, the needed reprints of Jessica's picture were ready, with her head facing to her left, as desired. I felt a bit devious, knowing the picture was really the same one, just flipped over. The bureaucracy seemed so ludicrous, and I hoped this would pass the requirements.

I took the public bus and entered the embassy at 11:40. They called my name almost immediately.

"Did you do the pictures yourself again?" Mr. Fraser asked. I shuddered.

"It is the only way to get a photo in less than twelve hours," I replied. "All of the shops require at least twenty-four hours to process pictures. Plus there is the time involved in getting an appointment."

He tucked the pictures into their envelope and said, "We will try to finish their visas before we go to lunch. Why don't you have a seat and wait?" I could have jumped for joy!

At 12:03, he called my name again and presented me with the precious documents. They were assembled into a sealed envelope whose corner had been cut away, and each one-page immigration visa was attached with a grommet from the outside to the documents on the inside. I examined the visa for errors and carefully tucked them into my thick binder containing all the children's documents.

I then explained to Mr. Fraser about our travel plans. Our flight on Saturday took us first to Schönefeld airport in the former East Berlin. But our flight from Berlin to America was the following day and from the airport in West Berlin, Tegel. Our daughters would need German transit visas since we were arriving from one airport and departing from a different one. We also planned to spend a few nights in our apartment in Berlin. As with the Turkish transit visa, a German transit visa for undocumented orphans could only be obtained from the minister of the Interior of Germany. His office was in the West German capitol Bonn.

"Uh," Mr. Fraser said, "I tried to reach the German embassy (in Ankara) to explain your need for transit visas for the children. The man you need to speak to is named Mr. Fassbender. But nobody answered. Then I remembered that their embassy closes at noon on Fridays." My heart sank.

I knew it would be impossible to talk one's way into an embassy when it had just closed, especially a German one, but I caught a taxi, nevertheless, and drove straight there. It was 12:20 p.m. when

I reached the massive steel gates surrounding the building. They had indeed closed at noon. A Turk with a handful of documents was trying to convince the guard at the giant gate to let him in. The guard opened the gate to let the man inside just as I approached the gate. I quickly stepped into the open doorway and explained briefly in German that I was there to see Herr Fassbender. The guard reluctantly let me in and, after a perfunctory body search, led me across a plaza to the building's entrance.

A second guard insisted on checking first with Herr Fassbender before admitting me. He returned a moment later and said I must come back later; Herr Fassbender was busy.

"This is urgent," I said. "We must have transit visas through Germany for tomorrow. Our plane departs from Ankara at 7:00 a.m." I was glad I had called Sultan Airlines that morning and confirmed the reservations. I had done it on the slim possibility that it really would work out, but I realized I might have to change them. I also reserved seats on the flight from Berlin to San Francisco on British Airways.

The guard returned and said I could come in. Relieved yet still full of disbelief that I'd get the visas, I climbed the stairs to the second floor and found the reception area for Herr Fassbender. He listened patiently to my saga. He said he understood our dilemma. He seemed genuinely sympathetic but said he couldn't single-handedly change the total German bureaucracy.

"You don't understand," he said. "Everybody here is finished working today. This embassy is already closed. And besides, it takes many days to process such a visa. We must have permission from the Ministry of the Interior since the children have no passports or birth certificates. At best, I could telephone them in Bonn and ask, but they also close at noon on Fridays." He paused and thought for a second. He remembered there was a one-hour time difference; hence, it was actually 11:30 a.m. in Bonn, while it was 12:30 p.m. in Ankara.

"Oh! It is actually only 11:30 a.m. in Bonn right now," he said with delight.

"I would be very appreciative if you tried to telephone," I said. "It'd be a miracle if they're available, however."

"You are right, there," he replied, "*ein Wunder*" (a miracle). Then he disappeared down the hall to his office.

He returned minutes later and said the specialist who handles these situations at the capitol in Bonn was not at his desk. If he called back in the next few minutes, we could perhaps do something; if not, then there was simply no hope.

I prayed as I waited. *Lord, it is truly unbelievable that I was even allowed into this building and that I have these US immigration visas! And that the pictures were completed in time. Dare I even ask that these transit visas be issued today?*

"By the way," Herr Fassbender began as he passed through the waiting room, "how long did you want the transit visas to be effective?"

"Four days," I answered optimistically. He rolled his head back.

"Four days!" he exclaimed. I knew immediately it was too much.

"That isn't a transit visa," he said. "Such a request is impossible to fill in such a short time. That will require an entirely different procedure."

"Well," I quickly responded, "if twenty-four hours is all that can be granted, then that's what we will work with. I will simply change the plane reservations. British Airways flies daily from Berlin to San Francisco." This seemed to satisfy him, and he disappeared again to continue working on it. Twenty minutes later, he reappeared.

"That will be sixty thousand Turkish liras," he said and laid two beautiful sheets of paper before me. Transit visas! I read them through quickly. This was fantastic.

"I have Eurochecks, Deutschemarks, and US dollars," I said. He looked at me disapprovingly.

"We do all our transactions in Turkish lira," he said.

"Hmmm," I replied. "I thought the embassy was a small piece of Germany."

"Well, I guess I will accept twenty Deutschemarks," he said good-naturedly.

I was on cloud nine as I left the building.

God, this is incredible! But I had to think fast now. Time was running out. If I didn't pay for and pick up the plane tickets before the travel agent closed, I would lose the reservations, and we'd have to wait a week for the next flight.

I scanned my map for the street of the British Airways office as I walked. Finally, a taxi came along, and he took me straight there. I entered a tall building and climbed to the fourth floor. As I sat in the plush office and spread out the immigration documents, transit papers, and our passports, I marveled that so much work could be involved just to make one journey. But then leaving Iraq with two undocumented orphans traveling through Turkey, then through Germany, and finally to the United States was no ordinary journey.

The travel agent listened to my request to change and pay for our reservations and checked his computer.

"That will be five thousand, two hundred and twenty Deutschemarks (DM)," he said. I had exactly 170 DM left in my wallet. However, I carried a twelve Eurochecks with me to handle unexpected expenses. They could be written for any sum, like a personal check. The bank insured each check for up to 400 DM, and businesses, therefore, never allowed them to be written for greater sums. I calculated quickly in my head. I could write all twelve checks for 400 DM each, which came to 4,800 DM. Plus I had the 170 DM in cash. I would still be short 250 DM.

I smiled nicely at the travel agent and asked if I could write just one check. I knew that amounted to a risk of 4,820 DM for British Airways.

To my complete surprise, he said, "Yes, that would be fine." I could hardly believe my ears. I remembered a travel agent in Berlin refusing Eurocheck payment and insisting I pay cash for a 1,500 DM ticket. But then I shouldn't be shocked. God was clearly in this!

With the flight from Berlin to San Francisco taken care of, I made my way downtown to the travel agent for Sultan Air. I needed to pick up the paper tickets for the flight from Ankara to Berlin. The agency was located in a decidedly older part of town; the building was badly in need of repair. I watched the exposed green walls and doorways go by as the antiquated elevator rose. I was heading for the fourth floor. Then without warning, the elevator stopped, and the lights went out. I was between the third and fourth floors.

There were no interior doors that automatically shut on this old elevator. A person had to be careful as the elevator went up, not to lean against the "moving" wall as the elevator climbed or descended. Now all that was visible was a narrow space at the top of the third-floor door and a narrow gap at the bottom of the fourth-floor door. I pushed the buttons over and over, but nothing happened.

"If you want these tickets, be sure and contact me before 4:00 p.m.," the agent had told me that morning when I telephoned. I looked at my watch. It was 3:40 p.m. I pushed the elevator buttons frantically. Nothing. After several minutes, the down button registered a dim light; then the cage shook violently and began to slowly descend.

At ground level, I considered climbing the stairs. But I was really short of breath. I decided to give the lift another try. This time, I pushed the third-floor button. The lift stopped correctly at the third floor. I opened the gate and then climbed the steps to the fourth floor to reach the travel agent's office.

A tiny rusted sign on the door was the only indication that I had reached the correct place. I rang the doorbell, knocked, and rang again. There was no answer. After an interminable pause, the door was unlocked, and an unshaven man answered. I looked at the rusty sign again to make certain this was the correct place.

"On Tour Travel?" I asked.

"*Evet*" (yes), he answered, and rubbed his eyes. He led me inside to an all but empty apartment. A telephone sat on the cluttered carpet. The only furniture was a coffee table, three chairs of various descriptions, and a plant, which was potted in a metal bucket. Several overflowing ashtrays sat on the windowsill. I wondered how long this man was planning to be in business or, worse yet, if his plane tickets were bogus. I was somewhat reassured to see a business license tacked to the wall.

"I'm sorry," he said after making a telephone call to check on our reservations.

He rubbed his eyes and said in a sleepy monotone, "Tomorrow's flight is overbooked. You will have to fly next week." I nearly exploded inside.

"You assured me this morning that you had seats for us!" I began. "You have no idea how important it is that we get those seats."

Then I proceeded to show him the binder of documents that I had assembled. I laid out the US immigration visas and the transit visas for Germany (which was only valid for the next three days). Finally, I showed him the overseas tickets and explained that I had paid over five thousand Marks for them. He was visibly impressed. And as he began to wake up, I realized that he truly wanted to help me.

He made another phone call, then asked me to wait for fifteen minutes for a return call. I then realized that the On Tour tourist agency had purchased a block of tickets on the Sultan Air flight and he was checking with other agencies to see if they had space in the blocks they had purchased. Finally, he quoted me a price, which I then bargained down 20 percent, and then he added our names to the bottom of a sheet of paper. I could see that there were thirty spaces typed onto the paper; he penciled in numbers thirty-one through thirty-four. Those were our seats. It was not a very secure feeling. I had been in enough Turkish airports to know that pushing and cutting in line were often more important in guaranteeing a seat on the plane than having a ticket. Several times, I had been at the check-in desk and witnessed screaming and shouting passengers when flights were overbooked. I asked the agent what time the flight left.

"Seven a.m.," he said.

We will get there at 4:30, I said. *I want the four of us to be the first passengers to board that plane!* But had On Tour Travel put us on stand-by? I had no way of knowing for sure.

"Jane," I said when I entered the apartment that night, "pack your bags. We are getting up at three tomorrow morning to fly to Berlin!" She was incredulous. And so was I, to be honest. Both girls were screaming, as was typical when I came through the door, so it was a while before I could tell her of the day's activities.

Fortunately, we had little to pack, but Jane was exhausted. We put the girls to bed, and Jane followed soon after. I finished up the dishes, cleaned up the living room, began packing and sorting our things, and woke Jane to finish the job. Finally, at midnight, we lay down for a short rest before the long journey.

"Dear Lord," we prayed, "you have been so good to us. You have led us so far, provided for all of our needs, and comforted us in times of distress. We trust and believe you will assist us as we pass the many passport control points in Turkey, Germany, and America. Please let it go smoothly."

Saturday, February 1, 1992

The kids were super when we woke them at 3:00 a.m. on Saturday.

"They always wake up at this hour, anyway," Jane reminded me. And, indeed, they did. Jane had the preferred side of the bed for that very reason; my side was against the wall. At least their digestion had cleared up this week. We had put the girls on yogurt instead of milk, and that did the trick. What a difference! We still packed three changes of clothes for Jessica in the carry-on bag; she usually managed to soil her outfits in spite of the two diapers she wore. Tasked with keeping the girls clean and happy, Jane had the far more difficult job of the two of us.

Once she was healthy, Suha was a bundle of energy
and loved to clown around. Ankara, Jan. 1992.

Meal time is happy time! Kirk and Nuha in Ankara, Jan. 1992.

The taxi pulled up in front of the apartment promptly at 4:00 a.m. Forty minutes later, we pulled up to the International Departure gate at the Esenboa Airport. I scanned the ticket counter for Hakki, the travel agent who had sold me our tickets. He had said he would arrive for check-in. He wasn't there. Other agents began arriving and checking in their passengers for the flight. I asked repeatedly, but nobody knew when he would arrive. At five thirty, he appeared and began preparing his desk for check-in. I was greatly relieved to see our bags disappear down the conveyor belt and to finally grip our own boarding tickets in my hand.

We decided it would be best to go through the passport checkpoint early since the girls had unusual documents. The paper issued by the Turkish Ministry of Foreign Affairs should suffice, as well as the US and German visas. However, this was Turkey, and one never knew for sure what to expect.

The woman at the desk was obviously new; she asked for assistance from her supervisor as each passenger reached her desk. After standing in line for thirty minutes, the girls had had enough. Delal was a normal two-year-old and intent on doing two-year-old things, and waiting in a long line was clearly not on her agenda. We had just about finished the bag of "bribe" pretzels when our turn finally came.

"Where are their passports?" the lady inquired.

I answered as confidently as I could. "They have no passports or birth certificates. We are adopting them in the US. Here are their immigration visas, transit visas for Germany, and the travel permissions from the Ministry of Foreign Affairs."

She knew immediately she was in over her head, so she called her supervisor again. He came and then called his supervisor, who led us past the checkpoint into an expanded hall to examine the documents more closely.

"This letter from the Foreign Ministry is not addressed to us," he said. "You must have a letter directed specifically to this office."

I thought quickly and said, "They assured us this would be sufficient to transit through Turkey. It states here that we may bring the children from Iraq through Turkey and on to Berlin."

"Your document must show that you entered here in Ankara in order to board the plane," he said.

I politely explained to him that the point of a transit visa is to allow people to enter in one place and exit in another. I tried to behave patiently but was exasperated inside. "We entered at the Habur border crossing near Silopi, and we are exiting in Ankara."

He repeated his comment in three different ways, and I repeated mine in three different ways. This seemed to be an essential part of persuasion in the Middle East. Frequently, a request is denied at first but later granted if one is persistent enough. It also gives people an opportunity to give *baksheesh*, a bribe, which I was not about to do.

The agent knew we were fully stressed out. Border guards have immense power, and they create pressure to elicit bribes. As the call for final boarding was announced, the agent finally let us go, and we hurried through the body searches and toward our gate. The cold morning wind whipped our faces as we walked in the darkness across the tarmac the one hundred meters to the waiting airplane.

"*Tiarra*" (airplane in Kurdish)! Delal exclaimed in glee. We had told her we would be flying in an airplane, and this time, she was clearly excited about it.

"Please hurry," an attendant said as we passed her on the tarmac.

"The plane is ready for takeoff," the captain announced on the intercom. There were no assigned seats, so we were spread out when we boarded. Later, we were able to shift about a bit and get seats together in the rear. I found it amusing that Turks are so organized about assigning seats on a long-distance bus yet so haphazard about airplanes. But chaos or not, we were elated when those wheels left the ground. An enormous load lifted from our hearts. I breathed a huge sigh.

Jane leaned across the aisle, took my hand, and said, "We did it!"

Chapter 17

"While We Waited"

Berlin, Germany, February 1, 1992

A s the wheels hit the ground in Germany, I turned to check on Delal. She was fast asleep. We had to wake her in order to disembark.

"After all these kids have been through, flying is nothing," I commented to Jane. The officials at the Schönefeld Airport in East Berlin were very courteous and efficient.

"It sure feels good to be in Germany, again," Jane remarked. There was an undeniable level of stress that one felt living in Turkey. It was oppressive. Our colleague Marcus Gladrow picked us up from Schönefeld Airport in East Berlin, with his VW transporter bus. It was the first time the girls had ever been in a car seat, and they weren't too excited about it.

"What do you think of Germany?" I asked Delal as we drove past street after street of five-story apartment houses. She had no comment, but she wanted a pretzel.

We spent the day Saturday visiting the Gladrows, who fed us generously, and then worked on preparing the apartment for an anticipated six-month absence. We quickly unpacked our things from our last four months in Turkey and Iraq, then began sorting out what was necessary to bring to America. We would have no time Sunday morning, as we had to leave for the airport at 6:30 a.m. Most of our valuables we placed in a small side room, which we could permanently close. We prepared the rest of the flat to receive guests of the OM team that worked in Berlin or perhaps another tenant. We put the kids to bed on a small mattress and in a playpen the Gladrows loaned us.

It was wonderful to be back in Berlin; we would have been quite happy to have just stayed on, but the transit visa gave our girls only twenty-four hours. So we sadly said goodbye and closed up our flat for another undetermined length of time. Our coworkers were also sad to see us go; they had a one-year-old girl too, and were anxious to spend time with us and get to know our girls.

Marcus teased me. "Now that you're all here, why don't you just stay? You'd be no different than the thousands of others that live here illegally." We laughed and said our goodbyes.

"It will be good to get back here and really set up this apartment," I said to Jane. But that was not going to be possible for quite some time. I had no idea how long it would take for the adoption process in California. I had optimistically booked a six-month return ticket to Berlin.

We were thoroughly questioned at the Tegel Airport in West Berlin, the morning of our departure. When they realized we had Kurdish children present, they became alarmed. They led us into a private room for interrogation.

"Where have you been traveling?" the stern guard asked. He was surprised at my answer.

"We will need the names and addresses of all the people with whom you had contact," he said. I couldn't begin to answer that one. I tried not to laugh; it was a ludicrous question. Over the next half-hour, I summarized our activities. We clearly did not fit in their box. It was a stressful interrogation, but I was strangely at peace. God had already moved a mountain. Finally, they released us to board the plane. The journey, though long and challenging, was nevertheless a wonderful experience. Our bodies were tired, but our hearts were lifted and we sensed a future full of hope.

Our arrival in California was a momentous event. Jane's mother, Eleanor Stevens, tells the story best, beginning in October 1991. Here is her account in full, dated March 1992:

While We Waited
by Eleanor Stevens[1]

In October 1991, Kirk and Jane returned to Silopi, Turkey, where they continued to work in the refugee camp. We enjoyed their letters explaining the various activities, situations, and their duties. Some letters made us laugh like the one entitled "101 Ways to Use Empty Plastic Water Bottles," describing their uses of the water bottles the US Army had left. Some made us cry. We read about people in the cold with no shelter, no toilets, and inadequate water, about a baby who died unnecessarily. We became more aware of the heartbreaking conditions that people were living in.

In December, we received a fax from Kirk. He and Jane were moving from Silopi across the border into Iraq. He explained about two small girls who would surely die if someone did not take them and care for them. They were very malnourished, had head lice, and one had a badly burned foot that was not healing due to the malnutrition.

At that time, my prayer was that God would help Kirk and Jane care for the children without becoming too attached to them, knowing that it would be hard to leave them. Wherever they left them, it was doubtful they would be able to survive.

It was a bit scary knowing that they were in Iraq. However, they were good about getting news to us whenever possible.

Due to the holidays, the last part of December went quickly.

I woke up early on January 2 with a bad cold and went downstairs to get a drink of water. It was 2:15 a.m. The phone rang. I was sure it was my number two daughter, Janet, as she was expecting to give birth any day to our second grandchild. It was not due until the end of January; however, the doctor said it was probably going to

---

[1.] Name changed

come early. Janet's son, David, had come to spend a few days with us, and so I had assured Janet that, whatever time the baby decided to come, she should call us, and we would leave for Sacramento immediately since she really wanted David to be there when the baby was born. David was excited about his new baby brother. David had even gone to a sibling class at the hospital.

Much to my surprise and delight, it was Kirk Legacy, calling from Ankara, Turkey. "Call me back at this number," he said. (It costs about three times as much to call from Turkey to the US compared to calling from the US.) I didn't have my glasses on and blindly wrote down the numbers. By now, Earl was up, so I called him to come and dial the numbers since I couldn't see. When Kirk answered, I picked up the extension. We had a good connection, so the three of us could visit.

Kirk explained that the father of the two girls whom they were caring for had asked Kirk and Jane to adopt them. Since there was no one to care for them outside the refugee camp, the father would have had to bring them into the camp. However, he could not care for them himself due to some physical problems from the war.

Kirk had spent the previous few days securing all the legal documents needed, such as the father's consent to adopt, the mother's death information, and identification records on the girls. This was very difficult since there were no records to begin with.

Kirk also told us he was in Ankara, ready to catch a flight to Berlin within the hour. He would be entering the hospital for a two-week tune-up treatment. At the same time, he would be working on getting the visas for the girls to enter Berlin. This is where the adoption would take place. It appeared that it would be a simple matter of finding the right procedures and some paperwork.

Jane was in Zakho, Iraq, by herself with the two girls. There was a friend, Bob, who would be checking on her each day and helping her when it came time to leave.

We were very excited at the prospect of two new granddaughters. We returned to bed, but who could sleep the rest of the night?

Later in the morning, Earl called Kirk's brother Doug and his wife, Dawn Legacy, because Kirk's parents were on vacation in Hawaii. Doug called Hawaii to tell them the news.

We were able to talk to Kirk almost daily while he was in the hospital. Jane was waiting in Zakho for permission to bring the girls into Turkey to travel to Ankara, where she would be met by other Operation Mobilization team members and she could wait for permission to go to Berlin. We were able to send fax messages to Jane (when the fax machine worked in Silopi) through Bob, who had an office in Silopi, Turkey. He lived in Zakho, Iraq, but went across the border almost daily. He was the one who checked on Jane.

Now a daughter is a daughter if she is nine years old or twenty-nine years old. But Iraq? That's the country we were just at war with. That's the country where all this pain and suffering started for the people Kirk and Jane had been trying to help. Kirk and Jane must know what they are doing, or do they?

Friends and relatives joined us in our excitement, calling and waiting anxiously for new news. From here, it seemed like an age as we waited to hear that Jane could take the girls across the border into Turkey. Nine days later, on Saturday January 11, we found a message on our answering machine. As we listened, we squealed with joy. We heard Jane's voice from halfway around the world. "This is Jane. I am okay. I have permission to travel across into Turkey with the girls. We will probably travel on Tuesday the fourteenth. Goodbye." (Tuesday morning for Jane was Monday evening here.)

So starting Monday evening, Earl started his announcements. "Well, Jane is getting up and getting the girls ready for the trip. Bob should be there to get them by now. They should be driving from Zakho, Iraq, to Diyarbakir, Turkey now." It is a five-hour drive. From Diyarbakir, they would take a three-hour plane ride to Ankara. Jane would be met at the airport in Ankara by some of her friends. Then it would be a one-hour drive to the apartment where they would stay. When we got up on Tuesday, we figured Jane would be arriving at the apartment. Earl couldn't wait; he called to see if she was there. She had arrived, and although she was very tired, she reported that all the travel had gone well.

It was wonderful to talk to her. Jane put Delal on the phone.

The first words we heard her say were, "Hi, Grandpa. Hi, Grandma. Be happy!" Now you'd think that put a lump in our throat and tears in our eyes! And then a few days later, she sang the song "Jesus Loves Me" loud and clear. She loved to talk. We could quickly tell she was a bundle of constant action. In the background, we could hear Jessica yelling. Jane said they were happy sounds; she had just finished eating.

Their head lice were gone, and Delal's appetite was good, but Jessica still had stomach troubles. Even so, Jessica had gained ten pounds and Delal eight. We got word from Kirk as well. He had been told by German immigration that the girls' visas would be in Ankara on Wednesday, January 22. So he left Berlin on Friday the seventeenth to join Jane in Ankara. He planned to pick up the girls' visas on the twenty-second, and then all four of them would leave for Berlin on Friday, January 24.

Kirk and Jane were anxious for both sets of grandparents to visit their new granddaughters. We decided it would be nice to go to Berlin, visit with the grandkids, and help do some remodeling to Kirk and Jane's apartment. Dave and Carolyn Legacy, Kirk's parents, bought tickets to fly to Berlin on January 25.

Both grandmas had done a lot of shopping for warm clothes for the girls. I took some clothes and a walker for Jessica over to the Legacy home on Tuesday for Dave to pack. (We felt that a walker would help strengthen Jessica's legs.)

We planned to go to Berlin later in February after Dave and Carolyn returned. Earl would continue with the apartment project with Kirk. Jane had some sewing for us to do and unpacking. They had moved to a larger apartment in the same building just before they went to Turkey and hadn't had time to unpack.

On Wednesday, January 22, Kirk called the German embassy in Ankara to arrange the pickup of the visas. He was told there would be no visas. Germany would not allow them to take the girls into the country to be adopted. They were shocked and frustrated.

So Kirk went to work inquiring about adopting the girls in Turkey. He found that Germany sometimes refused to recognize Turkish adoptions. At this point, Dave and Carolyn canceled their planned trip. The next option was to get permission from the US embassy to bring the girls to the US and adopt them here. Then they could become US citizens, get US passports, and go to Germany and anywhere else. Now we would have to do some waiting.

By the weekend of January 25, the what-ifs started to plague us. Earl especially was having trouble.

"What if the US would not let the girls come? What if they couldn't get them adopted? What if some authority wanted them sent back to Iraq? What would happen to the girls? Where would they go? What would this do to the girls as well as to Kirk and Jane?" By the end of the week, Earl was a basket case. He was also causing me to start thinking of things that I had not thought of. We were having a lot of sleepless nights.

Fortunately, Janet had planned to come down for the weekend of January 31 through February 1. Our third daughter, Janine, was flying up Friday night to visit, to see Janet, and to attend a shower we were giving their cousin Sandra. This would help take our minds off the situation surrounding Kirk and Jane.

Janet had some extra time, so she decided to come early on Thursday afternoon. On Friday morning, she asked if it would be okay to telephone Jane. That's all it took; Earl grabbed the phone and dialed Turkey. Janet started talking to Jane.

Jane said, "We have some great news. We are coming to the US. Here, Kirk will explain." Kirk explained that they had visas for the girls to come. They also had a travel permit for the girls so they could stop in Berlin for twenty-four hours. Once in Berlin, they planned to open Christmas presents, repack some clothes for the trip home to the US, and put all of their other things into one room of the apartment. That way, others could stay in their flat during their absence. Kirk gave Janet their flight numbers and the times of arrival on Sunday.

Janet wrote it all down and then asked, "Which Sunday, next week?"

"No. Sunday, the day after tomorrow," he replied. Wow!

We quickly called Dave and Carolyn. They had a weekend conference and were leaving within the hour to go to the Oakland airport. They planned on returning to Oakland on Sunday at one thirty. Great! They would drive across to San Francisco and meet us all there.

Janine arrived on Friday night. She was to return on Sunday evening, but after much debate about working on Monday, she decided to stay and go home on Monday night so she could see Kirk, Jane, and the girls.

Sunday morning, Grandpa Earl and David went to church. Janet, Ryan (her second son), Janine, and I had a leisurely breakfast and visit. Then we prepared the beds and closets and childproofed the house. Janet originally had planned to return home on Sunday afternoon. However, she decided to stay and go to the airport, visit with Kirk and Jane, and then go on to Sacramento when the rest of us returned to San Jose.

We rounded up two car seats and borrowed a van to go to the airport. On Sunday afternoon, February 2, we gathered at the international terminal—Dave and Carolyn, Doug (Kirk's brother) and wife Dawn, their children Abby and Nathan, Janet, her two boys, Janine, Earl and me. Excitement mounted as we stood in the observation area, looking through the glass down at the people arriving in the baggage area. Each of us waited for the first glimpse of Kirk and Jane. We watched one load of passengers arrive and get their luggage.

The room was almost empty, and we decided that it must not have been their plane. David, Nathan, and Abby started to play together and look through the glass at the customs area below. Another group of people started pouring into the luggage area, and soon it was full of people. Still there was no sign of Kirk or Jane. It seemed that everyone had come out. Then we saw a couple of people in wheelchairs come off and finally a group of stewardesses. People stood about waiting for their luggage, but no one else appeared. Dawn knelt on the floor in front of me and peered through the glass.

I leaned over and said, "They probably stopped in the restroom to comb their hair and brush their teeth!"

Laughing, Dawn responded, "That's probably right." Still there was no one in the arrival area.

Then we finally saw someone coming.

"It's them! It's them!" we yelled. Kirk was pushing a luggage cart with Delal sitting on the front. Jane was beside him; she was wearing a backpack with Jessica in it. They walked out to where we could see them and began waving to us. Kirk soon went over to watch for the luggage. Jane sat her backpack down on the floor (it stood up like a chair) so Jessica was out where we could see her and she could look around. Delal was waving to us. Soon she couldn't sit still anymore; she got off the cart and waved and jumped around. She went over to where Daddy was getting the luggage, and then they headed out to the immigration area. We all went downstairs to the arrival area and waited another forty-five minutes behind a wall for them to get through immigration. Kirk had a binder four inches thick full of documents on the children and a lot of patience.

After almost everyone had come out, Kirk and Jane appeared. Delal was at their side, and Jessica was on Jane's back. I was doing just fine until Jane hugged me, and then I came face-to-face with Jessica, and I started to cry. Her big black eyes sparkled as she looked right at me and smiled. It was like she was saying, "Here we are, Grandma!" Delal was jumping, running, and playing with her new cousins— Nathan, David, and Abby.

Kirk and Jane looked great. We visited together for a while; and then Janet, David, and Ryan headed off to their home near Sacramento. The rest of us returned to our homes in San Jose. Kirk, Jane, and the girls had been traveling for more than nineteen hours; so they were ready for their beds.

By April first, the adoption process was well under way and would probably be completed within three months. The girls were both doing very well. A wonderful pediatrician gave the girls free physical exams. Jessica had a slightly enlarged liver. However, he felt that it probably would not give her any trouble. She was happy and could finally crawl; her legs had gotten strong enough that she could use the kiddie walker very well. She loved the new freedom of moving around by herself. She was waking up almost every hour when she first arrived. Now she only awoke one or two times during the night. She loved her bath and played well.

Delal was very frightened of crowds of people when she left Iraq. However, she is doing very well now. She acts like a normal American girl.

She goes to Sunday school and plays with other children like a regular three-year-old. She talks from the minute she opens her eyes in the morning until she falls asleep at night. Her English is improving rapidly; she slips a Kurdish word in from time to time. She used to wake up in the morning crying; but now she gets up, comes out of her bedroom, and says, "Good morning!"

She used to wake up several times during the night, crying, "No! No!" Now she sleeps through most every night, and if she does wake up, you only have to let her know you are there and it's still nighttime, and she goes back to sleep. She is well-behaved, has good manners for her age, and is very loving.

Delal points up to the flag that hangs before our home and says, "It's America."

Chapter 18

Adoption and Citizenship

San Jose, California, February 1992

T he days went by quickly. To fulfill the legal requirements to adopt, we discovered we had to have a postplacement study. After which, the petition to adopt could be presented to the superior court judge. We were already familiar with the process for a home study, having completed that to satisfy immigration requirements. The postplacement study normally covers a six-month period; however, we were able to count the days we had lived together in Iraq and Turkey as part of the six months. That meant we could begin the six-month period on December 10, 1991, even though we didn't get to California until February 2, 1992. It could be completed any time after June 10.

In the home of Earl and Eleanor in San Jose, CA. Feb. 1992.

Multiple visits were made to see the girls in their environment by a social worker and to interview us. We were living in the spacious home of Jane's parents, Earl and Eleanor. They converted a large dining room into a private master bedroom for Jane and me, and the girls had a bedroom upstairs. It was a very generous and sacrificial kindness to us. Both of Jane's parents were overwhelmingly supportive and helpful. Once the placement study was completed, the adoption petitions were filed with the San Jose Superior Court. We were given a court date of June 30, 1992.

Delal and Jessica joined Jane and me in the chamber of Judge Donald L. Clark for a short hearing the morning of the thirtieth. Our attorney, Kerry Walter,[1] presented the judge with the two petitions to adopt. Judge Clark read them over, asked a question or two, and then decreed them to be lawfully our children. It happened so quickly that it was hard to believe it was true. They were officially our children! After a quick picture with the judge, we walked out into the California sunshine. We gave profuse thanks to Kerry for his help and drove home to Jane's parents' house in Almaden Valley.

---

[1] Name changed

We still had some hurdles to leap before we could return to our work in Germany, however. The girls needed US passports, and in order to get those, they had to become US citizens. They had been issued green cards shortly after arriving in the US but would need passports to travel with us overseas. I had investigated the process for them becoming citizens and had begun paperwork with the Immigration and Naturalization Services in San Jose. Now that the adoption was final, the INS had everything they needed from us. I was told one should expect to wait twelve to eighteen months in order for citizenship to be granted. But we had just thirty-one days before our return flight to Germany! I pleaded with the supervisor for special consideration. I explained my need to return to work and gave them copies of our plane tickets. Mercifully he scheduled his first available interview with an INS official. It was in thirty days.

The big day came. The sun was shining. The girls were wearing matching frilly dresses from Grandma Carolyn. Everything seemed to be running smoothly. There was a huge line stretching outside the INS building, but we had an appointment, so we wandered around the open plaza. Delal hopped and danced continually, and Jessica shrieked and laughed from time to time. We all felt a bit elated and at the same time nervous. Finally, our name was called.

The four of us passed through the Appointments Only door and followed a woman down a narrow corridor. She seated us at her tiny cubicle and began reviewing all the documents. Everything seemed in order. I looked at Jessica sitting in Jane's lap and Delal standing at my side. They had no concept of the significance of the transaction that was about to take place. People all over the world yearn for a chance to go to America, and a lucky few actually are able to become Americans. They were about to join those few. They would have freedom to travel, to live, to express their opinions without fear of government crackdowns or persecution, not to mention a quality of life and level of prosperity. I thought of their fate in Iraq. I looked again at the two precious girls and listened to the examiner.

"Take these documents to the outer room and have a seat. Your name will be called shortly," she said. We went back out into the sea of humanity that crowded the general waiting area. Minutes later, we were summoned to a small window. Two beautiful documents were presented for our signature. "Certificate of United States Citizenship" was written in calligraphy across the top. Each document had their picture attached. It was a bit overwhelming. On the one hand, we felt a great relief. On the other hand, we were booked to fly to Germany the next day and we still didn't have their US passports.

I knew that it took a month to get a passport when one applied at the San Jose central post office. We decided to drive to the main passport office in San Francisco that afternoon and apply in person. Then we could get them the same day. It was already noon, and San Francisco was at least an hour's drive. We left immediately.

Fortunately, we found a parking space in a garage right on Market Street. I begrudgingly paid the fourteen dollars to park for the day, and we headed up the stairs. Minutes later, we were standing in a long line in order to submit our applications, pictures, fees, etc. Finally, at two o'clock, it was our turn.

The official examined everything and said, "This all looks to be in order. The passports should be ready tomorrow for pickup."

"But I thought one could get a passport the same day if we came in person," I said. "We drove up from San Jose in order to complete these today." My attempt to elicit some sympathy failed.

"I'm sorry," he replied. "In order to get a passport on the same day, you must submit your application in the morning. It is already past two." But I was determined not to give up so easily.

"We have a plane flight to fly to Berlin tomorrow. My employment requires that we catch that flight. Isn't there any way this could be expedited?"

"You would need to document that, sir," he responded. Once again, I was glad to have hauled the big thick binder full of documents. I produced photocopies of our plane tickets.

"That should suffice," he said when he saw them. Of course, I had to also show the children's former identification since their old names were on the plane tickets.

"They should be ready for you in about an hour and a half," he said. "By the way," he added as we turned to go, "you will need to have the names on their plane tickets changed to match their passports." I hadn't even thought about that.

"Can I do that at the airport tomorrow morning?"

"No, it has to be done at the travel agency." I could just imagine us missing the flight because their tickets said Payman and Firmesk instead of Jessica and Delal.

So we looked for a pay phone to find the nearest British Airways office. I called the number on the plane ticket and discovered there was an office just two blocks away! We didn't even have to move the car. The agent was very helpful, and in no time, we had new tickets with their new names. It looked like we might soon get to return to our lives in Berlin!

God did the impossible! Citizenship and passports! June 1992.

Shortly before four o'clock, we returned to the passport office and collected their US passports. We drove home and rejoiced. It was with pure delight that the girls posed for a picture holding their passports and waving little American flags. Actually, I think they just liked the flags. It was, however, certainly symbolic of the freedom and security they now possessed—in stark contrast to the oppression and fear of Kurds living throughout the Middle East. It made me wonder what unusual plans God had for them. God's plans give us a hope and a future, the prophet Jeremiah tells us. But that is no guarantee there will not be adversity. And it wasn't long before adversity raised its vicious head.

Chapter 19

A Threatening Letter.
A Document Examined.

Berlin, Germany, June 1994

Our apartment in Berlin was now home to two rambunctious little girls. It was a two-and-a-half room apartment, which meant that it had a full bedroom, a living/dining room, a kitchen, and a half bedroom. The other half of that bedroom was part of the apartment next door. The building had been redesigned after WWII. Over half the housing had been demolished when Russia took Berlin from the Nazis, and so large apartments had been divided in half to house the population. What was once a large entry room was now two very skinny bedrooms that belonged to two separate units.

Jessica and Delal shared the half bedroom that was inside our apartment. We also had a full bathroom with a real tub. This was a big deal to us, since our first apartment in Berlin had a makeshift shower in the kitchen with a drain that flowed into an ice chest. Inside the ice chest was a sump pump. When we showered, we turned the pump on, and it pumped the shower water through a hole in the wall and into the back of the toilet. There was no bathroom sink.

The building was over a hundred years old, built when outhouses were located in the *Hof* (courtyard).

The living room carpet in our new apartment became their personal playground. I bolted some hooks in the high doorway and hung a swing for them. A modified stepladder and long board made a creative slide that ran down one wall of their narrow bedroom. We had to create play spaces for them inside since it was often too cold to go out of doors and since the neighborhood was dangerous. We lived in a ghetto, Kreuzberg, which was where many Kurds could afford to live. We wanted to meet them, eat in their cafes, and visit their cultural centers (sponsored by their various political factions.) So we chose to live in their neighborhood.

Our daughters were growing rapidly, and the side effects of malnutrition were long gone. Delal spoke English rapidly—and often!—and Jessica was learning words every day. Her first German word was *Kuchen*, which means "cake." It was quite fitting since it seemed to be her favorite food. Delal attended a German preschool that was sponsored by the German church we attended in Wedding. Wedding was the district to the north of the district of Mitte, and Kreuzberg was to the south of Mitte. Mitte was in former communist East Berlin and was previously separated from Kreuzberg and Wedding by the wall. We used to have to drive in a large semicircle to get from Kreuzberg to Mitte, or we could take the *UBahn* (underground), which passed under East Berlin. At each of the four underground stations in the East, there were armed guards to make certain the trains did not stop at the vacant platforms. We could then exit in Wedding and walk to church.

Most often, we traveled in an old VW bug that had been donated for our use. It had no heater, no defroster, and no third gear; but we were thankful to have this transportation. After we had adopted Delal and Jessica, we were able to purchase a (real) car with four doors and gears that worked.

I had agreed to write to Serwan periodically, whenever he would write and request an update. This was so he would know how the girls were developing and what their interests were. During the year since we'd left Turkey, I wrote him several times when I received his requests, and I told him of their progress. Having settled back into our daily ministry in Berlin, we were quite surprised to receive a threatening letter from him in early 1993. Serwan was angry because I would not give him our current address. He wrote me the following:

> Kirk—listen to me good enough. I want you iform me soon, about my kids, and send to me the true adress where my kids Living now. Look man—I never do anything bad along my Life. So—don't move me to do it. Be quick—I can not wate moor. Serwan 14/2/93

The letter was posted in Maastricht, Holland, on February 14, 1993. It seemed clear that Serwan was prepared to cause us harm, or "do something bad," whatever that could mean. I brought the letter to the German police, and they were convinced I should take the threat seriously. They blocked our names and addresses from the national information service, which is open to anyone who telephones looking for an address or phone number of a resident in Germany. At the advice from our adoption attorney Kerry Walter,[1] whom I telephoned, I did not respond to Serwan's threatening letter.

Then we received a disturbing phone call from the German Red Cross. Apparently, Serwan had researched us via the Red Cross in Holland.

"Is this Herr Legacy?" the woman began.

"Yes, it is," I answered.

"Did you adopt two Kurdish girls?"

"Yes, I did," I responded.

Certain that she was talking to the right person, she then asked, "Their birth father wants to visit you. Would it be possible for him to come to your apartment in Berlin?" A knot of uncertainty and anxiety formed instantly in my stomach.

[1.] Name changed

"No," I stammered. "We do not wish for such a visit." I could just imagine the ramifications if Serwan knew our whereabouts. *What kind of demands might he make? What might he do?* I worried.

The woman persisted, "Could he perhaps meet with you at some neutral location and be introduced as the girls' uncle or something?" I knew that such arrangements were very risky at best, and we were anxious how it would impact the girls. It seemed it could open a world of uncertainties.

"No," I repeated. "My wife and I feel very strongly that Serwan should not come here," I said. "And we do not want him to know our address or phone number. We wish to retain our right to privacy."

"The Red Cross does not divulge personal data. We merely try to arrange meetings," she said. Satisfied that she would honor my request, I concluded the conversation. But the knot in my stomach remained. And I knew it was the same for Jane. What would happen next? I wrote to our adoption attorney, Kerry, and explained the phone call.

In August of 1993, Kerry wrote us and explained that he had received a letter from the Dutch consulate. It was a request to have one of our adoption documents examined for authenticity. This was twenty months after Serwan had given up his children for adoption. It seemed that Serwan was contesting the affidavit of abandonment, which stated that he relinquished his parental rights and wanted us to adopt his children.

We knew of course that he *had* signed it. So it seemed like a logical thing to have it examined and its authenticity validated. Kerry said he would send it to the FBI. I had never had anything to do with the FBI, so it seemed a bit intimidating. Nevertheless, it was a genuine document, so it seemed right to send it off. Still there was the unanswered question in our mind, *How was the request initiated, and what was Serwan thinking and doing in all of this?* Kerry told us there would be a hearing later in January 1994 in San Jose in order to rule on the document. It seemed pretty far away, both in distance and in time, so we gave it over to the Lord and pressed on.

In January 1994, we moved from Berlin to a small town in the Black Forest called Kandern. It was located close to the Swiss border, where many Kurds lived in Basel. One of our teammates lived in Basel, and we also knew another couple who lived in Kandern. It seemed like a good place to locate to continue our ministry.

After the January hearing in San Jose (for which we were not present; Kerry represented us), the FBI returned the document (which was actually a photocopy) with the disappointing conclusion that its authenticity could not be validated. They did not say it was falsified, just that it was not possible to make a decisive ruling from a photocopy. Their finding was "inconclusive." They could not test the paper, the ink, and the depth of the pen impressions; and the quality of the copy was too poor to judge pen lifts, etc. We were disappointed the FBI could not prove its validity. However, we knew it was a valid document, so we didn't worry, either. Another hearing had been scheduled for April 1994, Kerry informed us.

Part 3

Chapter 20

The Phone Call. Forgery!

Kandern, a Village in Southern Germany, April 1994

The phone was ringing. "Are you going to get it?" I yelled to my wife after the third ring. She was busy tending to our two daughters; so I sprinted down the hall, burst into the office, and yanked the receiver from the cradle.

"Hello, this is Kirk Legacy," I said as calmly and smoothly as I could.

A scratchy voice said, "This is Kerry Walter calling from California." It had been two years since he represented us, in our adoption of Delal and Jessica. I was expecting his call, as I knew he would be representing us again in court. Serwan was claiming he had never given his permission for the adoption, and now the case was being dealt with in the court where the adoption took place.

"How did the hearing go?" I asked anxiously.

"Not like I expected," he replied.

That didn't sound so good. I pulled out the desk chair and sat down. "Why? What do you mean?"

"*He* showed up," Kerry said, emphasizing the word *he*.

"Who did?"

"Serdan, Serjohn…"

"You mean Serwan, the birth father?" I asked incredulously. "But he lives in Holland. You said today's hearing was between you, Serwan's California attorney, and a judge. How did Serwan get to California from Holland?" Serwan was unemployed and living on government assistance, having fled Iraq as a refugee. I couldn't imagine how he could afford a special trip to the States.

"I don't know," Kerry stammered. "He was there with some attorney, also from Holland, a woman who spoke perfect English. I had no idea he or she was going to be there."

"Were Earl and Eleanor there?" I asked. Jane's parents lived in San Jose. They had gone with Mr. Walter on two previous occasions when the matter had been postponed. Surely, they had come today, I thought.

"Yes, they came. They had to wait outside the courtroom, however. Just the judge, the two attorneys, and the district attorney were present. And, of course, Serwan and the woman from Holland."

"And what happened?" I asked again.

Jane had by now joined me in our guest room/office. She pressed her head close to mine to listen.

"It's Kerry, long distance from San Jose," I whispered to her, but her expression of concern told me she knew that already. She closed the door so the kids wouldn't hear. Kerry continued.

"Serdan—"

"Serwan," I interrupted.

"Yeah, Serwan. He talked and talked and told his long tragic story to the judge. And she seemed very sympathetic to his plight."

"What about the document?" I asked. That was the purpose of the hearing, to discuss the validity of the document. Serwan had contested his signature on this key adoption document, which was known as the affidavit of abandonment. In it, Serwan stated that he was relinquishing his parental rights and permitting his children to be adopted. But now Serwan was claiming that he never signed the document. And the FBI analysis had shown nothing.

"Did he sign it, Kirk?" Kerry asked flatly.

I was incredulous. Why was Kerry asking me *now* whether Serwan signed it? Of course, he signed it! Kerry himself had submitted the signed document to the court as part of the adoption petition. Did he now think that we had lied to him and given him a falsified document? He, obviously, had his doubts about the legitimacy of the document. I had assumed that Kerry understood that we were people of strong moral convictions. Generally, those who seek to live as Jesus lived aren't known for lying or falsifying documents. But then, how well did our attorney actually know us? It dawned on me that he didn't know us well at all.

Mr. Walter had been rather perfunctory when we first filed the papers and appeared in court for the adoption process. I remembered that he'd been in a hurry and had spoken very little to us. We'd given him thirty or so pages of background on our adoption, but now I wondered if he had read any of it. Then there was our home study and postplacement study documentation, which, if he'd read, would certainly have demonstrated our character and personal integrity.

"Yes, he signed it," I answered as patiently as possible. "I and two others witnessed him sign it in the notary public's office in Silopi, Turkey."

"Well, he is adamantly refusing to have signed it. And the judge was upset at the hearing. The district attorney took the document to have it examined by a handwriting analyst."

"Just a second," I said. I turned to Jane, whose neck had grown weary of trying to hear around my ear. She looked too shaken up to even formulate a question. With my anxiety level reaching the bursting point, I filled her in on the conversation, then turned back to the phone. Kerry continued.

"Serwan told the judge a dramatic story of how Saddam Hussein had bombed his village after the Kurdish uprising at the end of the Gulf War. He told about how his wife and parents were killed in the bombing and his house destroyed. The judge was really moved by his story. And who wouldn't be? It was truly horrible."

I could imagine the judge's emotional response. We were personally aware of the atrocities committed against the Kurds; we had seen and heard it ourselves.

"Was this the same judge at the last hearing?" I asked.

"No, a new judge was appointed to handle your case. A young judge named Cordell was the judge. After Serwan told her his tragic tale, she seemed genuinely sympathetic to him. She said she felt it was better for children to grow up in their own culture and with their own people."

"The judge said that in court?"

"Yes. She seems predisposed to annul the adoption and return the children to Serwan."

I couldn't believe what I was hearing. The girls had both been starving to death when we found them.

"She wants to annul the adoption?" As I questioned Kerry's words, I felt as if my heart were being torn from me. I tried to think. I had to focus on the facts. "Well, when the document comes back from the analyst and it is shown to be genuine, then everything will be all right, correct? It was after all a perfectly correct and legal adoption."

Kerry knew that California adoption law was among the most stringent in the world. And we knew without a doubt the document was genuine.

"Once the analysts showed the document is valid, everything would be fine, right?" I asked. Kerry wasn't so confident.

"I wouldn't be so sure, Kirk. Serwan said in court that he didn't understand adoption. And even if you were somehow able to prove that he did understand adoption, and I don't know how you could do that, he will say that his circumstances forced him into it. He had no other choice. And the judge is sympathetic to him and his plight. Kerry said it was the judge who suggested that it was his circumstance that had forced him into giving up his children for adoption."

Kerry's words didn't seem real. I didn't think judges, who are supposed to be objective, should make biased statements like that in a court hearing. But I could see no point in discussing it now.

"But what about the law? We've been a family together now for over two years, Kerry! How could a judge just decide to nullify our adoption? I thought adoptions were permanent." It seemed like everything I was hearing went contrary to logic and reality. Certainly, the law would guard the integrity of our family, I thought.

"California adoption laws are continually changing through legal precedents," he said. "Things just aren't the way they once were. And this judge is of the opinion that the children belong with their natural father."

I couldn't believe what I was hearing. Jane looked at me. I could see the agony in her face.

"Ask him what happens next," she said.

"Kerry," I began, "what happens now?"

"Nothing has been decided. Today was just a hearing to present information. Mr. Masters is going to have the affidavit analyzed and present the court with the findings."

"Who is Mr. Masters?"

"He's the district attorney. Bob Masters. He represents the children in court. The judge ordered him to have the signature analyzed." He added, "And try not to worry. You saw Serwan sign the document, so we know it is authentic."

Silently, I wondered if Kerry was really convinced that the signature was real.

"If it's real, then they'll come back and tell us it's real, and that should be the end of it," he concluded.

Nothing to worry about, I thought. Sure. We had heard that from Kerry before. But this was getting unbelievable. "When is the next court date?" I asked.

"Hmmm…" He paused a moment. "They didn't set one, but it should be this week sometime because Serwan has to fly back to Holland next Monday, and the judge would like to wrap it all up before then. I expect the signature analysis will be done early this week."

We wanted so much to put this legal thing behind us. Every postponement was torture. "The sooner, the better," I said.

"I'll call you after the next hearing. Can I reach you at this number?"

"Yes, this is our home number. It was just connected yesterday. Please call us whenever you have anything. Goodbye, Kerry. Thank you for helping us."

The next days were hectic. We were in the middle of moving from our apartment in Berlin, where we had been learning German and Kurdish, to a large apartment in Germany's Black Forest. It was a completely different world from the ghetto of Kreuzberg. We could walk up the hill and hike in a beautiful forest. The village was quaint and beautiful, more like the vision most Americans have of Germany.

Our living room was stacked to the ceiling with over one hundred boxes. German apartments do not have closets, so there was no place to put anything. I had no idea a family of four could accumulate so much junk. It was all necessary stuff, of course. But it's junk when you have to move it. It was impossible to concentrate on getting settled with this crisis looming.

"Where are the Easter Baskets, Kirk?" Jane asked. It was now April 16, and Easter was coming up.

Who cares about Easter baskets, I thought.

She continued, "Your mom wants to have them to prepare something for the girls." My parents, Dave and Carolyn, had recently moved to the nearby village of Holzen, where my mom was teaching for two years at the missionary school in Kandern called the Black Forest Academy. My father was leading the area teams of OC International.

"I have no idea," I said. "I haven't seen them. They're probably next to the can opener. I've been looking for that for three days and still haven't found it."

She shoved a box to the side and dug into another one. Before we could empty the boxes, we had to have shelves to put the things onto. But we couldn't put cabinets or shelves together, because the rooms still needed wallpaper and carpet. Every room in the apartment needed new wallpaper; the old stuff had atrocious colors and patterns from thirty years previous. We were half-way through the job when the phone rang. I was glad I had registered for it before our move. It sometimes took four to six weeks to get one hooked up. It was Jane's father, Earl, calling from California.

"Did Kerry call you?" Earl asked. Jane's father Earl was zealous about helping us.

Thank God it was Earl and not Kerry again, I breathed. Phew.

"Yes, he did," I answered. I relayed what Kerry had told us the other night about the hearing and the affidavit signature.

Apparently, Kerry had not told Jane's parents much of anything.

"You were at the hearing, right?" I asked. "What was your impression?"

"We met Kerry outside the courtroom just before the hearing began. He told us to wait outside. Since we weren't allowed inside, we don't know what they talked about."

"Kerry said Serwan was there. Did you see him?"

"Well, there was this slender man there who was pacing up and down the hall nervously where we were waiting."

"What did he look like?"

"Brown eyes, short black hair, olive color skin, kind of a large nose, well dressed—"

"How tall was he?" I interrupted.

"That's hard to say. Kind of tall, I guess."

Earl is five feet two, so that wasn't really helpful.

"Kerry said Serwan was inside and talked to the judge," I pointed out. "Was this guy out in the hall the whole time, or did he go inside the courtroom?"

"I don't remember. When Kerry came out, we tried to ask what had happened, but he just said, 'Come, we need to go right away,' and he quickly led us out. And then we learned the reason. He was afraid that his parking meter would run out and he would get a ticket. He didn't tell us anything except that the judge hadn't made a decision and there would be another hearing. He looked really shaken up."

"That's probably because Serwan was there," I said. Nobody expected that. I didn't even know he would be allowed into the hearing. "I wonder how he financed his trip from Holland to America."

We continued talking for a bit, and then I gave the phone to Jane. She greeted her dad and then spoke to her mom, sharing general news of the renovation work in the apartment and describing it a bit. Long-distance telephone calls from California to Germany were expensive, so we said our goodbyes, reassuring one another of our love and hung up.

As we prayed together that evening, we felt confident that all would work out; once the document examiner declared the signature to be genuine, Serwan would admit to signing it.

During the subsequent days, we worked from dawn until bedtime, stripping wallpaper, hanging new paper, and laying carpet. A week later, we had finished the bedrooms and were halfway through the dining room. Kerry called again. We both rushed into the half-finished office and closed the door.

"Kirk, I don't know what to say," he began.

I waited. It was immediately evident that our lawyer was distraught.

"The handwriting analyst completed her examination and found the—what's it called?—the affidavit of abandonment to be a forgery."

"What?"

Kerry was silent.

"How can that be? That's nonsense! I watched Serwan sign it. Two other men watched him sign it—"

Kerry interrupted, "The judge doesn't have that evidence. She has a statement from Serwan that he never signed the document and a declaration from the analyst that it is a forgery."

I was too dumbfounded to even think of a question to ask. I turned to Jane to tell her what Kerry had said. Her mouth opened wide in horror and surprise.

"Who analyzed it?" I finally asked Kerry, having absolutely no idea what it even meant to analyze a signature.

"An analyst from the US Postal Service who specializes in document examination," Kerry answered. "And based on the analyst's results, the judge made a finding today that the document is a simulated forgery. Then she granted Serwan temporary custody of the children. The hearing is set for a month from now on May 23, at which you and the girls are to appear in court and present their US passports. And she ordered the DA to begin an investigation to prosecute you for forgery."

Now it was my turn to be silent.

Jane's eyes filled with tears.

It was too much, too fast. I couldn't digest it. A thousand thoughts flashed through my mind at random. How could the analyst find a genuine signature to be a forgery? How could a judge take away custody of our daughters a full two years after we had adopted them? What were we to do? We had not broken any law. How could this be happening? How could a US judge order me to come back to the United States to appear in court? And to give up my children? How could such a thing happen? I was angry, confused, and terrified all at once.

"What does it all mean?" Jane whispered. I didn't know how to begin to answer her. I couldn't process it all.

"What happened at the hearing, Kerry?" I asked, trying desperately to get some information.

"I got a phone call in my office in Santa Cruz from the court clerk, wanting to know where I was. 'The judge is on the bench in the San Jose Superior Court, and issuing orders,' the clerk said to me on the telephone. When we recessed at the last hearing, the date hadn't been set, and I expected the clerk to call my secretary with the new date and time. I told the judge that I was in Santa Cruz in my office and that no one had told me the hearing was set for today. I told her that I wanted to be present. She asked how long it would take for me to get there. I said at least a half an hour. Then she put me on hold. A few minutes later, the clerk came back and said they had conferred together, and all agreed that I had been there when the date had been set. There was no excuse for my absence. Judge Cordell was going to proceed without me."

"So you weren't even in court?" I asked incredulously.

"They never told me when the date was. How could I have been there?"

I realized his absence at the hearing would have been understood as an admission of guilt. When an attorney has no hope of winning and wants to save face, he just doesn't show up in court. Then Kerry asked a question that caught me off guard.

"How long do you plan on staying in Germany?" he asked.

I wasn't sure what he meant. He knew that we followers of Christ, working in Germany with the foreign Kurdish population.

Jane and I generally worked overseas for two years and then spent about five months in the United States visiting our family, friends, and churches that had sent us overseas.

"What do you mean?"

"You could just remain in Germany," he suggested.

"You mean not return with our children for the hearing?" The thought of disobeying a US court order struck me as totally bizarre and absurd. "What do you mean, Kerry? Never return to the US? Are you suggesting we live as fugitives for the rest of our lives?"

"It would be one way of handling it, is all I'm saying. I'm not recommending it. I'm just saying it's an alternative."

I pictured myself fleeing from country to country, trying to eke out an existence under a false identity, living in a Mexican desert somewhere with a wife and two small children. I rejected the thought almost as soon as it had come.

"Kerry, we can't live our lives like that. And why should we? We have done nothing wrong. Why can't we fight it?"

"Quite frankly, I don't know what I would ask Serwan if he were on the witness stand. And besides, the judge has already made a finding. She has determined that the document is a forgery. Based upon that, she seems quite ready to nullify the adoption."

"Kerry, it isn't fair! It isn't right, or just, and it isn't fair!" I was almost shouting. My eyes were wet, and my voice filled with emotion. "Why should we have to fight this? We haven't done anything wrong!"

"No, it isn't fair," Kerry replied evenly. "Sometimes, the justice system just works out that way. The wrong guy goes to jail. The criminal gets off scot-free. A judge makes a bad decision. Sometimes, it just happens. Not always, and fortunately, the system still does work most of the time. But this time it isn't working fairly, and—"

"And it's ruining our lives," I finished his summary for him.

"Unfortunately," he replied.

And what were we to do? Just give in? The system had failed; we'd been duped. It's too bad. Nothing can be done. Kerry's words began to sink in.

I pictured myself in a US courtroom. I was handing my children's passports to the judge. The bailiff took my children and led them out of the courtroom. Away. Away from my wife and me. And there was nothing I could do. Nothing I could say to stop them. I was never going to see them again. Such imaginings were a nightmare—a nightmare that was to return to me over and over in the days and weeks to come. There was nothing I could do.

I asked Kerry to fax us a copy of the judge's court order so I could study it better, and we hung up.

My mind was too clouded and overwhelmed to make any decisions at the moment. It occurred to me that our lives were not the only ones to blow up as a result of this phone call. Two sets of grandparents' lives began to disintegrate as well. Maybe not as drastically as ours, but they, nevertheless, felt the pain and the crisis intensely. And the repercussions radiated outward to others, touching our extended family, our neighbors and friends, our coworkers in ministry, and the many Christians and prayer supporters around the globe who were involved in our ministry.

From April through May 1994, our family and friends asked us what they could do. We kept them updated by e-mail and via Jane's parents. People wanted to do something, to help somehow. We told them to pray, believing that God, who can change the heart of a king, could also change the heart of a California adoption judge by the name of Cordell. We also suggested they could write letters to the judge and to the district attorney, testifying to our character and expressing their outrage at the injustice that had been done.

And letters began to pour in. From countries all around the world. Expressions of support and concern came from psychologists, sociologists, teachers, mothers, and fathers, all people whom we had gotten to know in our many years of work abroad. We began to realize what an international community of supporters we had standing and kneeling with us as letters arrived from Africa, Asia, Australia, North America, Europe, and the Middle East. Indeed, a month later, the district attorney commented that we had the entire Christian community writing to him.

But a mountain of letters would not change the judicial finding or the reality of the impending May 23 hearing.

Jane's father, Earl, was on the phone nearly daily with us offering much more than support but a course of action. Sometimes, it was two or three in the morning when the phone would ring. It was easy to forget there was a nine-hour time difference between California and Germany when the issues were so critical. He and I would talk for sometimes an hour at a time, oblivious of the long-distance telephone charges. One cannot put a price on the value of the lives of one's children; it was ludicrous to consider finances in light of the gravity of the matter.

We had become e-mail users just eight months prior in September 1993 and now found ourselves exchanging several pages of writing daily as we thought through a plan of action.

I sat down at my computer during the day following the devastating phone call and began writing out the chain of events that had led up to the signing of the critical document. I tried to explain everything as thoroughly as possible. Twenty-six pages later, at 4:00 a.m., I e-mailed the whole thing to Earl and finally went to bed. The next day, I express mailed a copy of my missive to Attorney Kerry Walter in Santa Cruz. (For some unexplained reason, it took ten days to arrive.)

Earl advised me that we needed specialized legal help. Kerry would be unable to fight our case in court; he had said as much himself when he floundered over questions he could put to Serwan. We needed an attorney with a plan.

"Where do we go from here?" I had asked Earl. Kerry's wait-and-see attitude had gotten us into big trouble. And failing to appear in court had caused the judge to assume we were guilty. Without a plan of action, we were going to lose our children. Or maybe it was already too late. Certainly, Kerry made it sound like it was.

Earl got busy looking for other Bay Area attorneys. He followed every lead relentlessly. The search was consuming his every waking minute, and when he slept, he dreamt about it. He called everyone imaginable to try and get advice, ideas, help, or leads. Kerry agreed we needed more legal advice, and Earl pursued attorneys as far away as

San Diego. It was surprising how many attorneys there were but how few had had any experience with challenged adoptions. And fewer who had any experience with international adoptions. Someone suggested that what we needed was a good trial lawyer. Faxes flew back and forth between Europe and San Jose. More names. More phone calls. At the start of May, Earl found us a new attorney, a Mr. Terry Green.

I spoke with Mr. Green long distance as Earl sat with him in his plush office.

I trusted Earl's judgment in selecting him; I knew he was decisive and would hire only the best.

"At least, he has a plan of action," Earl had told me before the scheduled call. "We've got to do something!"

I could hear the desperation in his voice. How thankful I was that Earl was there in San Jose, giving 200 percent to help us. He had even taken an extended leave from his business.

But Terry had not been optimistic. He said that when a judge makes a factfinding of a forgery, there isn't any way to reverse that decision.

Indeed, nobody else Earl had talked to was optimistic either. A close friend from his church, who had worked half his life in the district attorney's office, spoke with Earl about our prospects.

"I wouldn't touch this case with a ten-foot pole. It's hopeless," he said.

Earl told me on the phone that Attorney Green considered opening the case up to media coverage.

"It could have a positive or negative impact," he cautioned. "Sometimes, this kind of thing can backfire. You think you have a clear case of injustice, but then some special-interest group latches onto the story and blows some aspect of it clear out of proportion." Still, Mr. Green thought that public opinion might be able to affect the outcome. We talked it over and decided to go public. At that point, we didn't have a lot to lose, it seemed.

Mr. Green had one further suggestion. He would prepare what was called a motion for reconsideration. It would provide, as he explained, an opportunity for the judge to change her decision without losing face. There was a legal deadline; after which, such a motion could no longer be filed. We had just a couple of days.

Two days after our long-distance phone call, Earl and Mr. Green met together with Kerry so that Mr. Green would have my twenty-six-page e-mail and the adoption records from Kerry's files. As they talked, Earl had an idea.

The phone rang in our little German apartment. It sent a shudder through me. It was that ring that had signaled the end of our peaceful lives; it was that phone that had brought terror into our home. I hated the sound of it, hated answering it, and feared the great unknown that lay in the messages it transmitted. Every time the phone rang, a knot would develop in my stomach. Just looking at the device made my stomach tighten up. Still, I put down the wallpaper brush and picked up the receiver. It was Earl.

"It's your dad," I said to Jane. Fortunately, the girls were already in bed, so we could talk freely. It had become more and more difficult to protect them from the news that might destroy their existence. News that, on the one hand, seemed certain yet, on the other hand, was too terrible to be true. There was simply no way a three- or four-year-old could comprehend what was happening, and we didn't want to alarm them. I gave my wife the telephone.

"You *have* to tell them," I could hear Earl's voice. A knot formed in my stomach.

"No way, Dad," Jane said firmly. Her petite frame belied her determination. "They simply cannot understand."

"But you have to prepare them. You have to tell them, or the shock of leaving you will be too great for them."

"But we don't know for certain that they will be taken away," she argued, wanting desperately to believe her own words. Tears began flowing down her cheeks.

"Jane, you've got to face reality."

"But the fear of being taken away from us could destroy them," she argued with her father.

"Dad, ever since we were in Iraq, the girls have asked us, 'Are we staying together? Are we staying together?' Neither of us can ever leave the house without the girls asking us that over and over. 'Is

Jessica going? Is Delal going? Is Mommy going? Is Daddy going?' They've only recently become confident that they're not going to be abandoned again. How can I tell them they might be taken away now?" By this time, she was sobbing. I took the phone from her.

"Earl, we'll try and prepare them. I don't know what we'll say, but we'll try and say something. But it's going to take some time."

"You haven't got any time, Kirk. Look, I know it's hard, but they've got to be prepared."

I didn't answer. I knew he was right. They could be taken from us any day, at any hour. Even here in Germany. I had asked my neighbor whether the German police could carry out a US court order. I wanted to know what the chances were of the local police showing up at our door with Judge Cordell's written order and taking our children into custody. The answer to my inquiry had only increased our anxiety.

"The German police will honor and carry out a US court order pertaining to a US citizen," my friend said. We could only hope that they wouldn't be too quick about it. Still, I realized that Serwan's Dutch attorney now had the legal ammunition she needed. She could force us via the German Child Protection Services to turn the children over immediately to Serwan.

Earl continued, "Listen, I want you guys to make a video."

"A video? Why?" I asked.

"A video. You need to tell your story. It doesn't have to be anything fancy. Just set up the camera, and film yourselves telling what happened. Your father is there, right? He can help you. Then you can DHL express mail it to me."

It sounded like Earl had already figured all this out, but it was a totally new idea for me. I was unprepared to deal with it.

"Earl," I began as I looked at the bucket of wallpaper paste and the wet brush, "we're in the middle of trying to wallpaper…" I no sooner said it than I regretted it. I knew how ridiculous it sounded. What difference does wallpaper make when your kids are about to be taken away from you? But, still, it was reality. We were up to our necks in paste, wallpaper, and the general mess of moving. "And it's ten o'clock at night, here," I added. "We're exhausted."

"Don't you realize your children's lives are at stake?"

I could hear the edge in his voice. No wonder he was exasperated; he was breaking his back to help us at his end. Why was I balking at such a seemingly simple request? So I agreed. I couldn't really see the point in it, but I agreed.

"Jane," I began after hanging up the phone. "Your dad wants us to make a video."

She was still trying to dry her tears.

My dad, Dave Legacy, at the time of the phone call, was at our apartment helping us finish the wallpapering.

"Earl suggested you might help us," I told him. "You know, just hold the camera." My dad had taken many home videos, and I knew it would be no problem.

"What are we supposed to say?" Jane asked.

"He said to just tell our story. Tell what happened leading up to the signing of the affidavit of abandonment. Tell a bit about our work in Kurdistan and about our interaction with Serwan. I guess I can use the long e-mail I wrote to Terry as a guideline." I sighed. It sounded so easy, but I was too tired to even think about it.

The apartment renovations had become a total chore, even with my dad helping. Wallpapering a complete room brought no gratification or sense of accomplishment. What was the point of a nice-looking apartment if there were no children? No giggling or laughter...?

Dave set up the camera, moved a few pillows on the couch, and adjusted the lighting; and we sat down to begin filming. I couldn't even think well enough to introduce ourselves and explain the purpose of the video. We were emotionally and physically drained. In complete resignation, I finally asked my dad to come back in the morning to give it a try. We were simply too far gone to be of any use. He agreed to come by at 9:00 a.m. the next day.

The next morning, we had no time to prepare or discuss what we would say. We knew we'd better just sit down and get started. Earl had made it clear that he needed the video immediately. He would try and show it to our attorney, to the district attorney, to anyone who would watch it. As Dave began to record our story, our minds went back to our first days in Iraq, to the time before we had even seen Delal and Jessica. We remembered the moment we first caught sight of the mountainous border between Turkey and Iraq—and later when we were first asked to check on Suha and Nuha. We told our story.

With that one phone call from Kerry, the relative security we had enjoyed as a family was shattered. Our ministry among Kurdish refugees came to a halt. Suddenly, the date May 23 was burned into my consciousness. It was the date Judge Cordell ordered us to present our daughters in court in San Jose, California. Should we return to the United States from Germany? If so, when should we leave Kandern? Should we all go, or just me?

We considered the alternatives. We knew that if we presented the girls with their passports, it could mean seeing them for the last time. Indeed, that was how the court order was written. If she had decided the document was a forgery, then the adoption would be annulled, their citizenship forfeited, and their lives changed forever.

So we tried to weigh our alternatives. Some advised us to keep our children in Germany and go without them and try and defend ourselves. That way they couldn't forcefully remove our children. But that seemed counterproductive. If we did not obey the court order, then I would find myself in jail, far away from Germany and my family. And if none of us appeared, then we would have to live as fugitives, as lawbreakers. For at the point we disobeyed the court order, we would be guilty.

At the same time, we knew the German police could come to our door in Kandern at any time, present the order granting custody to Serwan, and remove the children. The thought was terrifying. We were afraid to go outside or to answer the door. Yet we were ordered to fly home to San Jose. In my heart, I knew we would go. It was the right thing to do. And I have been taught that doing the right thing will yield the right results. But does it always? What if things, indeed, go wrong? Who says that life will be just, anyway? Why should I be immune to adversity and injustice? Surely, God wouldn't allow my children to be taken from us? Would He?

We put ourselves once again in the hands of God.

Chapter 21

Devastation. Visit with the District Attorney.

Even though the fig trees have no blossoms,
and there are no grapes on the vines;
even though the olive crop fails,
and the fields lie empty and barren;
even though the flocks die in the fields,
and the cattle barns are empty,
yet I will rejoice in the Lord!
I will be joyful in the God of my salvation!

—Habakkuk 3:17

Kandern, Germany, April 1994

The five weeks between April 18 and May 23, the date we were to appear in court, were agonizing. We were on the phone constantly talking to Jane's parents, Earl and Eleanor. They quickly realized how devastating it was for their daughter Jane, and so they sent reinforcements in the form of their second daughter, Janet Smith, who visited for a week. She was a real godsend. I could see why Muslim men enjoy having more than one wife. I told her husband, Dan, how great it was to have two wives. It was the only funny thing I had said in months. Janet was a real blessing. She cooked, cleaned, and kept the girls occupied, which allowed our household to continue while Jane grieved. And grieving it was. We grieved as those who've lost a loved one. Only our loved ones were still with us. We just didn't know how long it would be until they were taken. The girls sensed that something was wrong, only they had no idea what it was. It was impossible to hide our emotions from them, even if we didn't tell them what was actually happening.

Delal looked up at me and said, "Something sad has happened." It made me cry just to see her furrowed brow and look of deep concern. What could we say to her? She was just four and a half years old.

For a full week, Jane lay on the bed, sobbing and crying out to God. Over and over, the question—more of a statement really—kept entering her mind, *But adoption is forever.* Or so we thought. She was devastated. She wondered if she would still have daughters when Mother's Day came. She remembered her promise to Delal that she would bake her a cake on her birthday. But now we knew they would be gone long before her July birthday. How could we break a promise to our daughters? They had been abandoned once already and had been severely neglected. Long after we adopted them, they still battled the fear of being separated. What would another separation do to them? Would they ever trust anyone again? Jessica was just three years old. She probably wouldn't even remember us as she grew older and her childhood memories faded. And the thought of Serwan raising them seemed utterly disastrous. When we knew him, he was unable to take adequate care of himself, and he had such interpersonal problems with the other professionals he lived with that all of them moved out of their community tent. What kind of care would he give these two needy girls? These thoughts spun around in Jane's mind as we contemplated the court order.

Where could she turn for comfort and hope? It was the scriptures that ministered to her—in particular, Psalm 34 verses 15–19, "The eyes of the Lord are toward the righteous, and His ears are open to their cry. The face of the Lord is against evil doers, to cut off the memory of them from the earth. The righteous cry and the Lord hears and delivers them out of all their troubles. The Lord is near to the broken hearted and saves those who are crushed in spirit. Many are the afflictions of the righteous; but the Lord delivers him out of them all." Verse 22 continued with a promise Jane could take to heart, "The Lord redeems the soul of His servants; and none of those who take refuge in Him will be condemned." And a word from verse 1 of chapter 35 spoke volumes about the appropriate response in this conflict, "Contend Oh Lord with those who contend with me. Fight against those who fight against me." God was indeed our source of strength and our help in the midst of our troubles.

Jane began to recall Bible stories from her childhood. Moses had been taken from his mother. *Oh, how his mother must have grieved!* Joseph had been taken from his father and family and sold into slavery in Egypt. *What a horror. And then to be falsely accused of rape and thrown into prison!* Esther had been taken from Mordecai, her uncle, and sent to live in the harem of the evil king Xerxes. But in each of those situations, God had taken what was meant for evil and used it for good. This had to be our hope. God was still in control of this incredible adoption.

Ten days after we had heard the crushing news, Jane penned the following in an e-mail to her parents. It best expresses her feelings:

To Earl and Eleanor Stevens

Dear Dad and Mom

Thank you so much for all your support and work. It is an incredible comfort to me to hear about all the things you and others are doing to help. I feel very loved. Thank you also for being so willing to give of your savings on Delal and Jessica's behalf. Thank you for sending Janet and for coming here to visit me, Mom. I really need the company now more than any other time in my life.

To be quite honest, I feel paralyzed every morning. Getting up and getting going is very difficult. Facing each new day is a heavy load. I feel like every step is a big effort. In the mornings especially, I feel like I am carrying a bag of cement around, and it is tied to my heart. Breakfast is hard to choke down. Things get better as the day goes on. My brain always feels somewhat fuzzy.

Here is an excerpt from my diary:

4/22 Things have gone from bad to worse. So much injustice has occurred. Serwan lied about signing the affidavit of abandonment. Then an expert analyst stated that it was forged. It is an absurd lie. The judge gave custody of the girls to Serwan. Now what, Lord? My world seems to crumble. You lift me up repeatedly. I push myself through another day. Fix meals, play with the girls, brush their hair, kiss and hold them. They are simple everyday things. I try to act normal, constantly remembering that this may be our last normal day. The end of our family.

Delal talks about her birthday. It's one of her favorite subjects. I choke back tears, wondering if I will be able to keep the promise of a cake, a special meal of her choice, a gift.

I escape to the bedroom several times a day, lock the door, and cry out to my Lord on bended knee. "Save my family, O God. But even if you chose not to, I will serve you. I will praise you all the days of my life. Please do something great for your kingdom through this nightmare. I am your servant.

"You know what stress is, Lord. You sweat blood. You took a far heavier burden on yourself." My heart feels like a huge weight is resting on it. I make myself eat at every meal despite the nausea. Will my girls sit across the table from me giggling at mealtime next month? I never knew my eyes could produce so many tears. The only relief comes when I sing praise to God my King.

"Lord, you are more precious than my children. Lord, you are more costly than a home. Lord, you are more beautiful than a husband, and nothing I desire compares with you."

Shadrach, Meshach, and Abed-nego (Daniel 3:16) said, "Our God, whom we serve is able to deliver us…but even if He does not we will not serve any other gods." God chose to save them. He did not, however save Joseph from being sold by his brothers or falsely accused and imprisoned. He did not save Moses from being taken from his mother or Esther from her dear Mordeci. But He did use them all to bring glory to Him. He did have His hand upon all of them in a special way.

I never could have dreamed of all that has happened in my life. There is nothing I would do differently if I had the chance. I have followed the Lord. I have obeyed Him. We have always chosen the right way even when it was difficult. My husband (and maybe I) face arrest now, falsely accused of forgery. The man whose children's lives we saved (God saved them, He used us as tools) now kicks us in the face. *I forgive you, Serwan.* God Almighty is our righteous judge. Kirk and I have nothing to fear on that great Day. *"Thank you, Lord Jesus."*

Jessica woke up last night shaking. She was crying, "Mommy, Mommy!" I held her tight till she fell asleep. I wonder, will there be nights she cries out and I am not there?

"Oh God, prepare my children for what you have for them. They belong to you. Their little

mouths sing praises to you and declare thanksgiving for your daily blessings and your sacrifice for them. Are they the Kurds you sent us to reach?

"If it was for these two lives to save for eternity, that you gave life to me, Lord, it is worth the pain. You will wipe our tears away on that glorious day.

"This has been the hardest year of my life. More trials and tears are in store. But you, O Lord, are molding me, pinching me into the woman, the earthen vessel you want me to be. It hurts some-times—this maturing, this molding. My sole desire is to be the Bride you so deserve. Thank you for your dear presence."

Dad, please do not send this to anyone else.[1]
I love you.

Jane.
Good night.

When Janet went back to California after her week helping us, her mom came for a week. She, too, was a tremendous support as we faced our nightmare. And my parents, Dave and Carolyn, who lived just four kilometers away in Holzen, were a wonderful-sounding board and source of prayer. There was nothing like family to help in a time of crisis.

Jane's father began working full-time on our case in San Jose, trying every legal channel possible to help us. He "retired" from his role as the head of his company, Tractor Equipment Sales. He researched attorneys when it became evident that Terry could not handle the situation any longer. Our case had become too compli-cated for him. Terry recommended we find someone with experi-ence in international adoption trials. Earl was able to get the motion for reconsideration filed in time. Earl's D.A. friend said to him, "I see absolutely no way that the ruling can be changed. Judge Cordell has made a factfinding. That is irrevocable. It is an established legal

---

[1] Used with permission

fact that the document was forged." Earl was devastated. Still he did not give up. He talked to everyone he could in search of an answer. Someone suggested he try to see the current district attorney, Bob Masterson. Since he represented the children, it would not be permitted for the DA to meet with Jane or me, but he could meet with a third party like Earl.

So Earl called the office of the district attorney and asked for an appointment. To his surprise, he received a call offering him a 1:30 appointment on the following day! That night, as Earl lay in bed, unable to sleep, his thoughts kept returning to the upcoming meeting. What should he discuss? How should he present our side of the story? How should he describe what we had gone through? His first thought was to get eight-by-ten-inch enlargements made of pictures I had taken of Jessica and Delal during the first days we began caring for them. The devastating effects of malnourishment were more than evident. Mr. Masterson should know their condition caused by Serwan's abandonment and neglect. Earl got up and drove to a twenty-four-hour photo lab. He made the enlargements. But what else could be done to communicate the truth?

Fortunately, he had called and asked that I make a videotaped testimony with our 8mm videocassette recorder. We included footage of the girls playing at the playground down the street. They were well and active. Happy and energetic. When it was completed, we agreed it should be sent by express mail.

I drove across the border to Basel, Switzerland, and sent it off from the DHL office. That was at 1:00 p.m. on Monday. Earl's appointment with the DA was scheduled for Wednesday at 1:30 p.m., and he wanted to show him the videotape. Now Earl wondered if it would get there in time. All he could do now was pray.

At ten o'clock on Wednesday morning, the package with the video arrived. Earl quickly put it in his 8mm VCR, which had been malfunctioning, said a prayer, and hit the play button. To his amazement, the machine began working properly. Then he pressed record on his regular VCR and made a VHS tape. Of course, it took an hour to copy. Then he telephoned his office and asked an employee to run to the store and buy a portable TV/VCR. Then he called his sister, Betty, who had prayed fervently throughout our ordeal; and he asked her to drive to his office, pick up the new TV, and meet him in downtown San Jose at Mr. Masterson's office.

Exactly at one thirty, they stepped into Mr. Masterson's office with the large photographs and the TV/VCR. A kind but serious-looking gentleman, who looked to be close to sixty years of age greeted them as they entered.

After introducing themselves, Betty asked, "How much time do we have?"

"Just one hour," Bob replied. Earl knew the video by itself lasted an hour. "Would you like to see a videotape that Kirk and Jane made telling their story?" he asked.

"I certainly would," he replied, and they moved some of the piles of papers over to one side and set the small TV on his desk.

Earl then said, "First, I would like to introduce you to your clients," and he withdrew two of the eight-by-tens and laid them before Mr. Masterson. "This is what Serwan allowed to happen to his daughters," Earl said. Bob was visibly moved as he looked at the photographs of the emaciated infant, of the burned foot that wouldn't heal, of the hair loss caused by malnourishment, of Delal's edema in her hands and feet. Then they watched the videotape.

As the hour passed, Betty wondered if they would have any opportunity to talk. But she needn't have worried, for it was Bob who wanted to talk. He asked plenty of questions and gave every opportunity for Earl and Betty to explain our case. And slowly Bob began to form another opinion. He had been convinced the document had been forged. Now he was not so sure. There was definitely another side to the story other than the one Serwan had told at the hearing. After two and a half hours, Earl and Betty exited the DA's office, triumphant that everything had worked out yet cautious because legally nothing had changed. At least the truth had now been told to one of the key figures in the case.

Earl also sent a copy of the videotape to Judge Cordell, but we had no way of knowing if she viewed it or not. We would be seeing her soon...too soon. The appointed court date of May 23, 1994, was looming in upon us.

I was feeling poorly due to another lung infection. We felt it wise to take care of it before traveling to California for the hearing, so I began a two-week home IV treatment with antibiotics. I completed it just before we left Kandern, Germany, on May 14. I had no idea how long we would stay in the US, but I optimistically bought round-trip tickets with a return that was four months away. We flew from Basel to San Francisco, arriving to greet Earl and Eleanor, and Earl's sister Betty and her husband Darrell. We were greatly relieved to pass through customs and not be confronted by a social worker or police officer. It seemed quite plausible that Delal and Jessica could be taken from us at any time, since the court order granted "physical custody to Mr. Serwan."

We moved into Jane's parents' home in San Jose and shortly thereafter notified the court of our whereabouts. It was important for them to know that we were accessible and that we had come to comply with the court order. We wanted them to see this as an act of good faith, in spite of the unjust court ruling. Because of the motion for reconsideration and no doubt the influence of Bob Masterson, Judge Cordell altered the nature of the May 23 hearing. She called it a settlement hearing, at which time Serwan, Jane, and I would try to reach an agreement regarding the custody of our children.

Earl and I went to visit another attorney, Vanessa Zecker, who had just begun her own practice. She was a tall attractive woman with short brown hair. She had some experience in international adoption cases, was certainly intelligent, and came highly recommended. Perhaps most important at this point was her optimism: she truly felt there was some hope for our case.

Our new attorney, Vanessa, attended the May 23 hearing, the judge having decided in the end that we did not need to appear. The attorneys and judge would try and develop a suitable settlement for both parties. Serwan's legal counsel was also present. No agreement was reached, however, and so an additional hearing was scheduled for June 3, 1994. Serwan would be in attendance at that hearing via a live televised hookup. It was an expensive but effective way to converse without traveling across the ocean. Hopefully, we would reach an agreement.

June 3 came rather quickly. The hearing was held in the San Jose Convention center, since the courtroom was not equipped for a live connection. Prior to the TV hookup, we introduced Delal and Jessica to Mr. Masterson. He was pleased to meet them, and while they didn't really understand where they were or why they were there, they certainly liked the candy he gave them. Convinced that they were healthy and being well cared for, Mr. Masterson agreed to allow them to remain in our care so long as we did not leave the San Jose area. We were more than happy to agree to that! Grandma and Grandpa took them outside as the hearing began.

Chapter 22

Settlement Hearings.
Gathering the Witnesses

San Jose, California, June 1994

J udge Cordell surprised me by her approachability. She was a
tall slender woman with a determined look about her. She was
all business and yet not distant. She greeted us warmly and
explained how the hearing would take place. There would be no
sworn testimony; this was not the venue for bringing witnesses or
cross-examination. It was not a trial; it was a settlement hearing. She
would take the initiative and explain the history a bit, for the court
record, and so that everyone would be on the same page. Then she
would open it up for discussion. Serwan could see us on a TV screen
in Holland, and we could see him on a large TV positioned at one
end of a long table in the conference room. I could see he had his
legal aid present. I was told that she was an American but was living
in Holland. Apparently, she worked with a nonprofit group that provided legal aid to refugees.

The superior court had appointed a short heavyset man, Mr.
John Padilla, to represent Serwan in the California court. He was
seated across the table from me. He kept his professional distance
and never spoke to me. I found this unusual and a bit unsettling; I

am accustomed to greeting people and conversing at will. This legal protocol would take a bit of getting used to for us.

Although we could see Serwan on the TV, his expressions and facial features were hard to distinguish. The picture quality was poor and the sound even worse. Because the images took longer to transfer than the sound did, they were never matched exactly. Still it was better than a phone call. I watched as they positioned themselves before the camera and as they chatted back and forth. I wondered how well he could see Jane and me.

"*Tê Çawa nî?*" (How are you?) I asked him in Kuridsh. I hoped to somehow break the ice with a familiar phrase in Kurmanji. It didn't work. The icy atmosphere never went away.

When Judge Cordell asked what our wishes were, I explained that we wanted our family to remain intact. I was willing to arrange some kind of visitation if Serwan wished it, even inviting him to come to the US or Germany—wherever we were living—for annual visits. We had discussed this before the hearing, and although we were not at all comfortable with the thought, it was still better than losing the girls altogether. Unless the settlement hearing produced some results, we were going to lose our daughters.

I could see Serwan was thinking about our suggestion. There was considerable discussion between he and his Dutch legal advisor. She reminded him of the difficulties they had getting visas to come to the United States for the last hearing. She told him it would be no different than the current situation. We imagined that she had no doubt been convinced of the story Serwan had told her, just as Judge Cordell and Robert Masterson had been.

Serwan then said he wanted the adoption annulled. We tried to approach it from several different perspectives but to no avail; he was adamant. He wanted the adoption annulled.

I did not bring up the accusation of forgery at the hearing. I could not see that it would serve any purpose. I knew Serwan had sworn never to have signed the affidavit and would, thus deny it once again, even though he knew in his heart that he signed it. Since the document had been given to the US postal services document examiner and found to be a forgery, I felt that challenging Serwan on this point would be worse than just leaving it alone. It was clear, however, during the hearing that we were not going to get anywhere.

At this point, Judge Cordell told John Padilla to contact Serwan and convey to him the gravity of his position. She did not feel his position was tenable considering our relationship with the girls. This was encouraging. But I could see that the judge felt we, too, needed to modify our position. She wanted me to consider nullifying the adoption and having some kind of visitation rights or temporary custody or something. The thought of such an arrangement made me sick.

After we had completed the hearing and were standing outside in a corridor, our attorney, Vanessa Zecker, said, "I wouldn't want him visiting if I were you. I can see how unstable he is and unpredictable." Indeed, his difficult personality had become evident even through the TV monitor. I tried to understand his position; I assumed he had just changed his mind and wanted his children back. He had been moved from the refugee camp in eastern Turkey. Now he was living in Holland in better conditions. Perhaps he had become lonely, or maybe he was feeling the guilt from having given his daughters up for adoption. For the life of me, I couldn't figure him out. One had the feeling that he was constantly weighing his remarks based on what he thought he could get away with. He was a master of deception and manipulation. He certainly had manipulated the judge, the district attorney, his counsel, and the handwriting expert.

The hearing failed to bring about any settlement.

In frustration, Judge Cordell declared that the matter would have to "go to trial." That had such an awful sound. It would be final. Costly. Painful. Permanent. On the one hand, it would be the most difficult thing we had ever faced, but, on the other hand, Vanessa reminded us it would be a clean conclusion to the matter. It would seal our adoption and prevent any further intrusion. That is…assuming we were victorious. If we lost, it would be the greatest tragedy of our lives.

Judge Cordell announced that a different judge would handle the case when it went to trial since her opinions had been influenced by the three hearings. She recommended Judge Hoffman and

Mr. Padilla and Ms. Zecher agreed she would be fine. Then they discussed what witnesses would be called. Mr. Padilla said he could not commit to that yet; he would certainly call Sharon Mutton, the handwriting analyst from the postal service, Mr. Serwan, and perhaps some others. He wanted to confer with his client.

Ms. Zecher said she would call two witnesses from Turkey (the translator and the notary public), of course my wife and me, a document expert, and perhaps one or two others. It was felt that the trial might last for about two weeks. They would make a special effort to schedule it soon and not stretch it out in light of the travel involved for the participants.

The judge outlined two issues that would be tried. First, is the signature on the affidavit of abandonment document authentic, or is it a forgery? (That document stated that Serwan wanted us to adopt his daughters and he had relinquished his parental rights.) Second, did Mr. Serwan understand the meaning of adoption?

She told Mr. Padilla that the burden of proof would be upon his client if the adoption were to be nullified. She also said that even if the adoption were set aside, a separate hearing would be held to determine custody. While Mr. Masterson and Vanessa both felt the children would remain with us, Judge Cordell was not so certain. The two eyewitnesses in Turkey, who had witnessed the signing of the document, would have to demonstrate credibility on the stand. Otherwise, the opinion of the signature expert (who had made the forgery determination) would carry more weight. Finally, Judge Cordell announced that she would "stay" her previous court order granting custody to Serwan. This was a great relief. Still the battle was far from over.

The next few weeks were busy. We did have opportunity to get to know Vanessa better and found her to be very capable and thorough. She did not want to leave anything to chance. She was horrified at the way our case had been mishandled by Kerry Walter, in particular his negligence in missing such a critical hearing. And we learned that Judge Cordell should not have issued an order at a settlement hearing. But there was nothing we could do to change history. Vanessa was determined to do an excellent job—to save our children.

She was married to a judge and her mother was also a judge. She lived and breathed law. Whenever she was actually working on a case, her husband had to care for their two-year-old because she became so utterly wrapped up in her work. It was exactly the kind of dedication we would desperately need.

We had several immediate concerns. We had to find the notary in Turkey who prepared the papers for Serwan to sign. He would be a key witness. He had reportedly moved away from Silopi and been assigned to work in a town near Mt. Ararat. We also had to locate the translator who translated from English into Turkish for the notary. He was present when Serwan signed. I prepared a power of attorney for him so he could get the original affidavit of abandonment from the office in Silopi.

Then, of course, we had to arrange transport and visas for these two men. This entailed lots of long-distance calls to eastern Turkey, where an American friend of ours was living in Diyarbakir with his family. We hired him as an investigator to find the two men. To our utter amazement, he was successful in finding them! He then had to solicit their cooperation and handle the transfer of monies to pay their airfare and expenses to San Francisco. In addition, he oversaw the production of a videotaped testimony of additional witnesses from the refugee camp where Serwan had stayed in Turkey. His support was invaluable.

Vanessa, meanwhile, went to work locating other experts in the field of handwriting and document analysis. It was critical that we be able to refute the testimony of Sharon Mutton. We began assembling all the exemplars we could locate of Serwan's signature. We were getting quite an education in falsified writing. Exemplars provide a basis from which to compare a specific bit of writing. The analyst compares curves, loops, lines, etc. for similarities and differences of style. After Vanessa had collected two dozen signatures, she sat us down in her office for an update.

"It appears that one person has signed two of the exemplars, and all the others appear to have been done by someone else," she said.

"Which two look significantly different?" Jane asked.

"The affidavit of abandonment and this other document (*Relinquishment of Rights*) that grants custody," Vanessa responded. She continued to explain, "Serwan says that he signed the custody document but not the affidavit. What we need are any other signatures of his which would show he did not have a consistent signature, particularly from around this time period." I knew that would be very difficult. He was living in a tent in a refugee camp and had seldom if any opportunity to write.

We learned that at the time of the first hearing in April, when Serwan had flown to the United States, the judge had sent Serwan to the US Postal Service in person to provide some exemplars of his signature for the analyst. He was asked to write his name on three-by-five cards with a fountain pen. The signature in question had also been written with a fountain pen. Utilizing these signatures, created in April of 1994, as a basis, the analyst Sharon Mutton compared them with the signature from December 1991. She had other signatures of his available as well, from his passport, from letters, and from notarized documents.

Vanessa garnered as many signatures as she could and turned them over to a couple of different handwriting experts. We were all dismayed to hear that their first impressions were also that the signature was forged. But we were unwilling to give up. I knew it was an authentic signature. They studied the exemplars further and began to develop a case for authenticity.

As the days ticked by, we became increasingly anxious about our witnesses from Turkey. The notary public was Mr. Ahmet,[1] an older man with family and responsibilities. *Would he be able to come?* we wondered. The translator was a young handsome Kurdish Turk of about twenty years named Erdoğan [*air-doe-won*] Ercan.[2] He was tall, had short dark hair with a slender mustache, and an infectious personality. He spoke not only fluent Turkish and Kurdish but also Arabic (his father's language) and English. He was an English teacher

---

[1.] Name changed
[2.] Name changed

in Silopi, Turkey, and had been hired by the United Nations High Commissioner for refugees to work in the Haj Camp.

As the trial date drew closer, I became concerned about Erdoğan's sincerity in coming to the US. I learned that he hadn't gotten his passport. I was worried he might not come, so I telephoned him in his home in Silopi. I heard the line pick up.

"Erdoğan? Hello! This is Kirk calling from California."

"*Dide deke, keremke*" (one moment please), his sister answered in Kurmanji, the Kurdish language spoken in eastern Turkey. She told me to wait a moment as she went to find him. I was amazed that I got a connection and an intelligible one at that. I remembered the many times I had tried unsuccessfully to telephone from Silopi. After a moment, I heard Erdoğan's voice.

"Hello, Kirk! How are you?" We exchanged pleasantries. Then I got to the point. After all, it was long distance.

"Have you gotten your new passport?" I asked.

"I had some problems with that," he began. "I have to go all the way to Batman (a town in eastern Turkey) to apply for it.

I tried to be tactful. "It is very important that you come and testify Erdoğan. We must have your account as an eyewitness. We must show that the document is not a forgery." I knew that Erdoğan was angry with Serwan for claiming his signature had been forged. When Erdoğan had made a videotaped statement (for the investigator), he said he remembered the whole event quite well.

He looked into the camera and said, "Serwan, you are a liar. I witnessed you sign that. And when you claim it is false, then you are saying that I, too, falsified it. You are lying, and I would like to tell you that to your face!"

I didn't know if his anger would be motivation enough for him to come. Certainly, his honor had been attacked. Would he come to save his honor?

"The plane reservations are for next week," I told him. They were already paid for. "I have flights for you and for Mr. Ahmet from Ankara to Istanbul, and then from Istanbul to San Francisco." I hoped he would sense the urgency and my determination.

"I have a problem," he said. "I cannot get off work." His job with the UNHCR had him working sometimes seven days a week. There were always problems in the refugee camp that required his attention.

"Can you ask your boss for time off?" I asked. "I will compensate you for your lost time." I did not want his need for money to keep him from coming.

"I will try," he said.

It was a small assurance. I knew the UNHCR could be very stubborn. I also knew how difficult it would be for him to get a passport. On top of that, I realized that his promises might be empty. He might be just telling me what he thought I wanted to hear because he didn't want to disappoint me. In his culture, it is considered polite to answer yes to an invitation even when one cannot come. To reject an appointment would convey personal rejection. Countless times, Kurds would say they were coming to visit but then never showed up. Sometimes, they probably thought my invitation was not genuine, because I hadn't repeated it enough or said it forcefully enough. I didn't want to err on that side this time.

"It's really important for you to come, Erdoğan. We need you here."

"I will see if I can get the time off. The problem is they don't have anyone to replace me."

"I will call back on Saturday," I said. "And we will all be praying that you can get your passport and vacation time."

"Okay. I will talk to you later."

"Goodbye, Erdoğan." I hung up.

The trial was due to begin on the following Monday. There was no way he was going to be able to make the first flight we'd booked. I called the airline and changed the reservations to the following Tuesday, arriving on Wednesday. It seemed to be best for Mr. Ahmet and Erdoğan to fly together—especially since neither of them had ever been outside of Turkey and were unfamiliar with flying. And of course, Mr. Ahmet didn't speak English, so he would need Erdoğan's assistance if there were any problems. So I changed both tickets. That would mean that the trial would actually begin before they arrived in

San Francisco. But Vanessa assured me she could call other witnesses first. Erdoğan and Mr. Ahmet could be called later to testify. That is, if they came.

Chapter 23

Superior Court. Bob
Blincoe. Serwan.

San Jose, California, August 1994

The San Jose Supreme Court building, Family Court Division is a gray two-story concrete block building set adjacent to the downtown freeway. Shortly before 8:00 a.m., we passed through the security checkpoint and waited outside the courtroom. At the far end of the hall stood Serwan dressed in a mustard jacket and slacks. He looked very modern and well-groomed. He was conversing with his attorney, Mr. Padilla. We exchanged glances. My stomach was in knots, and I could think of nothing to say to him. Part of me wanted to reach out to him and befriend him, much as I had when we had first met in the camp three years previous. But I knew, on the other hand, that his was an adversarial situation and that to converse with him could jeopardize our case. Our adoption could be annulled. I could be convicted of forgery.

Vanessa led us into the chamber, and Jane and I were shown our seats. At the far end of the room was the judge's bench with the witness stand to the left and a table to the right. A long gray semicircle desk was placed around an open area right in front of the judge's bench. Behind this desk sat, from left to right, the court reporter,

Jane, myself, Vanessa, the district attorney, Serwan, and Mr. Padilla. Behind this long desk were rows of mostly empty chairs. Directly behind Serwan was a chair for the bailiff, and a few of the seats in the rear of the room were occupied by immediate family members. Earl and Eleanor took their places there. No visitors or witnesses were allowed to view the trial; they would be called to testify and then dismissed.

The presiding judge, Nancy Hoffman, entered the courtroom, and everyone stood to their feet. Vanessa said this was not always done anymore, particularly in the less formal family court. Nevertheless, I realized that showing proper respect was important. I placed a legal pad on the desk before me; Vanessa had said not to talk to her during the trial, instead I should write down comments or questions and position my notations so she could read them when she wished.

Vanessa requested that the witnesses be called out of the customary order of complainant first, followed by the respondent. This was due to the travel involved for the witnesses. Judge Hoffman agreed, and Vanessa called Bob Blincoe as the first witness. Bob was working in Iraq in the relief effort and was present when I found Delal and Jessica. He also had assisted Jane and the girls in their travel out of Iraq after the Turkish foreign minister had sent permission for them to cross the border. His family was in America for a visit at the same time as the trial. Bob's wife, Jan, and their three small children had left the previous day for the long journey to Europe. Bob would follow in a couple of days and join them.

Standing six feet five and speaking in his deep clear voice, Bob had a commanding presence. Vanessa sought permission for Bob to be accepted by the court as an expert in the Arabic language. He was questioned about his schooling in Jordan, and although he did not have written credentials with him, he was accepted. We were surprised and delighted. This enabled Vanessa to question him about the way Arabic is written. It is written from right to left—opposite the way English is written. This would account for the difficulty Serwan had in signing his name in English; he had all his life been accustomed to writing from right to left, and now he was writing from left to right. And much as a child who is learning to right cursive hesitates, then lifts their pen, and make frequent deviations in the shapes of their letters, Serwan had been challenged when signing his name.

Furthermore, there are several "light" vowel sounds in speech that have no written equivalents in Arabic. The short vowel sounds *a*, *e*, and *i* do not appear in Arabic writing, although they are spoken. Hence, for Serwan to begin to write his name using English letters, he would have to choose which English vowels he would use. He might write his name Sirwan or Sarwan, for example. This is in fact what he had done at the time of signing the two documents. The document signature was signed "Serwan," but all of his signatures from 1993 and 1994 had a dotted *i*—Sirwan. Bob explained that even Arabic scholars argue over how to spell their prophet's name, Mohammed. Is it Mohamed? Mahammed? Muhammed? It was not at all unusual for Serwan to have changed the spelling of his name.

Secondly, Vanessa was able to have Bob get accepted as an expert in the area of education in Iraq. This was granted to him due to the fact that his current residence was in Iraq and he was familiar with Iraqi public schools. This made him more knowledgeable than the average American, and since the questions were limited in scope, his testimony was admissible. He was able to establish that classes are taught in Arabic and that English is taught only as a second language in upper grades. Serwan maintained that his public school had conducted classes in English from elementary school onward. His command of English was quite good, and perhaps he felt he needed to concoct a reason for it; we were not sure. This showed a gap in his credibility. Vanessa was determined to show that to Judge Hoffman when Serwan's turn came to testify.

Vanessa expected that Serwan would be the next to give testimony, so I relaxed a bit; I was not eager to take the stand. The judge declared a recess for lunch, so we exited the chambers. None of us had much appetite; we were all too nervous. Still I was glad that I would likely not be called until the following day. But I was in for a surprise.

"I would like to call Kirk Legacy to the stand," Mr. Padilla intoned. In shock and amazement, I turned to Vanessa.

"I thought I wasn't on until tomorrow," I began.

"It's okay," she said. "He can call any witnesses he wants. I thought he would begin with Serwan, but it's all right. Just answer his questions." I walked to the front and faced Judge Hoffman.

"Raise your right hand. Do you solemnly swear to tell the truth, the whole truth, and nothing but the truth, so help your God?" she asked the familiar question.

Mr. Padilla began a lengthy line of questions. I could tell he was following my detailed account of the events that I had written the previous April. At the time, we had wanted only to get someone to listen to our side of the story. Now Serwan's counsel was using it as a basis for examination. Vanessa Zecher did not cross-exam me, nor did Mr. Masterson. They did not want Mr. Padilla to have any more information at that time than was necessary.

I was frustrated because there was much more that I wanted to say. I couldn't explain the context around my answers and was restrained to give a simple yes or no. But Mr. Padilla's questions were not designed to get the whole story. Rather they were aimed at making me seem devious and at damaging my credibility. I was glad to be able to finally step down from the stand. The intensity of testifying was very draining. To Jane's surprise, she was called next. Mr. Padilla used the same tactics with her, but she seemed to handle it much better than I did. Later, Vanessa cautioned me against becoming upset or showing my frustration to Mr. Padilla; it would only put me in a bad light.

Our second day in court began when Serwan was called to the stand to testify. His command of English was outstanding. He was questioned first by Mr. Padilla, then by Ms. Zecher and finally by Mr. Masterson. Serwan was very evasive when asked questions about his background.

"What do you do for a living?" he was asked. He didn't like the question. At first, he said he was a poet and a musician. Vanessa tried to be more specific.

"Are you paid for your music and poetry?"

"No," he retorted.

"Then how do you earn a living?" she asked.

He leaned forward, grew red in the face, and sputtered, "It is none of your business!" Vanessa took several steps back. In fact, she chose to remain behind her desk across the room for most of her examination of Serwan. He was simply too unpredictable and volatile. Judge Hoffman was disturbed by his attitude and tried to address his demeanor.

He angrily announced, "I will not be asked such questions!" This upset her even more.

She sat up to her full height in her tall leather-backed chair, leaned forward, and looked down at him.

In a commanding tone, she proclaimed, "You *will not* speak to me or anyone in this courtroom in that tone of voice, or you will be dismissed. It *will not* be tolerated. Do you understand?"

He was still livid but calmed down enough to answer between his teeth, "I understand." The bailiff moved around from his position at the back of the room and took up the space behind Serwan. Judge Hoffman called for a recess to allow him time to cool off.

Shortly after the recess, the line of biographical questions continued.

"Where did you attend school? When did you get married? Where did you live? Were you in the military? Had you ever been out of Iraq before the Gulf War?" With each question, he became more and more uncomfortable. I really could not understand why he was so upset.

Perhaps he objected in principle to having his fate rest in the hands of so many women. Women are not esteemed in Islam. Under Sharia law, if a woman is raped, for example, it takes the testimony of a man to confirm it. The judge, my attorney, the court reporter, the bailiff, the clerk, and both the handwriting analysts were all women. I knew this would be offensive to a Muslim from a male-dominated culture.

Or maybe he was worried that his military participation would make him an enemy of the US government, which would jeopardize his case. He didn't seem rational. Perhaps to someone unfamiliar with the US legal judicial system, such fears might be reasonable. We knew from our talks in the refugee camp that he had fought in the

Iran/Iraq war for seven years and that he had fought in the Gulf War. He was after all an Iraqi adult male and required to serve in their armed forces. Yet he denied ever having been in the military.

"What religion are you?" Vanessa asked. Everyone expected a simple answer. Vanessa thought he would say he was a Muslim, as are the vast majority of Iraqi Kurds.

But he said, "I am a Christian," his voice rising. Then he leaned forward in the witness stand. "But not like you are!" In spite of the intensity in his voice, I could see this amused Vanessa and Judge Hoffman. She asked him a couple more questions about his beliefs. He became evasive and upset.

"It does not concern you!" he shouted. Judge Hoffman interrupted his tantrum with another warning.

"I will not allow that type of behavior in my courtroom," she said, her voice rising. "You will not attempt to intimidate anyone here. If you cannot control yourself, you will be removed! Is that clear?"

"These questions have nothing to do with getting my children back!" he protested.

She responded with equal force, "You will answer the questions with a yes or no. You cannot choose which questions you will answer and which you will not. You must control yourself!" She paused to let her comments sink in. Then she continued in a more subdued tone. "Do you want to take a break? We can take a short recess if you need a break." He indicated he would like that. I wondered if he was going to make it through the trial.

Vanessa privately expressed to us her concern for her own safety. It was obvious that Serwan hated two people foremost, the judge and my attorney. The previous week, there had been a shooting in the family court, and any sign of anger or violence was cause for immediate concern. Because of Serwan's angry outbursts, Judge Hoffman arranged for his hotel to be "watched." In addition, she had a second bailiff on hand.

Providentially, one of the bailiffs spoke Arabic. He was able to converse in Arabic privately with Serwan during the recesses and breaks. That gave Serwan opportunity to express some of his frustrations, questions, and feelings in a more familiar language. When he first took the stand he had been given the chance to have all the testimony translated into Arabic for him, but he declined this, preferring to speak English during the trial.

That evening, the notary, Mr. Ahmet, and the translator, Erdoğan Ercan, landed in San Francisco. Earl drove the one hour to the airport and picked them up. They were all eyes as they drove down the big freeways and into the suburbs of San Jose. It was a completely different world than the village of Silopi in eastern Turkey! Even the older neighborhoods seemed like wealthy communities as compared to the simple flat roof stone houses of Kurdistan. Erdoğan was most amazed by the auto mall.

"I have never seen so many new cars!" he exclaimed. With his free time, he said he would rather walk through the car lots than visit the sights of the Bay Area. I asked him what it was like for him to leave his home.

"It was actually illegal for me to leave Turkey," he explained. "I couldn't tell you this on the telephone because our line is probably tapped." Then he told of how terrified he had been in the Istanbul airport, fully expecting to be arrested for attempting to leave Turkey without fulfilling his military duty. He explained how he had evaded arrest.

"I stuffed lots of documents into my passport, selected the most compassionate-looking passport agent, and strode boldly up to the counter. I asked the agent some mindless questions to distract him and said a prayer, and he let me through!" Erdoğan had legally postponed his military duty because of his work with the refugees. But he should not have been allowed to leave the country. After he left his home in Silopi to come to the United States for the trial, the authorities became suspicious. Turkish police came and searched his parents' home and interrogated the entire family.

But God was clearly in control. Erdoğan's testimony was going to prove critical.

Chapter 24

Serwan. Mr. Ahmet

San Jose Superior Court, August 1994

The third day of testimony began with a continuation of the cross-examination of Serwan. He was much calmer; apparently, Judge Hoffman's warning had had an effect. Certainly, Serwan's attorney, Mr. Padilla, made it clear to him that he only hurt his case and credibility by losing control. The district attorney began with a new line of questions.

"Tell the court how you came to Zakho with the children," Mr. Masterson asked.

"After our home was bombed in Kirkuk, I fled with the children. We walked much of the way and once we got a ride on a tractor."

"And how did you feed the children during this time?"

"People shared food with us as we traveled."

"How about milk for Payman? She was just a few months old."

"People gave us milk." The district attorney was establishing the fact that Serwan could have continued to care for them instead of abandoning them in Zakho.

"And when you reached Zakho, what did you do then?"

"I went to the church. No, to the *Mosche*. How do you say it?" Inadvertently, he had spoken the word in German, a language he claimed in earlier testimony that he did not know. I jotted a note to Vanessa.

I wrote on the legal pad "*Mosche* is German for *mosque*" and slid it over so she could read it.

Serwan continued, "I asked the people at the *Mosche* if my children could stay there while I looked for work. Many people were staying there because they were fleeing."

I could just imagine the chaos. Over one million Kurds had fled to Turkey. They had traveled with every imaginable means of conveyance, and when they ran out of fuel or when the roads ended, they walked. Some of them carried their aging parents on their backs and abandoned their precious possessions along the roadside when they became too burdensome for the journey. But they never abandoned their children.

"Children are a blessing from the Lord" is a common Kurdish proverb. Children are their future and their only hope. They protect, love, and care for them at any cost.

"Did they allow you to leave your children at the mosque?" Mr. Masterson asked.

"No," Serwan answered. "I then went from house to house and asked if someone, for the sake of Allah, would care for my children. I met a Mr. Abdul Rahman, and he said he would."

"For how long did you ask him to take care of them?"

"I don't remember," Serwan answered. Mr. Abdul Rahman had told us when we visited the children that Serwan had promised to come back in three days to get them. Abdul told me that Serwan was a complete stranger and that he had only done it for the sake of Allah. Of course, Serwan had never come back. Abdul had housed them with his other six children for well over six months.

Mr. Masterson entered into evidence a copy of a letter in Arabic that Serwan had written to Abdul. In it, Serwan expresses his thanks to Abdul for caring for the children and directs him to give the children to Mr. Legacy to care for. He makes no mention of the neglect, which would have been offensive. But, interestingly, he signed his name and spelled it just like he did on the affidavit of abandonment.

Bob then asked Serwan to judge the English translation of the letter for general accuracy. He said it was accurate. He was a bit perplexed as to how Mr. Masterson had gotten the letter. He did not know Abdul had given it to me in order to make a copy and that I had found someone in Zakho to translate it into English for me. It was just one document in a file of evidence I had assembled, the most critical of which was the affidavit.

The affidavit of abandonment was referred throughout the proceedings as #R-1; it was an abbreviation for "Respondent 1." It was the first document entered into evidence. In all, there were thirty-five documents entered. The other document of primary interest was #R-2. That was the document granting Jane and I permission to travel with the children and carry out all legal activities with the children. In effect, it made us legal guardians. Serwan never contested the authenticity of that document. But he claimed #R-1 was a forgery. Vanessa presented him with the documents one by one for identification. Then Vanessa presented him with a letter.

"Is this a letter from you to Mr. Legacy?" he was asked. He studied it carefully. I had saved the four letters he had written me; the third and fourth were threatening ones.

"I think so," he finally uttered.

"Is that your signature?" she asked. He looked at it closely as if he thought he was being tricked.

"Yeah."

The judge interrupted, "Either yes or no, Mr. Serwan. 'Yeah,' is not an acceptable answer." The court reporter as well as the court had to be certain that the answers were correctly recorded. I frequently made the same mistake and was just as often reminded.

"Yes," he said loudly.

Serwan painstakingly pondered over each exhibit, read through them as though he were seeing them for the first time, and then said he wasn't sure it they were from him or for him or genuine. Mr. Masterson then produced a two-by-three-foot chart and placed it on a trifold stand. On it were twenty-four enlarged reproductions of Serwan's signature. Each of the signatures was from authentic documents that Serwan had signed. Most of them had been signed during the past several months. Four had been signed at the time of #R-1 and #R-2. Serwan was asked, one by one, if he could recognize each signature as his own. There was no indication from the chart as to each signature's origin. One at a time, he studied the signatures, pausing to think before answering.

Twenty-one times, he said the signatures were maybes. He couldn't say for certain if he had signed them or not. When he got to the signature that had been enlarged from #R-1, he paused.

"That one I did not sign. It isn't mine." That exemplar was unique because one letter in his name had been partially left out. Two of the twenty-four, he said were his signature.

Vanessa continued with the questioning, particularly about the signing of #R-2, which Serwan agreed he had signed. That document was written in Turkish; and the notary (Mr. Ahmet), a different Arabic translator (the local Imam from the Silopi mosque), and myself were all present when Serwan signed it.

"Please tell us about this document, Serwan." He studied it for several moments.

"Mr. Legacy picked me up from the Haj camp, and we went to the office in Silopi." He continued to relate the chain of events that led up to his signing of #R-2.

"Who was the translator present?" Ms. Zecher asked.

"Erdoğan," he answered. I about fell out of my chair. I couldn't believe it. Serwan was saying that Erdoğan had translated for him at the signing of #R-2, when it was the Imam, a Mr. Ece (EDGE Eh), who was present. Erdoğan Ercan witnessed the signing of #R-1. This was a monumental mistake, evidence that Serwan was either woefully confused or lying. He was claiming Erdoğan to have been present at the wrong time. Vanessa asked him if he was sure, thinking he might recant or change his mind after thinking about it.

But he was adamant. "It was Erdoğan who witnessed it." She wanted the record to show that there was no doubt. Serwan had made a serious error. Hopefully, the judge would pick up on it. If not, at least the court reporter would have it recorded. At that critical moment Vanessa called Serwan's attention to the actual signature on the document.

"Whose signature appears on #R-2 in the translator section?" she asked. The translator had completed the lower half of the guardianship paper. It stated that the document had been dutifully translated (orally) into the language of the signatory (which had been Arabic in this case). Serwan studied the signature.

"I don't know," he answered finally. "But Mr. Ercan was there."

It was a small victory. Perhaps truth would prevail, I thought. But Vanessa put things back in perspective.

"Even the presence of eyewitnesses will not overrule the authority of Ms. Mutton, the signature analyst," Sharon said. "The fact-finding that declared the signature to be a simulated forgery carries at least as much weight as the testimonies of eyewitnesses." I was shocked. She continued, "We must demonstrate the signature on #R-1 to be authentic or at least create enough doubt about the abilities of the postal document examiner so that the judge rules in our favor." I could see the trial was far from being over.

After court recessed that afternoon, Ms. Zecher met privately with the notary Mr. Ahmet and with the translator Mr. Ercan in her office in downtown San Jose. Together, they reviewed what would transpire the following day when each of them took the stand.

We were in for some surprises.

The fourth day began, and I was again asked to take the stand. I was questioned first by Vanessa and then cross-examined by both Mr. Padilla and Mr. Masterson. Each detail of those crucial days surrounding Christmas 1991 was reviewed. Each conversation I had with Serwan came under scrutiny. The three hours we waited to see the notary the day of the Kurdish strike in Silopi were critical. My attorney wanted to demonstrate that Serwan had adequate time to think about and discuss his decision to proceed with the adoption.

Bob Masterson questioned me about each detail. As representative of the children, he was pulling for us 100 percent. We learned later that once he had viewed the video we had made, had met us, and then heard the whole story, he had been totally supportive of our case and done everything he could to help us. Vanessa referred to him as her "cleanup batter" because he would ask questions that she had forgotten or ask things in a way for clarification or emphasis. He was almost comical in his mannerisms and speech, giving a welcome relief from the anxiety and intensity of the trial.

Mr. Ahmet was the next to take the stand. For him to testify, we had to hire a translator for him. He spoke only Arabic and Turkish. His translator, appointed by the court, had to demonstrate that he could translate everything from English into Turkish and vice versa. When that was accomplished Vanessa began questioning Mr. Ahmet about his qualifications. Each question had to be tediously translated.

"Tell us about your education, Mr. Ahmet," Vanessa asked. He then explained some of the legal requirements in Turkey for him to be have his job in Turkey. The sign outside his office simply said, "Noter." I was shocked to discover that the rotund aging man, whom I had referred to as a notary, had in fact studied law and served as a lawyer for twelve years. Then he had completed the certification necessary to become a judge! Only then was he qualified to serve as a *noter*. Although the words looked similar, the Turkish word *noter* actually meant a lot more. Mr. Ahmet was the highest legal official in the region and had more clout actually than the mayor! I was impressed. His qualifications certainly increased the credibility and validity of #R-1, the document that gave us the right to adopt.

When Mr. Ahmet was asked why he had come all the way to San Jose to testify, he made even the judge laugh.

"In Turkey, we watch a television show called *Perry Mason*, and I always wanted to see a real American courtroom." I guess he was a bit disappointed that there was no jury. Later, Vanessa arranged a visit to another trial in a different division of the court system, one that had a jury, so he could see the "real thing."

She continued her line of questioning. "Tell the court about the specifics of #R-1 and #R-2, Mr. Ahmet." He remembered the occasion vividly and gave a detailed explanation. Apparently, he handled about six hundred documents a month. But ours was the only one he had ever had that dealt with an adoption. Most of what he worked on dealt with the transport of goods and vehicles across the border. Because of the international embargo against Iraq, the border was tightly controlled. Each vehicle, particularly trucks, had to have special authority to cross the Habur border just outside Silopi.

Mr. Ahmet handled all the paperwork for these vehicles. The United Nations was importing food, medicine, and building materials for the reconstruction effort in northern Iraq, so there was considerable traffic. Mr. Ahmet had to handle each of those documents.

"What is the significance of the number at the top of #R-2, Mr. Ahmet?" Mr. Padilla asked in cross-examination. There were several different numbers stamped here and there on the document, and I had paid little attention to them. The number 04335, made with a blue ink stamp, appeared in an upper corner.

"That is the number of the document," he said. "Each document is numbered in succession and entered into the register in order."

"And what is the registration number in the top-right corner of #R-1?" He was handed the affidavit of abandonment for examination.

"04388," he said. "So that means that there were fifty-three documents handled between the completion of #R-2 and #R-1," Mr. Padilla stated. And then skeptically, he said, "And they are dated just three days apart?"

"Yes," Mr. Ahmet responded with confidence. "I average about thirty documents a day. And I was closed for a day due to the strike." Mr. Padilla was caught off guard by the answer. He had thought he'd found a discrepancy in #R-1, because there was such a huge numerical difference between it and #R-2. But what followed was even more surprising.

"Tell us what happened when Mr. Legacy and Serwan came to your office on December 27, 1991," Mr. Masterson asked. I remembered how unfriendly Mr. Ahmet had been to me during my visits to his office, that day in particular. I wondered what he would say now

"There was a long line of people waiting to see me that day," he began. "Mr. Legacy brought a document for me to notarize. Erdoğan Ercan came to translate the document, as it was written in English. Erdoğan translates all my work when it involves English."

He continued, "Mr. Serwan said he wanted Mr. Legacy to adopt his two children."

"And what did you tell him?" Vanessa asked.

"I told him not to let his children be adopted." The courtroom was silent. I was shocked. He continued, "I said to Serwan, 'Your children will be raised in a different culture and will have a different religion. Don't do this. Don't sign this paper. But Mr. Serwan signed it, anyway."

Now I understood his attitude toward me. I remembered the two of them arguing on and on in the Arabic language, which I don't understand. I had no idea what their disagreement was and hadn't the temerity to ask. I knew Mr. Ahmet didn't like me and was eager to have everything completed.

He was adamantly against me adopting children from an Iraqi Muslim family. And even more important for our case, he advised Serwan against it! It could hardly be suggested that Serwan had been tricked into adopting or that he didn't understand the implications of releasing his parental rights. Mr. Ahmet had made it plain, clear, and simple. Mr. Ahmet, in opposing our adoption in 1991, had in actuality helped save the adoption. God's ways are indeed mysterious!

Chapter 25

Erdoğan Ercan, Ms.
Sharon Mutton.

Superior Court, San Jose, August 26, 1994

"Mr. Erdoğan Ercan, do you swear to tell the truth, the whole truth, and nothing but the truth, so help your God?" the judge asked. Erdoğan looked nervous; as well, one might expect since he had spent his entire life in Kurdish and Turkish villages and was suddenly thrust into a US courtroom. Yet he looked quite fine all dressed up in a black suit, his mustache trimmed, and his short black hair combed neatly.

"Mr. Ercan, would you please tell the court why it is you have come today?" Vanessa asked.

His answer came as somewhat of a surprise. "I came to preserve my honor. I came because when Serwan claims the document to be a forgery, he is calling me a liar. My name is on that document as a witness. And it is a genuine signature of his." He could not have made himself any clearer. At the same time, I was reminded how important honor is to a Kurd. They will endure incredible hardship, torture, even death to preserve their family or personal honor. I had always thought of the false accusation of forgery as a personal affront.

But it was also an affront to Erdoğan and to Mr. Ahmet. Their names were on those documents too.

"I do not want to take sides," Erdoğan stated emphatically. "I want to protect my integrity and the integrity of the Turkish legal system." He recognized that if #R-1 were indeed forged, it would have required some collusion in its preparation. It was typed with the same typewriter and stamped with the same rubber stamps as #R-2. In other words, Serwan was implicating Erdoğan in the alleged crime. Erdoğan's indignation was justified. Still he remained cool and collected on the stand, giving an excellent recollection of the events of December 1991. In my mind, nothing was more obvious. Here was an eyewitness to the signing of #R-1. That seemed like concrete. But Vanessa reminded me witnesses make mistakes and that the handwriting analysis was also like concrete. Refuting the work of the first handwriting analyst would be her next job.

So the fifth day began with a battle between the experts. Sharon Mutton, a middle-aged woman from the US Postal Service, was called to the stand. She was the expert who examined #R-1 in April of 1994 at the request of the District Attorney Bob Masterson. She had determined that the document was a "simulated forgery," meaning somebody had tried to copy Serwan's signature—just as he wrote it. Some forgeries are "falsified signatures," whereby no effort is made to actually copy the signature. In this case, Ms. Mutton maintained someone had deliberately copied Serwan's signature.

After reviewing her qualifications, she was asked about the deposition that had been taken. Our attorney, Vanessa, had done several depositions prior to the trial. These were done in her office, and while the witness was under the same legal oath as in court, no judge was present, just a court reporter. The witnesses were more relaxed in a deposition. Having their information before the actual trial enabled Vanessa to better prepare for questioning the witnesses when they were on the stand.

Sharon Mutton's deposition was quite extensive, ninety-two pages long, and covered everything from her education to her present work with all kinds of document analysis. It had been taken under oath, so Ms. Mutton's testimony today needed to be consistent with it. Mr. Masterson began with an interesting line of questioning.

"Ms. Mutton, you have determined #R-1 to be a simulated forgery. Is that correct?"

"Yes."

"Tell us, having reached that conclusion after your study, is there any evidence that would alter your assessment?"

"No, sir."

"What would you say if we were to show you a videotape of Serwan signing #R-1?" Mr. Masterson asked. "Would that change your opinion at all?"

"No, it would not," she answered. I was astonished. I couldn't believe she could be so sure of herself and her analysis. She wanted to prove to the court that handwriting analysis was a science, not an art. Bob continued asking about the nature of handwriting analysis. She was determined to show her expertise was in a proven science. Bob utilized her own weakness to demonstrate that her conclusions were based more on emotion than fact.

As he approached the witness stand, Bob looked down at the lapel of his navy blue suit. It was well-worn and probably hadn't seen the cleaners in a long time. There was a white speck that he flicked at with his finger.

He turned to Ms. Mutton. "Hmmm," he said, "it looks like there is a bit of birthday cake here." The bit of encrusted white frosting fell to the floor. "I guess it is from my granddaughter's birthday party last night. Now that was a nice event." Sharon looked at him with disdain. The judge smiled. The effect was timeless.

He continued with a hypothetical question. "Let us say that you received a personal check to be analyzed, Ms. Mutton, and the signature on the check was of the astronaut Alan Shepherd. After your study, you concluded the signature and the check were genuine. Are you with me?" Bob leaned forward and smiled.

"Yes," she responded, looking at him through narrowed eyes.

"However, on the date the check was written, Alan Shepherd was walking on the moon. Would that change your opinion any?" Ms. Mutton shifted uncomfortably in her chair.

"No, it wouldn't," she scowled at him.

This was great, I thought. *This woman is a fanatic.*

"If I determine it is a genuine signature, then it is conclusive." She chewed the words out. Bob let a moment pause to let the implications of her logic sink into the judge's mind. Mr. Masterson continued.

"Ms. Mutton, about how many times have you testified in federal courts and superior courts?"

"I would say about two hundred."

"And of those about, how many were for the defense?"

"Maybe four or five."

"And the rest of those trials, about one hundred and ninety-five times, you were testifying for the US attorney?"

"That's right, although with some of the smaller cases, as with stolen checks or whatever, they were prosecuted locally."

"In what percentage of the cases in which you gave testimony in court did you render the opinion that the handwriting was genuine, in other words, *not* a forgery?"

"About five percent of the cases. Maybe up to ten percent."

"And all the rest were forgeries?" Bob asked. The judge leaned forward. Ms. Mutton's answer was causing concern.

"Yes, that is right. I mean, they wouldn't be in court if they weren't guilty."

There was an audible gasp. Everyone in the courtroom was shocked by her answer, not the least of whom was Judge Hoffman. The judge interrupted Bob with a question of her own.

"I beg your pardon, Ms. Mutton? Do you want to explain that, please?"

Sharon continued arrogantly, "Well, the reason they were arrested is they committed a forgery. So, of course, that is my finding. That is why they are on trial."

"In our courts," Judge Hoffman began in rebuke, "a defendant is presumed innocent until proven guilty! Do you wish to rephrase your answer, Ms. Mutton?" Realizing the judge's wrath was about to descend upon her, Ms. Mutton backtracked.

"Well, what I meant was that, very often, because the people *are* guilty, they are in court, and in most of my cases, I also find the work to have been forged."

"No further questions at this time," Bob said and returned to his chair behind the semicircular desk. Ms. Mutton was clearly not having a good time.

Vanessa continued the questioning. "Ms. Mutton, in your deposition, you related how you obtained exemplars from Serwan."

"Yes."

"Do you recall anything he said to you at that time?"

"No, I don't. It seemed that there was a language barrier."

"You mean he did not speak English?"

"Yes," Ms. Mutton said. "He only spoke a word or two."

"Do you remember if he told you that he *did not* sign the document in question?"

"No. I don't."

"I would like to refer you to your deposition, Ms. Mutton. Do you have it in front of you?"

"Yes." Vanessa then directed her to the specific page in her deposition and had her read it aloud for the court. Ms. Mutton had clearly said Serwan had denied signing #R-1 when he came into her office to provide exemplars of his handwriting. Sharon was floundering.

"He may have said this, but I tried not to hear him, because I wanted to remain impartial."

"But you knew there was a document containing a signature that was in question, correct?"

"Yes."

"And you knew Serwan was voluntarily giving you examples of his signature so you could judge them against the document in question?"

"Yes, that is correct." Ms. Mutton sighed. She did not like the turn the questions were taking. "But I tried very hard not to learn about the circumstances of the signature until after I had made my finding," she added.

"Are there any other facts of which you have become subsequently aware, just in general?"

Ms. Mutton hesitated. "Facts…suspicions…not facts. I understand that the children were illegally adopted in this country based on #R-1 and that Mr. Serwan is attempting to, you know, to regain his children and take them to Holland to live."

"And who made you aware of that particular fact, do you remember?" Vanessa pressed.

"Bob Masterson. We discussed the case after I made my findings, and he came to pick up the evidence and receive my report. And I also pointed out to him the significance of the fact that the documents were typed on the same typewriter and stamped with the same rubber stamp. This indicated that they were prepared at the same time in Kurdistan, not later in this country, because that typewriter would not have been in this country nor the rubber stamp. So document #R-1 was done in that time and place."

"Okay. You said that after you rendered your opinion, you also had some suspicions. Did you have any suspicions prior to the time that you—" Ms. Mutton interrupted Vanessa.

"No. Bob Masterson and I discussed the significance of the timing of the forgery, in that it was planned at that time. And rather than coming to this country and coming to love the children and then adopting them, they planned it at that time. They went back to the notary; obviously, that was where the typewriter was. And of course, the horrible suspicion has to enter your mind as to why do they want the children? Maybe they did love them. I don't know. I hope that's why they wanted them." She was rambling and sounding more confused than ever.

"Any other suspicions come to mind?" Vanessa asked.

"There is always child abuse, you know, for unspeakable reasons. You have to consider these things, but that was later after I had rendered my findings."

"Did you have any suspicions before you rendered your findings?"

"No. I didn't. I thought…in the first place I was not sure I would be able to resolve the issue because it's a foreign script and a short name. So I wasn't sure I would be able to have findings at all or which way they would go." She then explained that although Serwan used the Roman alphabet, he had learned it abroad, where the old British system is used. It consists of more vertical lettering and spaces between letters in the middle of a word.

"So you get on very thin ice sometimes when you try to make an opinion about writing about a people from foreign countries, because you don't know what is unique to them or sort of kind of unique to them. But after finding the nature of the differences that I did find, I am sure it's a forgery."

Vanessa then asked her to delineate the similarities and differences in the handwriting that led her to her conclusion. She explained the significance of speed, pauses, pen lifts, rhythm, and letter formation in her analysis. In some cases, it was the fact that the signatures resembled one another that made her conclude one was copied. In other instances, it was the differences that caused her to conclude it was a forgery.

And then Vanessa asked an important question with a driving point, "If you were just to take the questioned document alone without any exemplars whatsoever, is there anything about the signature, the questioned signature, that, in and of itself, would say to you that it's *not* genuine?"

"No, there isn't. There is slowness (meaning the speed of the pen while writing) as I mentioned, but there are a lot of people that are not experienced with a pen who write like that, so I could well believe that this was a signature of someone who is not familiar with writing."

"I don't have anything further, thank you." Vanessa said and returned to her seat.

It was hard to tell if Ms. Mutton looked triumphant or just relieved that her testimony was over. She had twenty years of experience behind her, had published numerous articles on forgeries, had been a long-time member of professional organizations, and certainly had a high opinion of herself and her work.

On the other side of the battle between the experts were Nancy Cole and Lowell Bradford—two experts Vanessa had hired to present our defense. It was up to them to refute all the technical arguments Sharon had given about the signature itself. Without solid arguments against Ms. Mutton's conclusions, we would lose our girls. Nancy Cole had her work cut out for her. Fortunately, she had the weekend ahead of her. That gave her more opportunity to prepare. It was another sign that there was a greater hand directing all that was transpiring.

Chapter 26

Nancy Cole, Serwan's Friends. A Verdict.

Superior Court, San Jose, August 29, 1994

Nancy Cole's testimony began with a thorough evaluation of her background, her education, professional experience, and qualifications. She was subsequently accepted by the court as an expert witness in the area of handwriting analysis. Vanessa asked her about her first impressions of #R-1.

"Well, upon first examination, I thought the signature was a forgery. It has the telltale pen lifts that occur when someone attempts to copy a signature letter for letter. You can see these under the microscope."

"Why do you say 'your first impressions'?" Vanessa asked.

"Well, as I examined the document, I began to develop another opinion. I learned that the signer of #R-1 writes in the Arabic script most of the time. And this has an influence on his ability to write from left to write using the Roman alphabet."

"How does that relate to the pen lifts which occur on #R-1?"

"A person who is unaccustomed to cursive writing will often lift the pen as they prepare to make each letter or part of a letter. Only after one's writing style is more developed does the writing become more fluid. Also Arabic letters are formed individually when written, not joined together with connecting lines, as in a signature."

Mrs. Cole took into consideration Serwan's educational background, which consisted of high school in Kirkuk, Iraq, as well as other cultural and linguistic factors.

"Since he resided in the refugee camp," she explained, "he seldom had the opportunity to write anything and certainly didn't sign his name more than once every couple of months."

I had dug through my files and found two other examples of Serwan's signature from that time period. In both cases, interestingly enough, he had spelled his name like he had spelled it on #R-1 and #R-2. This supported the position that he later changed the spelling of his name. Vanessa asked that the chart with the twenty-four exemplars be once again placed on an easel.

"Please explain the variances you see in these signatures, Mrs. Cole," Vanessa asked.

"Serwan has a very variant signature, an irregular rhythm, and makes frequent errors when writing his name. However, we can see all of the variances are repeated in one or more of the other signatures on display here." She then systematically delineated each variable and pointed out which of the other twenty-five signatures had the same appearance. In some instances, she had made enlargements of certain exemplars, so the court could clearly see Serwan's use of the different letter formations.

She summed up by pointing out a single anomaly: "In the signature on #R-1, there is a portion of a letter missing. This one variable does not appear in any other signature that Serwan made, including #R-2."

"And how do you explain this?" asked Mr. Padilla on cross-examination.

"It is a mistake," Mrs. Cole stated simply.

"I beg your pardon?" said Mr. Padilla, trying to hide his amusement.

"Yes. All of us, at one time or another, make small mistakes when signing our names," Mrs. Cole continued. "It is not unlikely that someone who so seldom wrote his name would also make a slight mistake in writing it. Since he was using a fountain pen, he could not make any corrections. I consider this further evidence that the signature in #R-1 is *not* forged," she emphasized. "Someone who was carefully copying a signature would not be so careless to completely leave out a portion of a letter in the name. He or she would meticulously try and reproduce the signature in every detail. The missing line is simply a mistake made by Serwan when he signed his name."

"No further questions," said Mr. Padilla, and Mrs. Cole stepped off the witness stand. Vanessa was very pleased with the work Nancy had done. She had been thorough and clear in her presentation and had meticulously struck down each and every argument presented by Ms. Mutton. Vanessa then called Jane to the witness stand.

Jane was asked to explain our marriage, our interest in adoption, and how, why, and when we went to Turkey and Iraq. Vanessa wanted to make it clear that although we had an interest in adopting children, this was not our intention or plan when we flew to the Middle East. We were not "out looking for children" to adopt.

On the seventh day in court, Jane continued telling her story and was asked in particular about the incident in June 1991 when we were working in the transit camps of sixty thousand Kurds. She told of the six-week-old abandoned baby boy who had been brought to the camp from the mountains by Canadian medics. He was in perfect health. When his parents couldn't be found, we asked the UNHCR social worker if we could take care of the baby until a Kurdish family was found.

"We said we would even be willing to adopt him," Jane related. The social worker had looked at us with disapproval and denied our request to take care of the orphaned infant.

"You might bond with him and take him away," we were curtly told. The healthy boy was placed in a cardboard box in a tent, amidst seven typhoid patients. A week later, he was placed with a Kurdish family, but two days later, we were told he was sick. Kirk and Jane went to visit him in the morning at the military hospital tent. A US Army medic appeared at the tent doorway and told them with tears in his eyes how the infant had died in his arms.

"We accompanied the Kurdish family to the cemetery where we buried the infant," Jane concluded. The judge was deeply moved by the incident as evidenced by her countenance and by her personal remarks she made to us after the trial.

Jane was cross-examined, with particular emphasis given to each conversation she had had with Serwan. Mr. Padilla tried to make it seem like Serwan didn't understand adoption. But Jane recalled the dialogue clearly. "I was walking toward the building which we used to interview the refugees," she said. "Serwan came up to me and began asking again for help with his case. This was not uncommon. Everyone thought we were their ticket to the west, and we were inundated at every moment with people making pleas."

"And what did he ask?" Mr. Padilla inquired.

"Of course, I knew about his case because I had sat in his tent for over an hour and heard his story. He told me again about his kids in Zakho. We talked for a few moments, and I said he had to think over his alternatives. He wasn't willing for them to be brought into the camp. I asked him if he had considered adoption."

"And what was his response?" Mr. Padilla asked.

"He said it was a black sin."

"A black sin?" Mr. Padilla questioned.

"Yes. So I dropped it there. I didn't know what else to tell him."

Mr. Masterson then took over the questioning. Jane was exhausted but felt more at ease answering the district attorney. She knew he was pulling for us. Still she had to remain alert.

"I would like to enter into evidence a current photo of Delal and Jessica," Bob requested. He brought out an eight-by-ten-inch print that Earl Stevens had provided him. Mr. Padilla objected, reminding the court that the issue of what was in the best interests of the children was not at question. The only issues were the validity of #R-1 and whether Mr. Serwan had been defrauded.

"No one was questioning whether Mr. and Mrs. Legacy were good parents or whether the girls were being well cared for," he reminded the court.

Nevertheless, Mr. Masterson prevailed, stating that, "I as the appointed representative of Delal and Jessica have the right to at least let them make an appearance—even if it is merely via a photo." The judge overruled the objection.

"The picture depicts two children," Mr. Masterson began. "It does not show any parents or adults. It is just two children. I would like to remind the court that although the issue at hand is a purported forged signature, it really involves the lives of two small children." He carried the photo to the front of the courtroom and set it on the little ledge on the witness stand where Jane was seated.

"Can you identify these children?" Mr. Masterson asked. She looked at the picture of her precious daughters. Several moments passed. Tears welled up in her eyes; speech was impossible. The judge passed her a box of Kleenex.

Finally, she was able to say, "These are my girls."

August 30 began across town in a room set up for a video-conference. On the other side of the world, in a similar room in the Netherlands, sat Serwan's Dutch attorney with two of Serwan's friends from the Haj camp, Mohammed and Abdul. The first witness spoke about the poor living conditions in the refugee camp.

"It was cold and dirty. They did not give us proper heaters for our tents. The food was terrible." Nobody in court was contesting that, however.

"Do you have children?" Vanessa asked Mohammed.

"Why yes," he answered, obviously surprised by the question but nevertheless very proud. "I have four children!"

"Were they with you in the refugee camp?"

"Why, of course," he responded. "One of them was born in the camp," he said with obvious pride. That was enough to make Vanessa's point: Serwan could have raised his girls in the Haj camp. She then continued with a different line of questioning.

"What is your religion, sir?" Vanessa asked Mohammed. Again, he appeared surprised by the question. He looked to the right and the left as if to say, "Man, this is a no-brainer!"

"I am Muslim, of course."

"And how long have you known Serwan?"

"About three years, I guess."

"Do you know him well?"

"Why, yes."

"What religion is Serwan?" Again, Mohammed looked as if he couldn't believe the question. It was too easy.

"Why, he is also Muslim, of course!" Vanessa was poking more holes in Serwan's previous testimony. His words were not very believable considering all the discrepancies that were appearing.

"Tell us what Serwan did for a living," Vanessa asked Abdul. This question obviously made him very uncomfortable.

"He was a refugee. He had no work."

"I mean before he was a refugee," she clarified. Abdul uttered something in Arabic to which his translator responded without giving us the translation.

Before the discussion carried on any further, Judge Hoffman interrupted. "Translate the witnesses' testimony only. Do not talk or discuss anything. We must have all conversations on record." The Dutch translator appeared flustered. Abdul's discomfort seemed to increase.

"What was Serwan's employment before he became a refugee?" the judge asked.

Abdul's face made a few more contortions. He said something else to his translator. Finally, the translator said, "He doesn't understand." This obviously frustrated Judge Hoffman. She would not tolerate any games. If he understood what "work" meant a moment before, why then did he not understand it now?

"Work, employment, his job, what he did?" she stated. The translator repeated her words for Abdul's benefit. He gave her a puzzled look.

"I don't understand," he repeated.

"His Dutch is not that good," the translator said.

At this, Vanessa spoke up. "I suggest Abdul's entire statement be struck from the record. If he cannot understand the questions, then his answers cannot be reliable." Serwan's Dutch attorney agreed. Abdul looked greatly relieved. Serwan looked depressed.

We recessed for lunch. When we had gathered again, we heard the closing arguments from Mr. Padilla, Ms. Zecher, and Mr. Masterson. Judge Hoffman had taken copious notes and paid close attention to each closing statement. We had been told that it was not uncommon in a long trial for a judge to actually fall asleep on the bench. Fortunately, that had not happened in our case. Each attorney kept their statements brief.

Mr. Padilla was in a bit of a bind, however. His client maintained that he had not signed #R-1. The testimony and the eyewitnesses had shown, however, that Serwan did indeed sign it. So Mr. Padilla focused on the second part of the court's mandate. That was the claim that he did not understand the term *adoption*. But what sense did it make to claim that he did not understand the adoption document if he was saying he never signed it? Nevertheless, Mr. Padilla tried to demonstrate that Serwan did not understand the meaning of the word *adoption*.

It is difficult to prove that someone did or did not understand something. However, Vanessa pointed out that Serwan had used the word with its proper meaning in letters to me, as well as in statements he had made in the refugee camp. He also had been told bluntly by Mr. Ahmet not to let his children be adopted. And Serwan had gone to the notary the second time, specifically to grant the additional permission to adopt. So he knew it was more than just granting temporary legal custody. The first document (#R-2) had given legal custody only.

Judge Hoffman took a short recess after the closing statements and then returned to render her decision. She had not forgotten Serwan's angry outbursts and violent nature, so she arranged for a second bailiff to be present. He stood directly behind Serwan, just inches from his chair.

Her statement was quite lengthy, making reference to most every aspect of the eight days of testimony. In the end, she read forth her order.

Case: A13104

In the matter of Legacy

Based on the court's finding that the natural father did not meet his burden of showing the signature on Exhibit #R-1 as a forgery, the court finds Exhibit #R-1 to be a genuine document with a true signature of Serwan.

By clear and convincing evidence, the court finds the natural father understood that he was relinquishing his children and allowing them to be adopted by Kirk and Jane Legacy when he signed the document.

Conclusion: Therefore the adoption is not set aside.

To say we were relieved would be the understatement of our lives. *Oh God we thank you,* was our immediate heart cry. We felt overwhelming thanks to the dozens of people who helped us save our family. Our immediate thanks at the announcement of the verdict was to our attorney, Vanessa, who had worked so tirelessly and intelligently on our behalf. Without Mr. Ahmet and Erdogan's traveling to the US to testify we would have been sunk. Bob Blincoe had stayed in San Jose to testify of the educational system and the Arabic language. That too was invaluable. We could not begin to think of the many people to thank.

Judge Hoffman was very courteous and gracious to us following the close of the trial. She asked us to come to the bench and told us in her own personal way that she was honored to meet us, to hear our story, and that we had done a great thing in adopting Delal and Jessica. It was a great blessing to Jane and me to hear her words.

Our families and especially our parents had been so supportive and had sacrificed so much to help us. The Stevens and many anonymous donors had paid all our legal fees. And there were people who had written and prayed from literally every corner of the globe to whom we owed a debt of gratitude. It was extremely satisfying to be able to return to our work in Germany with our family intact. The real trial in our lives was not in the Superior Court of San Jose. It was in our walk with God. We had come to the place where we had put our precious children back into His hands. We would trust Him regardless of the outcome. For in spite of the evil in the world, God was going to use our broken circumstances for good.

Epilogue

Shock of a Lifetime

California, February 2018

Fourteen years went by and our daughters had grown into adulthood. The girls had been an incredible blessing to our family. Delal had become a gifted piano player and composer. She excelled in sales and planning events. She often sang at church and acted in dramas. She loved people and was gifted in creative arts. As a preteen, she brought us crafts she had made with tender words of love for Mom or Dad.

Jessica loved to sing solos, play with animals, was active in sports, and was a hard worker. Her favorite pastime as a little girl was doing cartwheels in the living room in winter and diving in the summer. One would never guess she had at one time been so close to starvation. She had an incredible ability to memorize and also perfect pitch. She too became an accomplished soloist. After leaving our work with Kurds in southern Germany, we continued to bring them with us in ministry. We ministered as a family in Spain, Mexico, Kyrgyzstan, Istanbul, England, Bosnia, Istanbul, and Croatia. We gave them an appreciation for the poor, for the unreached, and a deeper understanding of their national heritage as Kurdish Americans.

We did not hear from Serwan.

Then, in 2009, the unthinkable happened.

Jessica desired to participate in the Miss California USA beauty pageant. I thought it was a frivolous activity. But she really wanted to do it, so much so that she applied to become a contestant, was accepted, and then earned the $2,000 she needed to compete in Palm Springs, California. She bought a beautiful evening gown with lots of beads and lace. She had her hair specially curled. She bought shoes to accent her silver jewelry. She was jazzed.

Part of the preparation was an interview and a written history of each contestant. Jessica told them of her Kurdish heritage. Her candidate information was published on the website for the beauty pageant. News websites in Kurdistan, Iraq, regularly scour the Internet for news about significant Kurdish individuals or events around the world. They found the story of a young Kurdish woman in California who was competing for a famous beauty contest. It was a big deal.

They apparently dug deeper and found another article that had been published by a local news magazine years earlier. This small-town paper had been subsequently purchased by a larger paper, and so all the archives were now also available on the Internet. Delal had been interviewed when she was in high school. She told the complete story of how she and her sister had been caught in the chaos of the war in the Gulf and how her American parents had adopted the two of them. It was a moving story, and a follow-up piece was written by the same author some years later. Now the Kurdish news in Iraq picked it up and linked the lost-in-the-war story with the girl in the beauty pageant.

At the same time, Facebook was just taking off worldwide. Jessica had a Facebook account, and after the beauty pageant, she began getting "friend requests" from total strangers. They were mostly male. She told me about it.

"Look, Jessica," I said, "you are beautiful. Your picture has been published all over the world. These guys want just one thing. Trust me, you don't want to 'friend' these strange guys." So she just let it go. Then one man wrote her a remarkable message.

"Your birth name is Nuha,"[1] he wrote. We were shocked. This name had been never published. Jane and I and the girls knew their birth names. Serwan had told us their real names were Firmesk and Payman, Kurdish names. Nuha, however, was an Arabic name which Serwan had said was given her by Abdul. We were confused. Why would this stranger use the name Nuha?

Why would the Facebook "friend" tell Jessica her name was Nuha? Nobody in the newspaper interviews had been given the names Suha and Nuha.

"Jessica," I said with a degree of surprise, "this guy knows something about you and your history. You should 'friend' him on Facebook and find out who he is." Jessica wrote to him and he wrote right back. He told Jessica that her birth name was Nuha and her sister's name was Suha. This was too big of a coincidence to ignore.

He turned out to be a Kurdish cousin who was living in Europe.

Jessica wrote him again, and in his reply, he said, "Have you contacted your mother?" This was a shock! We all knew the girls' mother had died. Serwan had told us that repeatedly, even swearing to that fact before two judges in two countries. Jessica wrote her cousin several times and finally wrote to a woman in Iraq.

It was indeed her mother! Her name was Riza. She was alive! Very much alive. In fact, she said she had been looking for her two babies for eighteen years!

Eighteen years! Riza[2] had traveled all over Iraq and asked everyone who would listen, "Where are my daughters?" She explained to us later how her daughters had been taken from her home by her husband, after a heated argument. She and Serwan had had a marital dispute about how best to leave Iraq. She wanted to wait and emigrate. He wanted to leave with the flood of refugees. In anger, Serwan said he would leave with the exodus of refugees; he took the girls with him.

Riza thought that when Serwan left their family home in Mosul (*not* Kirkuk), he would take them to the home of Serwan's mother

---

[1] Nuha means "intelligent, educated, and intellectual."

[2] *Riza* (name changed for privacy) means "satisfaction."

in Kirkuk and then return the next day after he'd cooled off. But the girls had disappeared with her husband, and she'd never heard from them again. She'd been devastated. She couldn't eat or sleep. For the past eighteen years she had been an English teacher in a nice city and had a steady income. She had a nice home with property. But she had no husband and no children. She'd lived without joy or happiness since her daughters had disappeared in July of 1991. But she did not completely lose hope; she believed they were alive somewhere.

Even more amazing, Jessica had always believed deep in her heart that her birth mother was alive somewhere. Jane and I considered this the dream that every adopted child has. It's the belief that life is better elsewhere. "My *real* mother wouldn't discipline me like this and make me sit on my bed!" So we took such fantasies in stride; we knew from Serwan that their birthmother (whose name Serwan said was Kurdistanê) had died in the violence when Saddam had attacked the Kurds. We let it rest. He said all the relatives were dead. But now we knew different!

Riza wanted to come to the US to see her daughters. But how? We had no idea how such things were done. In the fall of 2009, our daughters were adults. Jessica was eighteen, and Delal twenty. We told them it was their decision to make. We would support them, give counsel if they sought it, and help them when needed. But they would have to decide what they wanted. Together, they decided they wanted to invite Riza to come to the United States for a visit.

Delal undertook the paperwork, the writing to embassies back and forth, the faxing of documents and letters of invitation, and the assurances of a hosting family. It was a big job for a young woman. But she and Jessica were determined. And Riza, on her end, was doing everything possible. She endured multiple five-hour trips to Baghdad where she sat and waited, pled her case, asked for understanding, pled again to this office and that, was rejected, reapplied, and finally was approved for a thirty-day visit. She was elated.

Riza had never been outside of Iraq. She had never flown on an airplane. But in June 2010, she left her home in Mosul, boarded a plane in Baghdad, and began one of several flights that would bring her to San Francisco. It was a frightful experience for a fifty-three-year-old woman but one that was full of unimaginable anticipation.

At seven thirty on a warm June evening in 2010, our family waited just outside the security gate at San Francisco International Airport and looked through the crowds for Riza. Jessica says now that she was a bit anxious, very excited, and somewhat relieved to finally meet her. We had no picture of her and were unsure what to expect. Several minutes passed after everyone had exited security. Riza was the last person to come through the gate. She seemed small and timid as she made her way across the carpet toward us. Beside Jane, Jessica, Delal, and me, there were Delal's husband Ed. It seemed like the whole airport was empty but for our little group. Riza walked toward us. She wore a head scarf, horn-rimmed glasses, had an oval face, had olive skin, and stood about five feet high. Her face was wet with tears.

Jessica and Delal stepped forward from our group for long hugs. They shed tears and whispered quiet welcomes into Riza's veil. It was a moment captured in eternity. Life seemed to flow in slow motion—like something in a movie.

Can this be really happening? was on all our minds. It was totally surreal. For eighteen years, she had been dead. And yet here she was. It was a rebirth.

I gathered up her simple tattered luggage. No wheels, no fancy leather, or pull-out handles. Just a simple cloth suitcase with a handle. It was heavy. We walked toward our cars.

What do you talk about when you haven't seen your children since they were six months old and almost two? Where do you begin? Who is this young adult that stands before you? Yes, you are related, but who are they? They were beautiful, mature, and healthy. And Delal was married. The girls had interesting lives, were gifted musically, had a good education. And they are Christians. Of course. Riza is a devout Muslim. They are Americans and reflect that culture but also Kurds. And they were born in Iraq. One cannot begin to imagine the questions, the tensions, and the emotions that coursed through Riza's mind. There was so much to process.

And there was a lot for us to process as well. We learned from Riza that they had not fled the war. Their home had not been bombed and none of their family killed. Serwan had taken the two babies after their tense argument and said he'd flee the country. Riza had not believed him. But he had left, indeed. We learned that their original names had not been Kurdish but Arabic. Their mother, Riza, is an Arab, not a Kurd. Jessica's real birth name is Nuha. Delal's real birth name is Suha. Their birth father Serwan was in fact Kurdish. (This much of what he told us was true.) It is most unusual in Iraq for a Kurd to marry an Arab. They lived in Mosul (not in a small mountain village near Kirkuk as Serwan said). Mosul is noted for the fact that its population is almost half Arab and half Kurdish. A small percentage were Assyrian. Mosul had seen some of the worst fighting and racial tension in all of Iraq for this reason. The girls were born in Mosul, we learned—not in an impoverished mountain village.

Their home, the home where Riza now lived, was a middle-class home, not a primitive house. Riza had a good job as an English teacher in a high school and was college educated. There were no men in her extended family since they had all died in the Iraqi wars, beginning with the Iran-Iraq war. Known in Iraq as the First Persian Gulf War, it lasted eight long years beginning in 1980. At least a million people died in the conflict, half of whom were civilians. The dispute was over territory; the end of the war brought the border back to its prewar line. Many of the men in Riza's family had died in those battles, leaving many widows. It was in that war that Serwan was injured. Riza's only hope for the future was in her children. And her children had disappeared in 1991 with Serwan.

Finally, the girls learned their real birth dates. Delal was born in June in 1989. We were not far off when we had guessed July. Jessica was born seven weeks earlier than the doctor had estimated; she came into life in Mosul in November 1990. That meant that her weight of eleven and a half pounds (when we found her in Zakho) was even more frightful. She was thirteen months old when that weight had been taken.

In short, we learned that every detail Serwan had given us when we met had been a deception. He simply did not want their true identity to be known. He did not want them to go back to Mosul to their mother. He would have succeeded in his lie had it not been for the Internet and Facebook. And a beauty pageant. And a determined mother. And a God who cares about the widow and the orphan.

Riza spent a month in the home of a Kurdish family that had settled in Pleasanton, California. It was a long commute for them to come and go, to visit Riza in Pleasanton, and they each had jobs they needed to keep. But they managed to have many precious times together. The host family spent lots of time explaining Kurdish and Arab life to Delal and Jessica. They mostly just sat and talked. *How can you make up for eighteen years of life?* Riza showered them each with gifts: a GPS, a laptop, and lots of clothing from Iraq. That's what was in the heavy bags. Riza, Delal, and Jessica spent hours strolling through malls and doing memorable mother-daughter things, looking in Best Buy, drinking lots of Jamba Juices.

Jessica learned how Muslim families lived, as prayers were made five times a day toward Mecca from a carpet in the family room in Pleasanton. Arabian food was served, Arabian TV played, and the home was like a microcosm of Mosul. We thought of all the years of the girls' lives Riza had missed. I made DVD copies of videotapes we had taken as the girls were growing up. Riza appreciated receiving those.

It was going to be sad for all of them when she departed SFO and flew back to Baghdad. Jessica says she felt a great closure in her life. The girls made strong memories of her visit that will remain with them forever.

Riza wanted them to travel to Washington, DC, to the Iraqi embassy. She wanted them to obtain new Iraqi birth certificates. Then she hoped they would come to Mosul and see all their cousins. She had dreams of them becoming Arabs again, of leaving their American culture and their faith behind.

While Riza was here in California, Jane and I drove to Pleasanton to meet with Jessica, Delal, and her husband, Ed. We wanted Delal and Jessica to have a clear understanding of the ramifications of going to the Iraqi embassy and of visiting Mosul. We sat in a booth in a Denny's restaurant and had a serious talk. I shared with them some of the realities of life in Iraq. We explained that there were still honor killings for girls who had strayed from Sharia law. Marriage of Iraq girls to foreign men was forbidden.

"What would that mean for the nine-month-old marriage of Delal and Ed?" I asked them. "The Iraqi embassy in New York is actually Iraqi territory," I explained. "Once you are there, you are no longer under any protection as US citizens. You were born in Iraq, so by American law, you are Iraqis first. Your US citizenship carries no authority in Iraq." They needed to understand that they could be moved to Iraq from the Iraqi embassy against their will—or that if they decided to visit Iraq, their US passports could be taken from them and they'd never see it again. They would be unable to prove their identity or travel.

I also explained how marriages are arranged in Iraqi culture. Many first cousins are selected for young girls to marry. We wanted to help them see the risks and realities of the decisions that were before them. But we told them in complete honesty, it was their decision to make. They were adults.

"Basically," we told them in all seriousness, "if you leave and we say goodbye to you, we will in our hearts know that it's a real possibility we may never see you again."

It was a serious decision for them to make. They had to choose between the life that they had and the unknown life that was in another country where they were born. They knew their US adoptive parents; they had only just met their birth mother. They also learned that their birth father, Serwan, had visited Iraq since he had moved to Holland back in 1991. They realized that there was a lot they could not know and that they might be deceived. We knew what that was like.

They decided to stay in the US. Riza returned to Mosul when the month was up.

They still e-mail, Skype, and text Riza in Mosul. It is a city that's always in conflict. For several years, Mosul was the capital of ISIS in Iraq, the Islamic state. Riza sent texts to Jessica and said they were "dying slowly." It was dangerous for her to use the Internet when ISIS was in power. Water and electricity were rationed. The government was oppressive. Women had to be completely covered and were beaten mercilessly when seen in public unescorted or not properly covered. Markets remained closed. Life was unbearable. She, too, was caught between Iraq and a hard place.

I made a trip there in March 2015 to survey the work being done by nongovernment organizations in Iraqi Kurdistan. Jessica (accompanied by a friend) made her own journey there a year later to visit her mother. She stayed in Erbil, the Kurdish capital city, and Riza traveled up to visit with her. Riza's home in Mosul had been ransacked and ruined by the retreating ISIS army as the city was being retaken. She temporarily moved in with a relative further south in Baghdad.

Jessica thoroughly enjoyed her visit, met a dozen other relatives, and decided she would visit again. As of this writing, Mosul has been liberated by the Iraqi army, the Kurdish peshmerga, and the US Special Forces. Riza can now return home to Mosul to rebuild. The region has become inundated with refugees from Syria and Iraqis who are "internally displaced." The Kurds—who for so many decades were the victims of genocide and had lived as refugees in Turkey, Iran, and other lands—are now hosting Yezidi Kurds, Assyrians, Turkomans, Armenians, Arabs, and other Muslim Kurds. They have established refugee camps, and converted malls and schools that have been transformed into living spaces, sheltering over two million people.

The Kurdish government is democratic, has an established parliament, provides freedom of religion, and enforces the rule of law for all its citizens. Iraqi Kurdistan is religiously and ethnically diverse and holds regular democratic elections. In a referendum on September 25, 2017, in Kurdistan, the citizens voted to leave Iraq and form their own country. Israel was the only country in the world that accepted their declaration. As of this writing, an independent Kurdistan is still a dream. They are still caught between Iraq and a hard place.

Coming Soon

Scars that Tell Stories

This new book is a collection of thirty-seven stories of "scars": physical, emotional, and mental, from the author's life. They represent but a fraction of the illnesses, surgeries, and injuries he has sustained in his sixty-one years of life. They are funny, emotional, sometimes tense, fascinating, and each brings glory to the God who sustains us "through it all." Look for it in the spring of 2021.

About the Author

Kirk Legacy is a retired pastor, overseas Christian volunteer, and teacher. He has ministered in over forty countries, mostly in the third world. He and his wife, Jane, are passionate about sharing the love of Jesus with the lost, especially where Christ is not known. His friends know him as the "miracle man" because of the countless number of times doctors have announced the likelihood of his demise. He has been hospitalized over one hundred times (in nine countries). He had a heart-double lung transplant in 1997 and several open-heart surgeries since then. He loves music and plays his trombone in a big band, a jazz band, and a worship band. He loves to learn how to build or fix things. In 2011, he and a friend finished a complete frame-off restoration of a 1936 five-window coupe. You can write Kirk at 1936gasser@gmail.com.

CPSIA information can be obtained
at www.ICGtesting.com
Printed in the USA
FSHW010544121019
62911FS